Ishmeet Kaur Chaudhry teaches at the Centre for English Studies at the Central University of Gujarat, Gandhinagar. She is the editor *Patrick White: Critical Issues* (2014), co-editor of *Violence, Subversion and Recovery: Women Writers from the Sub-continent and Around* (2019, with Rachel Bari) and the author of *Texting the Scripture: Sri Guru Granth Sahib and the Visionary Poetics of Patrick White* (2016).

BLACK NOVEMBER

Writings on the **SIKH MASSACRES OF 1984** and the Aftermath

Edited by
ISHMEET KAUR CHAUDHRY

SPEAKING TIGER BOOKS LLP
4381/4, Ansari Road, Daryaganj
New Delhi 110002

First published by Speaking Tiger Books in paperback 2019
Anthology copyright © Speaking Tiger Books 2019
Introduction copyright © Ishmeet Kaur Chaudhry 2019

The copyright for each piece vests with the individual authors, translators, or their estates.

Every effort has been made to trace individual copyright holders and obtain permission. Any omissions brought to our attention will be remedied in future editions.

ISBN: 978-93-89231-45-8
eISBN: 978-93-89231-46-5

10 9 8 7 6 5 4 3 2 1

All rights reserved.

No part of this publication may be reproduced, transmitted, or stored in a retrieval system, in any form or by any means, electronic, mechanical, photocopying, recording or otherwise, without the prior permission of the publisher.

This book is sold subject to the condition that it shall not, by way of trade or otherwise, be lent, resold, hired out, or otherwise circulated, without the publisher's prior consent, in any form of binding or cover other than that in which it is published.

Dedicated to all the innocent victims across the world
who have survived their times, despite all oppression and exploitation,
and still have the courage to fight endlessly against injustice.

For my daughter, Harsheel Kaur,
who will grow up to read these stories of survival and strength

Contents

Introduction   xi

SECTION I
THE SURVIVORS SPEAK

Interviews and Personal Narratives

'Our House Was Full…': Shakuntala and Harbans Singh   3
     interviewed by Ishmeet Kaur Chaudhry

'Chaurasi Cannot Be Forgotten': Attar Kaur and Relatives   11
     interviewed by Ishmeet Kaur Chaudhry

'The Children Are Already Watching…':   20
Cheeja Kaur and Relatives
     interviewed by Ishmeet Kaur Chaudhry

'We Always Gave the Vote to Congress': Phanda Singh   29
     interviewed by Uma Chakravarti

'Badshah…Maintain Our Honour': Balwant Singh Granthi   39
     interviewed by Kulbir and Anil

31 October 1984   63
     Jarnail Singh

'Now the Tears Have Dried Up'   71
     Dhiren Bhagat

'I Could See Houses Burning, Taxi Stands Burning':   75
Manmohan Singh and Gursharan Kaur
     interviewed by Daman Singh

'Had Sardarji Lived…'   85
     Harsh Mander

Affidavits Filed with the Nanavati Commission

Gurmeet Singh S/o S. Mohan Singh	97
Satu Singh S/o S. Sunder Singh	99
Wazir Singh S/o S. Dharam Singh	101
Surinder Singh S/o S. Ajit Singh	102
Smt. Joginder Kaur W/o Late S. Amrik Singh	103
Piara Singh, S/o S. Ajit Singh	107
Jitender Kaur W/o S. Gurcharan Singh	109
Sharanjit Singh S/o S. Mohinder Singh	111
Amar Singh S/o Late S. Ram Singh	113
D.P. Gulati s/o M.D. Gulati	114
Harbans Singh S/o Late Niranjan Singh	116
Bhagwani Bai W/o Sh. Sewa Singh	118
Manbhari Kaur W/o Late S. Kuldeep Singh	119
Phota Singh S/o S. Doonger Singh	120
Khushwant Singh S/o Sardar Bahadur Sir Sobha Singh	121

SECTION II
SHORT STORIES

The Fiery Embrace by Parvinder Mehta	127
It Doesn't Matter Either by Rachel Bari	140
Sweets of Mathura by Harish Narang	145
Another Kharku by Harish Narang	153
Eyes Don't Lie by Jyoti Verma	165
When a Big Tree Falls by N.S. Madhavan	170
Dear Friend, the World Is an Enemy by Satya Vyas	184

SECTION III
Plays

The Old Man Speaks by Gursharan Singh	195
Seekh Kabab: A Tragicomedy by Kuljeet Singh	210
One Day from Chaurasi by Harvinder Paul Singh	233

Section IV
Poems

AJMER RODE

    Trilokpuri 1984

The Pond in My Soul	251
Bones in her Hands	252
The Sixth Finger	253

BISHNU MOHAPATRA

October-November 1984	254

PASHUPATI JHA

A Riot Victim	256
A Godless Country	257
Idea-Obsessed	258

HARNIDH KAUR

Eighty-Four	259
Fleeing	260
The Portrait of a Man	262
Bargain	263
Muscle Memory	265

Jagjit Brar
When the Sky Darkened in Shame — 266

Gurcharan Rampuri
Dwarf Heads — 268
Duryodhan Still Rules Hastinapur — 269

Parvinder Mehta
Shadows — 270
Smudges of History — 272
aphasia — 273

Manroop S. Dhingra
A Moment — 275
Mother — 276

Gautam Vegda
Cinders — 276
Inside the Borders — 277

Ishmeet Kaur Chaudhry
Rest in Peace — 279
A Chapter in Indian History — 280

Notes on the Contributors — 282
Acknowledgements — 290

Introduction

Following the assassination of Indira Gandhi, the Prime Minister of India, by her own bodyguards on the morning of 31 October 1984, innumerable innocent Sikhs were humiliated, beaten, lynched and burnt alive over three days. New Delhi in particular, the political centre and capital of the nation, became the site of uncontrolled civil unrest and violent mayhem against many ordinary citizens whose only fault was that they belonged to the same Sikh community as the assassins.

Nearly thirty years later, in April 2014, as we walked into the Tilak Vihar Widows' Colony, which had been established in 1985 to house the widows and families of the Sikhs killed in the 1984 pogrom, we felt innumerable eyes upon us. The sight of our tripod was scoffed at, with onlookers saying, 'They have come again—no one does anything, they just hold their cameras and walk in.' We had been taken by a contact, a person who worked in my cousin's office, whose family had been victims of the pogrom. We entered a house and I was immediately overwhelmed by the stink of the moisture from the walls. The walls had been covered by tiles so that the seepage wouldn't be visible, but it nevertheless made itself felt. The drawing room had three sofas, and four women were already assembled there, waiting for us. A curtain hung at the entrance of the adjoining room and I could hear the voices of some young people inside. It seemed to me that a young man had just returned from his office. He chose to remain aloof. A kitchen adjoined the room on the other side, with an open shelf on which utensils were neatly arranged. The women seated themselves on the sofas and I was given a chair to sit behind my camera and the tripod. They were keen to talk to us, unlike the onlookers outside. They began narrating their woeful tales and as we heard story after story, we began wondering how these women had endured all that they told us. I only wished it was an exaggeration, but the truth couldn't be denied. Every word that they spoke was truth that they had lived through.

As they spoke, it seemed that their lives had been spent in a quest for justice, in pursuit of which they had grown old. This quest was their only motivation for enduring the manifold challenges of their lives. For them, going on strikes (dharnas) had become a common routine. Many of them recounted that their children would naturally accompany them to the dharnas and, in turn, realize the wrongs done to them and the need to seek justice. The dharnas bore little outcome, as, even after thirty years, the women had only received petty jobs and compensation worth rupees six or seven lakhs.*

The women narrated their struggle, often remembering their past and returning to the present like the sway of a pendulum. They recalled how their lives changed drastically overnight. Ever since, they have been haunted by the senseless murders of their husbands and other family members. Most of the men had left their homes in the morning following the routine of jobs or school, but that evening they never returned. The women said that each time they heard an account of how someone else had been killed, they felt that the same thing might have happened to their loved ones. The gruesome nature of the pogrom has left its ghost behind to haunt the survivors. Many of the women recounted how they still wake up and panic about the safety of their families, even now.

The women we spoke to had several stories to share about the night when the mobs returned to rape them. The electricity supply had been cut and the men lit candles, found women and young girls, and raped them. One woman recalled that they tried to cover their girls with dupattas but, as one man was followed by another in a continuous chain the whole night, the coverings wouldn't stay in place for even a few minutes. Afterwards, many women thought of committing suicide, however, ultimately they had no choice but to continue living and look after their children. They recalled how they saw each other

---

* Cheeja Kaur and Relatives.

the next day, and shared their grief and suffering, realizing that they were all the same. This, in a way, allowed them to carry on. One of the survivors, Kulwant Kaur, remarked that they could continue living only because they saw each other as all victims of the same fate.[*]

While recalling these events, the survivors began expressing guilt, either for having survived, unlike so many others they knew, or for not being able to save others. They spoke about how they continue to live with this guilt, and continually justify their survival to themselves, by holding themselves accountable for their children or old parents or even siblings. Alongside this, they tend to examine the reasons why they were attacked, looking for ways to say that the violence was or was not their fault.

Whether they followed the Sikh religion or not, their cultural affiliation to Sikhism was clearly the overwhelming cause of the killings, and so, unsurprisingly, the survivors spent a long time in defining their relationship with the religion. They begin defining a separate Sikh identity for themselves, in the manner in which they were othered. Many of them recalled their childhoods and how they grew up with Sikh sentiments of brotherhood. One common narrative described how it used to be difficult to differentiate between Sikh and Hindu families, as there was a long-standing tradition of mixed families: Hindus and Sikhs used to be members of the same family. For example, one survivor in Ahmedabad, who wishes to remain unnamed, recalled that his grandfather had eleven children. Out of eight sons, four were brought up as Sikh and four as Hindus. Two of the daughters were married to Hindu men and one to a Sikh man. The speaker recalled how, during the pogrom, the Sikh brothers had been targeted while the Hindu brothers remained safe. His grandmother began doubting her decision to bring up the sons with different religious identities after the pogrom, though at the same time, she was proud of how her Hindu sons had helped several Sikh men, not only their own brothers. He remarked that he could never understand the concept of a separatist Sikh identity in the context of his mixed family.

---

[*] Cheeja Kaur and Relatives.

He said that he felt as confused as his grandmother when suddenly Hindus began considering Sikhs to be of another religion, and vice-versa. His conclusion was that we have all been victims of politics and politicians, who had fooled the general public.

The conversations at the Tilak Vihar Widows' Colony also emphasized the fact that the nature of the pogrom was political and that it had been instigated by members of the Congress Party. Some of the speakers described this as an open secret, and others reported seeing senior leaders of Congress Party during the violence. They also recalled that the mob comprised of people of all communities and all castes. One speaker suggested that it would be wrong to examine the events on the basis of a simple Hindu-Sikh divide.* Throughout her conversation with us, she continually underlined the political nature of the pogrom. She spoke about how her own family had been loyal to the Congress Party as they had got loans to build their business and houses during the tenure of the Congress. She now lives with a sense of betrayal, and questions any affiliation of any one at all to any party.

For a while now, the Sikh community has been used as a pawn both by political leaders and the Sikh leadership itself. In their bid for votes, political leaders prior to 1984 had tried collaborating with religious leaders, neither party realizing that their involvement would compromise the sanctity of the most important Sikh shrine, the Golden Temple, or lead to the post-assassination pogrom. After the carnage of 1984, the Sikh leadership turned a deaf ear to the pleas of the survivors and did not take any strong measures to either rehabilitate them or fight for justice. In the past thirty-five years, the voices of prominent Sikh leaders remained silent. Despite the substantial membership of Sikhs in the Congress party, it too, ignored the survivors of the 1984 violence. Ironically, when Dr Manmohan Singh was prime minister, he apologized to the Sikh community in 2005. This apology was received with mixed feelings of relief, anger and pain, particularly as it was a Sikh Congress leader apologizing to the Sikhs, while many of the other senior leaders who had instigated

---

* Attar Kaur and Relatives.

the violence remained free and unrepentant till date.* The only impact that this apology had was that it acknowledged that the Congress party was complicit in the violence of 1984. The community has felt threatened and suffered at the hands of its own people and from the ones to whom they provided security in the past.

Moreover, there is a sense of utter betrayal due to the complete breakdown of the judicial institution when it comes to justice for the survivors. Over thirty-five years, a total of four commissions, nine committees and two special investigation teams (SITs) have been appointed to investigate the anti-Sikh pogrom. However, many of them do not seem to have served any purpose; nor have substantial policy changes been made based on the few recommendations that have been submitted.

The first of the commissions was the Marwah Commission, set up in 1984 to investigate the role of the police in the violence. The inquiry is said to have been stopped in mid-1985 and this commission was replaced by the Mishra Commission in May 1985. In February 1987, this commission submitted a report recommending that three more committees be set up to investigate the role of the police, the registration of cases, and to determine the total number of killings. The Mishra Commission stated that it was constituted only to verify whether the violence had happened and not identify the perpetrators. However, it gave a clean chit to Rajiv Gandhi and H.K.L. Bhagat. It also documented the delay in the response of the Army against the violence, and that cases against politicians or police officers had not been registered.

Thereafter, a series of committees attempted to work on the issue. In 1985, the Dhillon Committee was constituted to look into the rehabilitation of the survivors. It mandated that Rs. 10,000 be given to each family that had lost their dear ones and that insurance be given to those who had lost their property in the violence. Later, the

---

* Dr Manmohan Singh in his tenure had promised that the cases would be reopened and justice meted out, but despite the fact that he remained prime minister for a decade, nothing was done in this matter.

government rejected this recommendation and no insurance money was paid. The Kapur-Mittal Commission was constituted in 1987 to look into the role of the police. They submitted their report in 1990, but not a single person was dismissed. The Jain-Banerjee Committee was constituted in 1987 to look into the registration of cases but was quashed in 1989. The Ahuja Committee was formed in 1987 to assess the number of people killed. It submitted its report in August 1987, recording 2,733 killed in Delhi alone and 3,325 across the country. The Poti-Rosha Committee was formed in March 1990 and expired in September 1990, without any significant contribution.

In 1990, the Jain-Aggarwal Committee recommended the registration of cases against some prominent Congress leaders, like H.K.L. Bhagat, Dharam Das Shastri, Jagdish Tytler and Sajjan Kumar. This was followed by the Narula Committee in 1993, set up by BJP leader Madan Lal Khurana, the then Chief Minister of Delhi. The committee also recommended the registration of cases against Sajjan Kumar, H.K.L. Bhagat and Jagdish Tytler in its January 1994 report.

In 2000, the Nanavati Commission was formed after a unanimous resolution was passed in the Rajya Sabha. Notice was issued by the commission to H.K.L. Bhagat, Sajjan Kumar, Jagdish Tytler, Dharam Das Shastri and Kamal Nath. Though the committee dismissed allegations against Rajiv Gandhi due to lack of evidence, in its report of May 2005, it also recommended that an anti-riot police force that remained free of political influence be established. This has not been done so far.

The Mathur Committee was set up in December 2014 after an announcement of giving Rs. 5 lakh to the victims by Home Minister Rajnath Singh. The committee noted that proper investigations had not been conducted and recommended an SIT to inquire whether cases closed by the police needed to be reopened. Its recommendations were implemented in 2015 and innumerable cases were reopened under a central government SIT. Having convicted Naresh Sherawat and Yashpal Singh, the SIT later closed 186 cases in December 2017 without an investigation. Finally, the apex court decided to setup its own SIT, orders for which were given in January 2018. Its report is still awaited.*

In 2018, Sajjan Kumar was convicted of instigating the mobs, setting a gurdwara on fire and killing five members of a family in Raj Nagar. He has been given a sentence of life imprisonment. This took place in the run-up to the national elections of 2019, when the Congress Party was winning in three states. Ironically, Kamal Nath, another of the suspected perpetrators, was sworn in as the Chief Minister of Madhya Pradesh at around the same time. It is clear that such piecemeal justice cannot substantially heal wounds that have been seeping for the past thirty-five years. Many of those who lost their families and livelihoods have passed away or are on the verge of death, waiting for justice knock at their doors, maybe, someday.

~

After our interviews, we were taken to Gurdwara Shaheed Ganj Sahib in B block of Tilak Vihar Widows' Colony. A room adjoining the main hall is full of photographs of the men killed in the pogrom. Some have been stuck on the walls, while many others are still lying in piles due to paucity of space. The women accompanying us pointed out their relatives, eagerly saying, 'That's my son, that's my brother, that's my brother's brother-in-law, my sister's husband, my husband's brother….' The list seemed endless. We were soon surrounded by more women, who also started showing us the photographs of their relatives. Every woman had many photographs to show us, and it was clear that every family had borne the loss of several members. Later, one couple showed us death certificates for eleven of the sixteen members of their family who had been killed in those three days. A photograph of a six-year-old boy struck me speechless. What harm could anyone imagine that this boy would bring to them? How could the mob have had the appetite to lynch him?

---

* Deeksha Bharadwaj. '4 Commissions, 9 Committees & 2 SITS-the long road to justice for 1984 Sikh Killings.' *The Print*. 16 November 2018. https://theprint.in/india/governance/4-commissions-9-committees-2-sits-the-long-road-to-justice-for-1984-sikh-killings/150166/

As I saw the emotional responses of the visitors to the gurdwara, I began to question the memorial site being built at Gurdwara Rakab Ganj Sahib. That 2,500-square-foot space would be in stark contrast to this tiny gurdwara built by the survivors themselves. Once again, the role of the Sikh leaders came into question: Why couldn't these women be given a respectful place to display the photographs of their loved ones? Why couldn't this gurdwara itself, an actual memorial to the events of 1984, be expanded and made into a formal memorial site? And, hovering around these, the larger question of why substantial efforts had not been made in the past thirty-five years to give these women and their families a better life? Serious deliberation on the policies related to the rehabilitation of survivors, their education, and access to the basic, necessary facilities to live a decent life is required. Perhaps had such policies been available to the survivors residing in Tilak Vihar Widow's Colony, they wouldn't have lost their children to drugs and petty crime.

It was while entering this gurdwara that we heard some women objecting to us, saying that everyone walks in with their tripods and no one does anything. Having seen the photographs inside, I could now understand why they said this. They have lived lives full of betrayal and unbearable pain. Their losses have been irreplaceable, but the least that they expected was justice—which has *never* come their way. It was quite understandable that these women felt that they were now reduced to products or stories for journalists, who came by, every now and then, but whose questions and articles led to no change for them. At that moment I felt the pangs of guilt: Why had I come to record them? Why couldn't I just leave them to fight their own battle of life? If I was not there to help them, at least I shouldn't disturb them. I began feeling like a criminal. These questions lingered on in my mind for a long time after that visit.

~

After much thought, I decided that I must compile this anthology, for several cogent reasons. First and foremost, my personal experience as a six-year-old child who had witnessed the '84 violence began to resurface in my memory. At the time, we used to live in Shimla, where the intensity of violence was much less than in Delhi. Though a small mob approached us, we were saved by our Hindu neighbours, particularly veteran journalist Ravinder Randev, who scared the mob away, as they were worried that he might recognize them and publish their names. Around that time, my father's best friend had begun to tell him that there was no need for Sikhs to wear turbans, as they were no longer soldiers, and that Harmandar Sahib in Amritsar had actually been a Hindu temple and should be re-consecrated as one. I also remembered how, after we had shifted to a new house in 1985, my eight-year-old neighbour had remarked that she hated me from the day we came to live nearby. I understood that, despite growing up together, we never became close, primarily because of the impressions that she had about Sikhs, after the assassination of Indira Gandhi. Having visited Tilak Vihar, I realized that I had been privileged, but despite that, the memory of '84 was embedded in my being. In Ahmedabad, I met a few students who narrated their experiences of the Godhra violence in 2002. Their fear of speaking out, even after many years, touched me, and my own half-buried experience of the menace in the air in '84 returned to my mind. If we, the fortunate ones, could feel so othered and afraid, one could almost imagine the magnitude of the fear and alienation amongst those who had lost almost everything in their lives. If they were not able to speak, or if their voices remained unheard, it was up to us to lend our voices and amplify them. The main purpose of this book is to voice the concerns of those who had suffered.

Secondly, in our secular nation, the whole idea of nation had been compromised in the three–four days of mayhem. There was a complete breakdown of security and all institutions had crumbled. The training of people in these institutions, ever now, is questionable. Why do doctors or policemen (among other institutions, like the judiciary itself) retain their communal identities when it comes to performing their duty? The victims were denied medical treatment, the police failed to protect them and, in thirty-five years, injustice continues to prevail. In certain places, the police had even asked Sikhs to hand over their weapons, collected them in the gurdwaras and fired at them. No official record testifies to these incidents, except for those of the survivors. Their narratives serve as testimonies to the past. Surely, they have not been sufficient evidence in the court of law with the exception of the sentencing of Sajjan Kumar.

Thirdly, it was important to devise a methodology to read and write violence. Violence can never exist in isolation, therefore, in order to understand violence, it is important to study experience. There can't be a better way than to bear witness to the first-hand experience of the survivors. Thus, first to understand the consequences of violence, it was important to read what was available. Unfortunately, there seemed to be a disturbing silence around the events of 1984. Within weeks of the violence, the People's Union for Democratic Rights (PUDR) and People's Union for Civil Rights (PUCL) had published a joint report. This report was translated into Punjabi by the Association for Democratic Rights (AFDR). Later, a new edition was published by AFDR in 1985. Interestingly, the report recorded several narratives by Hindu families describing how they had rescued Sikhs during the pogrom. But Jagmohan Singh, its publisher, was charged as an 'antinational' and the book still remains banned.[*] Though journalistic and prose writing provided a substantial (but still not adequate) political analysis of the pogrom, writers were not able to do justice to the subject in literature. The scanty literature available on the subject was also scattered, both across languages and regions.

The earliest book, *The Punjab Story*, was published two months after the Operation Blue Star in June 1984. It was authored by eight veteran writers: Amarjit Kaur, Lt. Gen J.S. Aurora, Khushwant Singh, M.V. Kamath, Subhash Kirpekar, Sunil Sethi and Tavleen Singh. The book critically evaluated the roles of the Sikh leadership and the central government. It was republished in 2004 (Roli Books). In 1987, a remarkable collection of first-hand interviews with the survivors of

---

[*] Amaninder Pal Sharma."30 years on, book on 1984 victims still banned" *Times of India*. 3 Feb. 2014. https://timesofindia.indiatimes.com/india/30-years-on-book-on-1984-victims-still-banned/articleshow/29793487.cms

the carnage was published by Uma Chakravarti and Nandita Haksar. Two of the interviews from *The Delhi Riots: Three Days in the Life of a Nation* (Lancer International, 1987) have been included in this book.

Amandeep Sandhu's article in *The Hindu*[*] provides a quick and a comprehensive reference list of works in Punjabi, Hindi and English literature on the 1984 violence till 2014. He points out how some of the Punjabi stalwarts had failed to address the subject until the late nineties. Thereafter, he lists the significant work of Ajit Rahi, Buta Singh Saad, Ninder Gill, Jaswant Deed and Manmohan Bawa on the topic. It is important to mention the contribution of historian Ajmer Singh who has provided a comprehensive understanding of the subject in his three volumes of historical study of the subject: *Vihvi Sadi di Sikh Rajneeti: Ek Gulami ton Dooji Ghulami Tak* (2003); *Sikh Rajneeti Da Dukhant: Kisbidh Ruli Paatshahi* (2007); *1984 Unchitviya Kehar: Na Mamanjog, Na Bhulanjog, te Na Bakhshanyog* (2009).

In Hindi, an anthology of short stories edited by Surendra Tiwari, *Kala November*, appeared in 1987 and was translated into English by Saroj Vashisht (Rupa, 1995). The title of the present anthology has been inspired by Maheep Singh's story, 'Kala November' which was published in this collection. Unfortunately, since copies of this book have been hand to trace, this story could not be republished in this volume. Two other regional language works are also immensely significant: one an Assamese novel by Indira Goswami *Tej Aru Dhushorito Prishtha* translated as *Pages Stained in Blood* (Katha, 2001) by Pradip Acharya, and the other a short story by N.S. Madhavan, 'Vanmarangal Veezhumpol' translated as 'When a Big Tree Falls' by K.M. Krishnan and later also by N.P. Ashley. Madhavan's story was later made into the Hindi film *Kaya Taran* and Ashley's translation of it has been reproduced in this anthology.

However, until relatively recently, there has been a general silence in English writing about the events of 1984. Preminder Singh

---

[*] Amandeep Sandhu, "The Carnage that Shook Society". *The Hindu*. 01 Feb 2014. https://www.thehindu.com/books/literary-review/the-carnage-that-shook-society/article5834658.ece

Sandhawalia wrote *Beyond Identity* (Singh Brothers) in 2007. The novel reveals the conflict faced by numberless Sikhs in political asylum and how they live with changed identities in diasporic spaces, giving rise to several separatist movements that follow. Amandeep Sandhu's novel *Roll of Honour* (Rupa, 2012) is situated around the time of the actual crisis. Set in a military school, it describes the political situation in Punjab and its impact on the youth. Jaspreet Singh also locates his novel *Helium* (Bloomsbury, 2013) in India around the carnage of '84. He suggests that the personal cannot be separated from the political. Vikram Kapur's edited volume *1984: In Memory and Imagination: Personal Essays and Short Fiction on 1984 Anti-Sikh Riots* (Amaryllis, 2016) also attempts to address the issue through the genre of short fiction. Vikram Kapur also wrote *The Assassinations* (Speaking Tiger, 2017) in which the transformation of an individual, caught in the political machinations of the times, has been dealt with very sensitively as part of a love story. *The Year of the Hawks* (Speaking Tiger, 2017) a novel by Kanwaljit Deol located in the premises of Golden Temple on the fateful day of June 6, 1984 is a moving account of what the young generations went through in Punjab in the early 1980s.

Apart from short stories and novels, Tariq Ali also wrote a playscript *The Assassination: Who Killed Indira G?* in 2008. The third instalment in a series of unpublished television film-scripts, it suggests the intrusion of foreign forces in the assassination of Indira Gandhi for their vested interests, and shows how her political strategies resonated with the manner of her own death.

Interestingly, while many of these writers depict the horrific nature of violence and inhumanity of humankind, at the same time these stories are not bereft of the human ability to feel love, compassion and kindness. It is this ability to display hope even in the most sombre conditions or forbidding times that keeps humanity alive. It is also this sentiment that made this work possible.

It is an effort to recall, revoke and remember the past. Remembering is important largely for two reasons: One, that the past needs an assessment so that it doesn't recur in the future. Second, recalling is an attempt to address many of the questions that have remained unanswered for the last thirty-five years. These questions are related to the nature of violence, community differences, identity crises and political assertion. But they become prominent primarily because none of these cases have been given justice. Thirty-five years down the line, the survivors are on the verge of meeting the ends of their lives and still await justice.

Fifth, literary spaces offer a form of activism and a space for representation. Writing about the past doesn't merely remain a space for nostalgia, but transcends its dimensions to become a space for resistance. The process of writing offers different perspectives which, in turn, suggest a broad version of the truth.

Literature has the ability to recreate time and demonstrate its truthfulness. A piece of work may be fictionalized but the experience relocated by it is real in all aspects. This reality has been depicted in various forms, genres and narrative styles. This form or style is particular to the context. The literature of the margins has been highly experimental in writing styles, use of language, theme and context. Often, writers face a dilemma in depicting violence, and so they tend to employ various experimental forms such as life-narratives, diary-writing, conversation or even interviews and oral narratives. Experience has been central to these writings. Writing experience doesn't allow the writers to just represent themselves, but it opens the possibilities for recreating the history and experiences of their people. These literatures are expansive in nature;they reach out to a wider public and are impactful in bringing shame to the perpetrators.

In light of the above, this book is an edited anthology of oral narratives, affidavits filed by the survivors, poems and short fiction on the 1984 pogrom. They analyze the situation from various perspectives emerging not only from literature, but also from major socio-political concerns, studying them from historical, ethnographic, archival and representational aspects.

~

The present anthology is divided in four sections. The novelty of this volume is the first section, 'The Survivors Speak' in which the experiences of the survivors have been retold, for the most part in their own words. Some interviews have been reproduced from an earlier anthology, *The Delhi Riots: Three Days in the Life of a Nation*, and depict the immediate impressions of the pogrom on people's lives. The newer interviews, recorded thirty years later, in 2014, depict a long history of injustice. These thirty-five years have been too long for the survivors, who have struggled every single day, while at the same time, this period seem to have been too short for the courts to punish the perpetrators. Excerpts about the events of 1984 from Jarnail Singh's autobiographical book, *I Accuse...: The Anti-Sikh Violence of 1984* (Penguin, 2011) and Daman Singh's book *Strictly Personal: Manmohan & Gursharan* (Harper Collins, 2014) have also been included, as well an article by Dhiren Bhagat on the political impact of the pogrom in its immediate aftermath. Finally, Harsh Mander's life narrative from his book *Fatal Accidents of Birth: Stories of Suffering, Oppression and Resistance* (Speaking Tiger, 2016) has also been reproduced in this volume. The narrative is the personal life-story of Lachmi, who was widowed during the pogrom, and her struggle to bring up her children thereafter.

A collection of fourteen affidavits filed to the Nanavati Commission in 2000 by the survivors of the pogrom has been reproduced. The selection process for this section has been extremely complicated as we were able to include only fourteen out of more than 3000 affidavits. Care has been taken to reproduce these affidavits, which seemed to have been written by the survivors themselves. In the course of reading these affidavits, it became evident that template-type affidavits were distributed to many women who were asked to fill in the number of deceased in their family and demand compensation worth the loss of material objects looted or burnt during the course of the pogrom. Many people refused to fill them up and chose to write their own accounts, some of which have been reproduced in this section. Many of these affidavits were written in a technical, official language. The criteria of selection favours those with more information recorded in them, as these have been important legal statements.

The second section of this volume is a collection of short stories where time is an important dimension. Parvinder Mehta's 'The Fiery Embrace' depicts the strength of friendship, while straddling the razor's edge between the roles of perpetrator and victim. The delicacy with which the sides turn in this story is remarkable. Rachel Bari's story 'It Doesn't Matter Either' is a collection of serialized episodes that connect to each other, revealing the role played by the police in the abduction of a young girl around the year 1984. It powerfully opens up the 'in-between' layers of the clandestine nature of those who exercise power and the vulnerable, particularly women who bear the brunt of any kind of conflict.

'Sweets of Mathura', a story by Harish Narang, is about what happens during a train journey when the death of Indira Gandhi is announced. A mob walks into the train in search of Sikhs and is unable to reason that many other communities also use Singh as a surname. A second story by Harish Narang, 'Another Kharku', is a moving account of post-carnage times; how the image of Sikhs undergoes a transition and how an innocent man is treated as a terrorist because of his religion. The story is particularly relevant in today's milieu, when Islamaphobia, both in India and abroad, has led to similar incidents being reported on a regular basis.

Jyoti Verma's experimental story focuses on an individual family, building a mysterious aura around the image of the protagonist's young brother, at a time when young turbaned Sikh boys were considered terrorists by the police in Punjab. The story makes a connection between June 1984 when operation Blue Star was conducted and October-November 1984, during the anti-Sikh pogrom. The plight of the family is representative of many survivors of these two events.

The violence spread to different places throughout India but much of the literature has been centred in Delhi. Thus, an excerpt from Satya Vyas's Hindi novel, *Chaurasi* set in Bokaro, Bihar, and a short story, 'When a Big Tree Falls' by N.S. Madhavan written originally in

Malayalam, have been included in this volume. Vyas's novel explores the violence from both within and outside the mob, while Madhavan's story addresses the fear felt at the time by locating it in the interiors, both in terms of physical and psychological spaces.

The third section is a collection of three plays. 'The Old Man Speaks' is by veteran Punjabi playwright Gursharan Singh, who critiques both the political and the religious structures of society. It points out the weaknesses of an institutional religion vis-a-vis the political manipulations of the nation state. The second play, 'Seekh Kebab' by Kuljeet Singh, is a tragi-comedy set in the late '80s, after 1984. A man comes to a police station looking for help in finding his son, but the police are hell-bent on proving the son a terrorist. The third play 'One Day from Chaurasi' by Harvinder Paul Singh is a musical play situated in the present. It recalls the events of Chaurasi to a new generation and emphasizes the idea that 'justice delayed is justice denied'.

The fourth section is a collection of poems written by Indian poets within the country and in the diaspora. Ajmer Rode, Jagjit Brar, Gurcharan Rampuri, Bishnu Mohapatra, Pashupati Jha, Harnidh Kaur, Parvinder Mehta, Manroop S. Dhingra, Gautam Vegda and this editor have contributed to this section. The poems in this section correlate the experience of suffering with that of other communities and hold a sense of both catharsis and resistance.

~

No matter how many systemic attempts are made to erase the memories of violence, no matter how much time is taken to deliver justice, no matter how many blankets are distributed, no matter how many votes are pleaded, every act of violence announces itself as a shameful blot on the society where these incidents occur. This violence reverberates across communities and across time. Unfortunately, in India, all ruling parties have instigated as well as supported such instances of violence. The Congress was the ruling party in 1984, and many perpetrators of the carnage were its supporters. Similarly, when the Bharatiya Janta Party ruled Gujarat in 2002, many instigators of the post-Godhra violence were again supporters of the ruling party. In both cases a complete breakdown of the institutional machinery was evident. One fails to understand why our citizens remain so divided in the name of religion, community, caste and region that they forget their constitutional duties and responsibilities towards each other in times of conflict. During both these events the police remained inactive. In 1984, the divide between the Sikhs and the Hindus surfaced between the policemen themselves (as recorded in one of the affidavits included in this anthology). Also, many doctors refused to treat the deceased as they didn't want to compromise their own safety, or they chose to remain divided on the basis of religion itself. Moreover, the judiciary took years to close certain cases and it still hasn't been able to resolve all the cases yet. The witnesses have passed away and a generation is slowly coming to an end, having led a miserable life awaiting justice. It is evident from this that the institutional training in our country is flawed.

The impact of the 2002 pogrom in Gujarat is still visible in the eyes of the survivors who resist speaking about the incident. It may not be an ideal or utopian idea to presume that strict action during 1984 would have perhaps prevented the 2002 pogrom. If nothing else, perhaps, had justice for 1984 been dispensed in time, the examples would have set precedents for Gujarat in 2002 as well. Moreover, in 2012, the sight of Sikhs sitting in dharna to support Muslims as their cases were being heard and resolved was heartwarming, as well as painful. It was encouraging to see that communities could empathize with each other, but painful because the most gruesome experiences had brought them together. Similarly, recent months have seen Sikhs coming act in support of Kashmiris when Article 370 was abrogated. It was heartening to see that an official statement from the Akal Takht was issued, urging Sikhs to protect Kashmiri women. The acting Jathedar, Giani Harpreet Singh, said that some politicians have made derogatory statements pertaining to the honour of Kashmiri women; similarly 'Sikh women were attacked by people of the same mentality

in 1984 and no Sikh will let this happen to Kashmiri women'.*
Many Sikhs have also equated the situation in Kashmir to the years
of insurgency in Punjab. One wonders what lessons we learn from
our past.

Ishmeet Kaur Chaudhry
October 2019

---

* https://www.thequint.com/news/politics/article-370-jammu-kashmir-punjab-sikhs-narendra-modi-hindutva

SECTION I
THE SURVIVORS SPEAK

Personal Narratives and Interviews

'Our House was Full...'
SHAKUNTALA AND HARBANS SINGH

This interview was recorded on 3 April 2014 at Tilak Vihar Widow's Colony, New Delhi by Ishmeet Kaur Chaudhry. The speakers narrate how sixteen members of their family were killed in the violence after the assassination of the prime minister at the time, Indira Gandhi. This is an eye-witness account of their experiences and those of their family members. Harbans Singh narrates how he escaped the mob by hiding, and also accompanying the mob, walking with them to save himself. He talks about how he had to cut his hair and remove his turban to hide his identity. Shakuntala remembers the torture borne by her sisters-in-law and the children in the family. She shared images of the debris of her house and the cremation of the partially burnt bodies of her family members in the house itself. They refuse compensation or monetary help in the name of their dead.

SHAKUNTALA: My father's name was Mangal Singh. This is Mangal Singh's family that was finished.

Q: What is your name?

SHAKUNTALA: My name is Shakuntala.

Q: And what is your husband's name?

SHAKUNTALA: Harbans Singh...(silence)...We have never spoken to anyone. We are scared, we think if we say something, they may kill us. Three–four of us, the only ones who are left. One: my sister-in-law. When my sister-in law came out, she asked for water.

They said urinate in her mouth, don't put water in her mouth. None of their children should be spared, none of their women should remain behind, kill all of them. Two of my sisters-in-law were killed by them. One, who came out, died and the other, was burnt inside. And, the one who came out, she was killed horribly, one man pulled one leg, and the other person, pulled the other leg, she was ripped apart from the centre. We have seen all this with our eyes (weeps inconsolably). She had been married fifteen days back. Fifteen days are not enough for marriage (a long pause, remains silent, weeps, tries to gather herself.)

Our Vicky was of this age (points to a boy of ten or eleven years, her grandson), whom I carried with me, wandering in streets, one after the other. His pant was hanging loose.

HARBANS SINGH: He didn't have shoes on his feet.

SHAKUNTALA: He was just like him (points to her grandson).

HARBANS SINGH: If we went to someone's house, they refused to let us in.

Q: Did you wear a turban in those times?

HARBANS SINGH: No, I had got my hair cut; everyone had cut their hair, except my father. He said even if I die, I will not cut my hair. I don't care.

Q: Did you cut your hair during the violence or before that?

Voice in the background: He cut his hair during the violence.

HARBANS SINGH: We had just cut our hair and then the violence (kand) broke. We had come to know that kand is about to take place.

Q: So, you cut your hair because you anticipated that the kand was sure to happen?

HARBANS SINGH: Yes, because the kand would happen, to save ourselves we cut our hair.

SHAKUNTALA: Everyone started saying, 'Cut your hair'.

HARBANS SINGH: Neighbours in the street started saying that

you get your hair cut, don't speak Punjabi. Sit indoors, we are with you, we are with you. When, in the morning at 8 a.m., the mob with so many people came to kill us, there was a huge crowd—we couldn't identify who is who—then no one from the neighbourhood came out. They said they were with us but no one came to save us. When this kand happened, someone was holding a lath* or maybe even a glassy,† or something else. Sixteen-seventeen people from our family had died that time.

Q: Who all were the dead?

HARBANS SINGH: (Asks Shakuntala) How many of your brothers?

SHAKUNTALA: I had six brothers, four passed away.

HARBANS SINGH: Two sisters-in-law; five nieces; one nephew; one father; means a total of sixteen–seventeen people of our family died. Me and my brother-in-law, elder to her (points to Shakuntala) were sitting on the roof in front of our house. Our children were with us, it was cold and we had just one blanket. They came to us and said, 'Bole So Nihaal', I said 'Yes tell us, we are Hindus, we are sitting at our home, we are here at our houses with our children, we are sitting here.' 'Is there any sardar here?' they asked. I replied, 'No there is no sardar here.' When they went away, we were relieved and grateful that we were saved. If anyone would have pointed towards us that we were children of the sardars they would have killed me. Once they went away, we also left that place, anticipating that they may return to kill me, as one of their men stayed behind to watch us.

When I ran away from there, my elder son Vicky was four years old. He ran behind me and fell down the stairs—all were kachcha construction. His legs were injured badly.

SHAKUNTALA: He still has scars of those wounds on his legs.

---

* Lath is a thick lathi, a very thick and solid stick used by weight-lifters or wrestlers.

† A small steel glass—if the attackers couldn't find anything else, they used these to hit people.

HARBANS SINGH: He ran behind me and I pushed him, I said let me go...then I ran away. A-2, no I went to somebody's house in A-4. He also started saying, 'Harbans don't come to our house. They are saying wherever we find a sardar's son, we'll burn that house.' I said, 'Look, I match you all, my hair is already cut.' I was saved there. Then I returned at 9 a.m. back to my house to check if my children and family had been killed or were saved. She wore a neighbour's dhoti; my son had long hair, we opened it and made him wear a cap. Then I took her with me to the same house. I spent the night there. Those people then cut my younger son's hair. They asked me, 'Should we cut his hair?' I told them to cut it. He [the son] took a photo of Baba Nanak, cut his hair and handed it all to me. (Harbans makes a cup of his palms as one does when receiving prashad). Then, I immersed it sacredly in the flowing water. She stayed inside the house.

Then we kept wandering in the streets. On 3rd November, the buses were back on the road. Her massi's daughter stays in Filmistan, so on 3rd November we went to Filmistan.

SHAKUNTALA: We walked. On the way dead bodies were lying. My sister-in-law was killed in front of my eyes, all of them were killed in front of me.

HARBANS SINGH: They pulled her and took her away, said that whoever serves water to her, we'll kill that person too.

SHAKUNTALA: My younger brother was climbing up the stairs with others, they pulled him down by his leg, pulled him down and he was beaten and was bleeding all over. (Weeps)

He had five daughters and one son, he went to Sis Ganj barefoot and prayed for a son. After five daughters he got a son.

HARBANS: His girls were all killed and so was his son.

SHAKUNTALA: One of my brothers, he stays in Jahangirpuri, his wife was killed most horribly: her one leg was pulled by one person and the other leg by another person.

HARBANS SINGH: It was only fifteen days to his marriage.
My brother had an attack, he forgot everything, so he is a little better now. He had no job, nor pension, nothing, poor man; one doesn't know how he survived.

HARBANS SINGH: That time, our condition was pathetic. We were saved, that's it.

SHAKUNTALA: Our house was full, but everything was burnt. My mother's name was Lajwanti Kaur; she was not given any compensation for her loss. They only paid her for those who died but after a lot of struggle.

HARBANS SINGH: The government announces compensation but it is not easy to get it. They say go there, go there...

SHAKUNTALA: We have struggled immensely, ...

Q: Do you expect money from the government? It is thirty years now, all members of your family have expired. You must be doing some work...

SHAKUNTALA: We work...

HARBANS SINGH: We haven't got any job, nor money. The only house we have got is her mother's. In a family where two houses...

Q: After the death of sixteen people, you have got one house?

HARBANS SINGH: Yes, one house. After that, a house that you burn, where sixteen–seventeen people die, didn't it have any stuff? Was there nothing, weren't there any utensils? Haven't we suffered any loss? The government gave us nothing. They say bring us the proof. Where do we get the proof from? We left home without anything. We were barefoot when we left our houses. What we were wearing is what we brought with us.

SHAKUNTALA: I didn't even wear my chunni. My head was bare. I didn't have chappals on my feet. We wandered street after street barefoot.

HARBANS SINGH: Mother died there. She used to keep her gutthi* in

---

* Money folded in a piece of cloth or handkerchief.

her string around the salwar. The neighbours knew she kept her gutthi there.

SHAKUNTALA: They broke her string, she was short…

HARBANS SINGH: To snatch her money, they broke her string. The salwar fell down and our mother stood there naked.

SHAKUNTALA: Then they hit her head.

HARBANS SINGH: There was a deep wound on our mother's head. (Shows with his hand) We began crying and yelling and we said that our mother is dead. But Sache Patshah* saved us.

SHAKUNTALA: My mother finally passed away in the year 2000.

HARBANS SINGH: They took the gutthi away.

SHAKUNTALA: She was lying on the road, naked. They were beating people and throwing them there. All this happened right in front of us, they brought these big barche [spears] (makes a gesture of measuring her arm), knives, someone held a thing, the other person something else… We didn't even cry, we just said 'Hai'.

HARBANS SINGH: We watched from the house we were in. There were windows and ventilating windows with nets. We were seeing through those nets. I saw my mother through that, I couldn't go to help her. Had I gone out, they would have killed me. What could I have done? I couldn't gather the strength to go downstairs.

SHAKUNTALA: No one could gather strength to go. Someone said if you allow them we'll kill every child of theirs, if someone asks for water, pour urine in their mouth (weeps), my sister-in-law came out from inside, she was burning, she fell down and cried 'Water, water'. They said don't give her water, urinate in her mouth, then someone pulled her leg…they killed her horribly. We saw all this with our eyes. If someone asks us, we shut our doors, we are scared someone may kill us if we say something about someone.

HARBANS SINGH: I can't tell you, we were treated very badly, we say that enemies should also not go through what we went through.

---

* The true king i.e. God

SHAKUNTALA: We have never gone to anyone to say anything. If someone asks us if we'll speak something, we tell them, what can we say. We are unable to speak. We begin crying much before we speak.

HARBANS SINGH: Whenever she speaks, she falls sick. A person in front of whom so many people of her family have died, what can that person do? It is thirty years now.

SHAKUNTALA: They killed our little children. They were sleeping inside, no one knew that someone is coming to kill them. (silence, weeping)

Q: Do you have any expectations from the government?

HARBANS SINGH: What can we expect? It is already thirty years past now.

SHAKUNTALA: We have never asked anyone for anything. We work hard and earn to eat. (weeps)

HARBANS SINGH: Those who have killed people are wandering around.

SHAKUNTALA: The day our shop remains closed we have to struggle for a meal.

HARBANS SINGH: If we don't run the shop, what should we do? Where will the children go?

SHAKUNTALA: But we don't get justice, where do we get justice? Those who have killed are wandering free, enjoying.

Q: If they can punish even a few, will you get some some solace....?

SHAKUNTALA: They don't punish anyone...

HARBANS SINGH: If they punish, then the whole problem is resolved, but they don't punish anyone. They didn't give us any money for our loss, nor any compensation. They ask for proofs. Your name doesn't appear in the list. I asked, 'Was I supposed to write the name?'

SHAKUNTALA: When we all gathered in one house, all of them were sleeping together (makes a gesture with her hands as if the children were sleeping in a line). We couldn't be told so as to pull our children out from there (weeps), the children were sleeping inside, they burnt the house.

HARBANS SINGH: They burnt the house, both the houses were burnt. We don't know from where they brought the powder. They would ignite it and throw it in the air as if a cylinder was bursting. I was so stressed, I thought I should go down. How are they killing them in front of me?

Voice in the background: What could a man do all alone?

HARBANS SINGH: Where they killed so many, what could I, one man, do? They will kill me. Then I decided to stay strong at heart. It is evening right now, how should I tell you what I felt. I was scared someone may point at me, someone may tell them, I kept sitting like this (sits bent with folded arms). When the mob went away, when it was at a distance from me, I felt relaxed. Then I was scared they may return, then I thought I shouldn't stay here, what if someone points at me? I thought I should move away from here, they won't spare me and I left that place. I was saved. I thought I'll jump from the back of the house, but doing that I would have fractured my leg or arm.

SHAKUNTALA: (showing a photograph of her house) My mother collected the leftover bones in her lap from here. She searched for them and cremated them.

HARBANS SINGH: We went through the worst. Wish it never happens to any of our enemies ever.

SHAKUNTALA: (showing a photograph of the place where her mother cremated the bones) The collection was this big (points to a height of about four feet with her hand) at the place where it was burnt within the house.

HARBANS SINGH: Show the death certificates.

SHAKUNTALA: I have eleven, the rest are with my brother's children.

'Chaurasi Cannot be Forgotten'

Attar Kaur and Relatives

This interview was recorded on 2 April 2014 at Tilak Vihar Widows' Colony, New Delhi by Ishmeet Kaur Chaudhry. The speakers narrate eyewitness accounts of how their children and family members were killed and how the women around them were captured and raped. It highlights the post-event trauma, focusing on the hopelessness of the survivors and their struggle to get justice. Their struggles make them believe that they will never get justice and they continue to search for a justification for what was illegitimately done to them. They relate the cruelty meted to the values of Sikhism that functions on equality for the entire human race. Despite their traumatic experiences and loss, they continue to pray that such an event never repeats itself, irrespective of caste, religion or region.

AK: I am Attar Kaur. We used to stay in Trilokpuri and after the pogrom we came to stay here.

Q: Since when had you been staying in Trilokpuri?

AK: We used to stay in Kastura Nagar and then we shifted to Trilokpuri. We stayed in Trilokpuri for ten years, then the violence broke out. During the violence my husband died, my nandoi was burnt in the gurdwara, three sons of my jeth were killed, my chacha was killed, my son-in-laws were killed, our sons were killed, many members of our family were killed. We lost our mama, sasur, his sons. The situation was really bad for us.

Q: How many members were there in your family?

AK: I had seven children and my mother-in-law stayed with us. We had employed servants at home, we lived well. We always voted for Indira Gandhi, for Congress; she brought us to Trilokpuri from Kastura Nagar, gave us loan, gave us a house, a plot, we stayed there for ten years. In those years we were flourishing, we had prospered.

Q: What was your husband's occupation?

AK: My husband used to give cycles, autos on rent, (a relative sitting next to her: 'He had a small business.'), if TV didn't work, he repaired it.

Q: So, he had a repair shop.

AK: Yes, repair business of small things. When '84 happened…

Q: How grown up were your children?

AK: My daughter was one month old.

Q: Where is she now?

AK: My daughter is very unhappy, she is married now.

Q: So, your daughter was one month old, where were the other children?

AK: That daughter was very small, other sons were this much (raises her hand to suggest ten to eleven years old); they met a mussalman friend, he took them to their house. What did we know this will happen! He hid them by cutting their hair. My jeth had a son, he was also turned mona,* my sons were made monas. The children were little, they were not saying anything. We went inside, we were hiding. Then, it was evening, we didn't know that there will be such a carnage. When we came out, we saw they were burning them with tyres, they burnt them alive.

Q: Where are your sons now?

AK: My sons? They are here, they ride autos. Two of my sons studied at Baru Sahib.†

Q: How did your sons go to Baru Sahib?

---

* Mona: A Sikh boy who has cut his hair.
† Baru Sahib: Akal Academy, a school for Sikh students near Solan, Himachal Pradesh.

AK: The Sikh forum people sent twenty-two children to Baru Sahib.

Q: Are your boys gursikh* or mona? Did they grow back their hair?

AK: Yes, my boys became gursikh again.

Q: What was the effect on the children?

AK: Oh! A tremendous effect on children...they couldn't get their father's love. Now I have grandchildren, I married off my two sons and three daughters. I worked for twenty-five years and am retired now for the last three years. My son is injured, his heart was operated, my granddaughters are very little (raises her hand to indicate a young girl of about seventeen or eighteen years), she studies in a college.

Q: How did your husband die?

AK: We had a storehouse of ropes, there were many. On finding out that our nandoi was burnt in the gurdwara, he went there. Having gone there, someone told him that his shop was also burnt. When he was running from there, he was burnt...They have done a lot of injustice to Sikhs, bahut julam hua.

Q: Then after that did something happen with you?

AK: What we have seen, the whole day they kept killing our sardars. Then in the evening, all women were collected. Someone was falling on her son. Little children, they were opening their clothes, if it were a boy, they killed him. If a woman fell [down], they tore her clothes, they lit candles at night and took [raped] the daughters and daughters-in-law.

Q: Where are those women now?

AK: Three days, three nights...(pauses) after three days, the military came, we are thankful to it. After they came, they handed our children to us and asked us to take care of them, someone was looting, someone killing, bahut julam hua.

Q: It is thirty years now, justice hasn't been done...

---

* Gursikh: Following the edicts of Sikhism; in this context, it means, 'Are they turbaned, with unshorn hair?'

AK: No justice was done to us, they did nothing. It was our sardars who in chaurasi* took us to the camps, they gave us sewing needles, threads, old salwars, whatever...our sardar brothers helped us a lot. Even now, they help us if someone's daughter is getting married, if there is someone in need, if someone is sick, they help us, our sardar brothers. Bahut julam hua. Rajiv Gandhi said, when a tree falls, the earth shakes. For his mother, the earth shook. But for us, for so many of our brothers who were killed, nothing happened for them (sobs). This Congress, everyone knows how these sardars were killed, women were raped (cries). They know everything. Rahul Gandhi says, 'I am sad for my grandmother'...but...so many mothers were raped, sisters were dishonoured, daughters-in-law were dishonoured... No one saw that? What happened to Sikhs, no one was saving them. They were roaming like beggars, poor fellows, kept wandering for three days with a child, to Chilam Gaon.† Here or there, someone is giving them roti like alms (continuously weeping). Did Congress do less with us? Kitna julam hua.

Q: Did you see what happened to women?

AK: We saw what happened to women (weeps), they were burning like logs. Initially they didn't say anything to children, then they started saying that these Sikhs are snakes and their children, the children of snakes. And they said 'Saliyon, you will be our daughters-in-law now' and that they [the Sikhs] are cutting the chests of Hindus in Punjab and sending here, they were abusing endlessly... Who got this done? Congress did this, Congress knows all, how they raped the women, how they burnt men alive, we feel so sad (weeps bitterly).

Q: If Chaurasi did not happen, then how would your life have been?

---

* Chaurasi: The number 84 in Hindi and Punjabi, which is now used to indicate the anti-Sikh carnage of 1984.
† Chilam Gaon: a village in the suburbs

AK: If Chaurasi didn't happen we would have been happy, we would have been sitting at our homes. One actor, Salman Khan, killed a deer, they take him again and again to the court. We go to Geeta Colony and say, 'He murdered our men, he murdered our men': no one listens to us. Police killed us, they said, 'Sit inside, nothing will happen to you', the government got this done. Even now the situation is such that there are such women who don't have food to eat.

Q: Do you trust the government?

AK: (Shakes her head in negation) I don't trust anyone.

AK's Relative: How can we trust the government? No justice has been done to us in these thirty years.

AK: The rest, what happened with us in Trilokpuri...we say they should have killed us, even the women and the children. They say, 'Forget it'. What? Is Chaurasi forgettable? Chaurasi cannot be forgotten.

Q: How old were you then?

AK: That time I was thirty–thirty-five years. In our family, they marry us at a young age. We had children in the first year of marriage, all children were very small (gestures with her hand to show heights ranging from four to ten years of age). When I shifted here, I used to watch my kids and sleep. Once, one of my children went to someone's house. I told a lady, I can't find my child, I shouted to find him. These women make fun of me even today, they say that this woman counts her children before sleeping. He had gone to watch TV at someone's place. In those times there were no TVs, no cameras.

Q: After 1984, what happened with you in the initial four–five years, those must have been years full of trauma, and to overcome that trauma would have been...

AK: (interrupts) We didn't know anything, our life was written such, we didn't know whether we'll stay alive or we'll die. We didn't know where to go...

Q: Do you feel that your being saved was a blessing?

AK: No, not at all. My daughter-in-law told me that my granddaughter was inquiring about this photo of her grandfather that hangs on the wall. The child asked where is my grandfather? Where did he go? What do we tell these children? Every year he was one of the paanjpyaras.* We found a photo from somewhere and framed it. Our house was looted...who looted our house, who killed us? (Weeps)

Q: When the Sikhs were being attacked, when people were being killed, did you recognize some of those people, who were attacking you all?

AK: We don't know where they all came from. We don't know, people from every caste had joined hands, people from all castes and communities were attacking...

Someone adds in the background: There was no light and water

AK: They had disconnected our light and water. Then they lifted them as if they were lifting animals, as if lifting sheep and goats, they took them in that manner, everyone was saying run, run... no one was saving us.... We were trying to enter the Hindu houses, but they were pushing us out...

A voice in the background: Hindus said that if we hide you, they will kill us too.

AK: Such a Chaurasi should never come in anyone's life. We watch TV and if something happens somewhere, we start crying, our hearts begin to pain.

Q: After Chaurasi there were riots in 2002 in Gujarat, what did you feel then?

AK: (Nods) We felt very bad, we felt very bad...but in Chaurasi,

---

* The paanjpyare represent the five Singhs who were ready to sacrifice their life for the Sikh faith. They symbolically hold the highest position amongst Sikh clergy and are considered sacred.

they [the victims] said 'Rajiv Gandhi, teri boti boti hoyegi'* Rajiv Gandhi got this done, Rajiv Gandhi got this done.

Relative: When there is a mixed riot, it doesn't hurt so much, but when people of a single community are attacked it is very painful. When there are riots then all seven religions participate; Hindus, Muslims, Sikhs, Christians, all are involved.

Q: Sardars involve all religions...

AK: (interrupts) We feel pity on the Sikhs. Sardars are supposed to be kind. They are kind, at present too, they are kind, why not? They are still very kind.

Voice in the background: They can't bear people suffering.

Q: Do you have any bitterness towards any community, towards people of any caste?

ALL TOGETHER: We don't hate anyone.

AK: We say that whoever: Hindu, Muslim, Christian or a Bihari, whoever is at a loss, we feel sad about it. We have endured it, we have endured it

Voice in the background: They are also human beings like us.

AK: We have faced the music, the manner in which our men were burnt, our neighbours, how Trilokpuri was destroyed.

RELATIVE: This is a consequence of politics, not of religion.

AK: Where did the leaders go then? Janta [the public] was also there, where did they go all those three days? They say 'Dilli dilwalon ki hai,'† this was the capital city. Here in this capital city, women, daughters-in-law, daughters were raped, sardars were killed, where were the Hindus then in this Dilli? If someone's wife or daughter is raped in the present, what happens? They show it on the media, nothing happens...

Q: Are you hopeful that justice will be done to you?

---

* 'Rajiv Gandhi you will be cut into pieces'
† Delhi is a city of kind-hearted people.

AK: No, we won't get justice.

Relative: No, we won't.

Q: Did you register the FIR?

AK: Yes, very much, everything. Our files have been documented in Karkarduma, we get summons. I still have the summons.

Relative: Everything…every person's FIR was registered; FIRs were registered in the camp for a full year…

Q: In which year was your FIR registered?

Relative: In 1984 itself…

Q: In 1984?

Relative: Yes, in the camp itself, our FIR was registered in the camp.

AK: We still receive the summons, we go there, to Karkarduma.

Relative: Everyone's FIR is registered. There was a camp, and in the camp, everyone's FIR was registered. They registered loss of home etc.

> *Voice in the background: They took everyone to Kalyan Puri Police station.*

Relative: Whatever they have given us, almost nothing, works on the FIR. Even now, they work on the basis of FIR. Every house has death registration certificates.

AK: Today, it's three years since my retirement. I've been sitting home for three years. My son is a heart patient. My daughter is studying. Everything is on me. I get a pension, what comes of the pension? Nothing.

Q: What were you working as?

AK: I went to a school in Janakpuri, I did a job in Janakpuri, we carried post to offices.

Q: (to the relative) Did you work too?

Relative: I still work, I work at Delhi Secretariat.

Q: There are influential people in the Secretariat, you didn't seek help from them?

Relative: No, I work there. Now I won't ask them for help. I won't say that I don't have anything. You help me.

Q: No help, not of this kind but help for justice...

Relative: No, no one helps this way. They say they have jobs, why do they need help?

AK: Initially, when we came here, trucks full of things, groceries came from Bombay. Thing were inexpensive then, we started working in 1986, we got six or seven hundred rupees as salary. Now the salaries have increased, now we get Rs. 30,000, Rs. 36,000.

Voice from the background: They said, not more than Rs. 25,000.

AK: This was for those who worked in the hospital.

'The Children are Already Watching...'
Cheeja Kaur and her Relatives

This interview was conducted on 2nd April, 2014 by Ishmeet Kaur Chaudhry. Three women together share their experience of the 1984 anti-Sikh violence and its after-effects. They describe how Bura Singh, their family member, was killed, and the struggle for survival that his wife and other relatives have had to face. They describe the present state of affairs and talk about togetherness and how this togetherness enabled them to move on ahead in life. They are extremely worried about their children, and the difficult circumstances in which they live, without decent jobs.
Cheeja Kaur is referred to as CK; Attar Kaur as AK; Kamlesh Kaur as KK and Janak Kaur as JK.

~

There is a photograph of a young Sikh man hanging on the wall with the caption 'Sh. Bura Singh'.

Q: What was his age?

CK: He must be twenty-two or twenty-three years old. This picture is from 1984.

Q: What did he do?

CK: He drove an autorickshaw. He had got a license made from someone, that person had brought a passport-sized photo. Nothing was left in our house, everything was stolen in the loot. That man who made the license came later and gave us this photo. We enlarged it and hung it here.

Q: You didn't have a photo?

CK: Nothing was left in our house, nothing. My daughter was one and a half years old, my son was five–six months old. He must be twenty-two or twenty-three years old, not more than this.

I was twenty years old, though my age was registered as more than that. I was twenty years old, very young. This sister-in law (points to the relative) has seven children; she got my marriage fixed with him.

Q: Where do you belong to?

CK: We are from Jamnapaar, all of us were together. We were from Trilokpuri, my sister-in-law was from Mangol Puri. Two of my brothers were killed, my brother-in-law, my husband, my nandoi—all members were killed.

Q: So, you were twenty years old then…

CK: Yes, not more than that… He was just two years elder to me, we didn't have much difference in age.

Q: What was your husband's name?

CK: His name was late Bura Singh, it has been written on the photograph (points towards the photograph).

Q: So, you got this photograph from somebody and got it framed.

CK: Yes, we got it from somebody and then framed it. Me and my sister-in-law, we went. Her husband worked in DTC and my chacha-sasur also worked there. Even they didn't have any photograph, both of us brought it from there.

Q: Why did you go to get the photograph?

CK: (Responds promptly) Because we didn't have one. Our children, grandchildren should know him.

Q: Do you think your children should be told what happened with you?

CK: We now tell our children what happened with us. Now our children have grown up. My elder daughter is handicapped. Now the children weep profoundly, they didn't get their father's love. A lot happened with us.

Q: Your life must have changed completely…

CK: Yes, our lives completely changed.

Q: Can you share with us, what the children feel now?

CK: We don't share details with children so that they don't feel too much, they don't get a shock, and they don't do anything. That's why we don't tell them much. But the children know, now they are grown up.

Q: But they might get to know the details from outside.

CK: They know everything, they know everything. They are all Chaurasi wale,* this colony is full of Chaurasi wale.

KK: In the gurdwara there are photos of all those killed. It is Shaheedan da Gurdwara.†

Q: Is it the Singh Sabha Gurdwara?

CK: The photographs are there in the gurdwara. (Wipes her tears)

Q: Is it the Singh Sabha Gurdwara?

CK: The gurdwara is here in the colony. It is our gurdwara.

Q: Are you aware of what happened to your husband?

CK: There was a gurdwara in 36 block. They had burnt people of that side. Our people saw that they came in a bus. They began hurting people, they came into our houses. The police came and said, get inside the houses, there won't be any fight. They sent them to the side and then took our weapons from our homes, asking us to hand them over as there wouldn't be any fight. They took our weapons. We didn't know that this would happen to us, that they would kill us in our houses.

Q: What kind of weapons did people have?

CK: They had weapons, like everyone had kirpans.

Q: Were there sufficient weapons, how many weapons were there with people?

CK: They had weapons. We were many people, they had attacked and encountered them, but the police came and took away everything.

Q: No, but my question is that does a common man, like us, have weapons at home, and how many?

---

* People who were affected by the 1984 pogrom.
† Literally translated as 'Gurdwara of the Martyrs'.

CK: No, Women also encountered the mob, they stoned the public that came to kill us. Their attempt was unsuccessful, but later the government got it done again in every house.

KK: We trusted the police.

CK: The police got us killed. We trusted the police.

Q: Would you like to say something through, this medium, that is, in this recording which you'd like to convey to the government?

CK: We want justice. For those who died, those who were killed, we want justice. The government is not doing justice to us. No one will do justice to the Sikh.

Q: Do you think that you'll get justice in your life time?

CK: Thirty years have passed, we kept watching. It is not just one day, it is thirty years. Many widows have expired. At least fifty to sixty widows have died. Some of them are left, some old women are left, like our mother. She died suffering for her sons, for us, for her sons-in-law. Her mother-in-law has passed away, (points to her relative and then to another woman and says) we are sisters, we are cousins.[*] We had four brothers, we are four sisters, sons of two sisters were killed. We are four sisters who were widowed, four of my sisters-in-law[†] were widowed.

Q: So, there must be very few men in your family?

CK: There are no men now. My chacha's two sons, and my two brothers, the count is equal. Five from my chacha's house and five from my parent's house were killed. We were one family, what is left now? Poor chacha expired, chachi expired, my mother expired. My mother and her mother were sisters. (Points towards another relative).

KK: Five from a family, six or seven from different families.

CK: My jeth, nandoi, they killed families, full families...

---

[*] i.e. chacha's daughter.

[†] i.e. Brothers' wives.

Q: Do you want to say anything for your children, maybe if someone sees this recording after twenty-twenty-five years.

CK: Our hearts are so cold now, that we don't want to say anything to anyone. We cry, fill our eyes with tears, and give ourselves some relief by crying.

KK: What we have gone through in these thirty years…we sat on so many dharnas, no one listened to us. … Only the government can do something. … We have spent days on dharna and nights on the roads.

Q: Like now you have lived so many years, life is drawing to an end…

CK (Interrupts): Our life is finished, we have grown old earlier than it would have happened because of stress and tension. My age is not as old as my body is.

KK: What more is suffering than what we have seen? The person whose entire family is finished, neither is her husband alive, no one is around. How much can a mother earn for her children? A little girl widowed in an early age, how will she look after her children. Neither children, nor brother…no one.

CK: If a brother would have been left, there could have been some solace. But if every man around you expires… We were widows, our sisters-in-law were widows, there aren't enough jobs…

KK: Our children don't have enough jobs.

CK: How much can you earn in a private job?

AK: What is the life of those people who have lost their families, their paternal as well as maternal families? If there is a single widow in any family, she feels that her family members are there, her sasuralwala and mayekewala* are there for her. Now in our situation, where do we go, to whose house? We are living in our house and we are dying in our houses. No brothers, no in-laws, my mother and father would suffocate in their pain. Where could we have gone?

---

* Husband's family and her own family.

KK: I had seven children, I was seven months' pregnant in 1984, he was born later. We married at a very young age. In those days, once a child was one and a half years old, another was born. I was married when I was fifteen years old.

JK: In Rajasthan, there was a tradition to marry girls at a young age, between fourteen to fifteen years. If they didn't do so, they couldn't find a match.

CK: Look at our age now, are we that old to be retired?

AK: When Muslims turned us out from Pakistan, they didn't kill us. They made us sit in the ships.

CK: My mother told us.

AK: They didn't kill us, they turned us out alive. Mussalmans didn't kill us.

CK: Now, it is the government who did this to us—no one came from outside. They did so in a manner that we cannot forget.

AK: Congress did it. Vehicles full of people.

JK: They say Hindus are brothers, Hindu-Sikh are brothers. So a brother kills a brother? If brother only kills, then who will save us.

CK: Is there anyone to help us?

AK: If Hindus only kill us then, what will remain of us? What will remain in the country?

Q: Would you like to give a message to the succeeding generations, the new generations would hardly know anything about 1984. So would you like to give any message to those children?

CK: Our children are already watching…

Q: That is right. Your children are watching, but people of my generation also do not understand 1984, as we were children or not yet born when the event occurred. Children born now will have no clue about the event…

AK: To children, we say, don't trust the police. Don't trust the government, the government got them killed, the government betrayed us. Now it is Janta [BJP], Janta also knows but…

KK: Our children know everything. The moment they turn seven–eight years old, they get to know everything. As we go to sit on dharna, our children also come and sit with us. They realize what is happening with us and what their mothers are going through.

JK: Is there any hatred in the hearts of the children?

AK: Yes, there is hatred. Towards the government, yes. My daughter's son has a lot of hatred. He says 'The manner in which they killed our nana, if we find them, we'll also kill them the same ways.

JK: Yes, there is a lot of hatred, this happened to us for three days.

KK: We left everything of ours—shops, houses, everything

JK: … If someone comes to kill you, won't you hate that person? Won't we get angry that they have come to kill us?

BSW: My sister-in-law is suffering from so many diseases, sugar and whatnot. Her eyes have been operated twice. Nobody was left in her family, she lost all. I became a widow, her younger brother-in-law was killed.

JK: I recently met with an accident and my body is damaged.

BSW: My younger brother died.

JK: When I see myself, when I see her, my sister-in-law, she and I have experienced the same, our suffering is the same…don't I feel sad?

KK: How have we lived? How have we remained alive? We are alive seeing each other, watching each other, empathizing that 'I am a widow, she is also a widow.' We talked together, we remained together, there is no one in our family to share our suffering. We have lived supporting, seeing each other. We brought up our children this way, seeing each other. Watching and seeing each other, we are tending our households. Someone's child is employed and in someone's house there is not even a single person who earns. I have three daughters. Amongst my sisters, one has died, two more are widows. All discussing together about all the men who died and no one is left to take care of the families.

Q: When you sit on dharna, do you get a response?

KK: It is only when we sat on dharna that they declared a compensation. But once they declare any compensation, they don't provide that compensation. Only when we sit on dharna they give us something.

JK: We sit for two–two days together. We say give jobs to our children, we talk about employment.

KK: All children are unemployed…no one is employed in Trilokpuri.

JK: Our children don't get jobs, they are growing old and they are thirty years old now. They don't have jobs.

AK: When we were in the camp, the government gave us ten–ten thousand rupees. Our houses were badly looted, so we got five–five thousand.

KK: I got two thousand.

CK: Arre, I got one thousand. Can you buy things for the house in one thousand rupees?

AK: After that, when I came to Trilokpuri, I got ten thousand and then after a year three lakhs and thirty thousand and then three and a half lakhs. I received a total of seven lakhs.

CK: In thirty years…this much amount is insufficient for the weddings of your children too.

AK: What would come of such money? Now they say, we'll get five lakhs. They have got the forms filled…we don't know what will come of it.

Q: Do you need such money?

AK: What are we to do with such money? We ask for jobs; such handsome and good boys are driving autos.

CK: What do we do? Do we fetch daily food or send our children to study?

Q: What about the Sikh bodies, like the gurdwara committees, did they do something for you, like setting up of schools, or fetching jobs for your children? Did you get any help from the Sikhs?

JK: The gurdwara walas helped us, they helped the women to get jobs, they took the responsibility of helping us.

AK: The outside Sikhs helped us.

CK: I will tell, there is Sardar Dr Samlok Singh, he was in Hari Nagar Deen Dayal Urban Hospital. There was another Dr Lakhani in Safdarjung Hospital. They helped all of us, we ate food because of them.

AK: Now they are sitting in Baru Sahib. His wife was also a doctor of the eyes. They have left their jobs and are serving in Baru Sahib now. Two of my sons have studied from there. Now they have been polished, he is very good now.

CK: They worked very hard with us…even our brothers may not have been able to work so hard as they did. They took the responsibility of our children, that they need to stand on their own feet.

AK: We feel if someone can support our grandchildren, we'd like to send them too.

Q: Do you think that the children who went to Baru Sahib, their life was saved? They didn't get spoilt, so it was good that they went to Baru Sahib?

AK: Yes, I had sent them as small children (raises her hand to about three feet to indicate their height).

Q: They were little children, so you must have missed them around you?

ALL TOGETHER: We missed them for sure, yes.

'WE ALWAYS GAVE THE VOTE TO CONGRESS'
PHANDA SINGH

Interviewed by
UMA CHAKRAVARTI

Phanda Singh was interviewed in 1985, a year after the violence. This interview was first published in Delhi Riots: Three Days in the Life of a Nation *by Uma Chakravarti and Nandita Haksar (1987). His interview draws a connection between forced migration during Partition and in 1984. He narrates how he escaped from the mob and, while he was on the verge of being killed, he recognized familiar faces in the mob. He also talks about feeling a sense of utter betrayal by the Congress leaders.*

Phanda Singh is an old man who does not know his age but looks as if he might be about seventy years old. He remembers Partition very clearly and described it vividly, as if he was talking about a recent event in his life. He sees his life as one long struggle for survival, marked by endless migration which appeared to have ended finally in Trilokpuri. Following the riots, in which he lost two of his adult sons, he has moved once more and he lives now in Tilak Vihar where he runs small tea shop.

Q: Since you are one of the older Labaniya* Sikhs here, do you remember your days in Sind and can you tell us about your migration to India?

A: We lived in Sind in the villages around the small town of Shikarpur. We were farmers who had some land which we farmed. We didn't

---

* Labaniya or Labana Sikhs are originally from Sind and do not speak Punjabi. They are mostly engaged in carpentry, iron work or charpai making. There was a heavy concentration of Labaniya Sikhs in the resettlement colonies of Trilokpuri and Sultanpuri.

know anything about the Partition or the beginning of riots. There was no trouble in our area. The people around would not let anything happen to us. Independence came and went, but we stayed on as before. Even after Muslims from India came to Sind and described the riots, our neighbours and other villagers did not do anything to us. They told those who had come from this side that we were their brothers. We stayed on. Then Gandhiji was killed. After that, Pandit Nehru came to Sind. He told us, 'I have come to take you to that side. Come there and we will give you land to farm.' So we agreed to move, all of us were taken to a camp at Shikarpur, then from there to Hyderabad—not the Hyderabad of this side but that of Sind. From there we went to Karachi in a train, then they put us in a jahaj and took us to Bombay. It took us four days to reach Bombay. We lived there in a camp but no one liked it. Some people left. My brother went away but I stayed on.

Q: How old were you when all this took place?

A: I was a jawan. I was engaged but not yet married. Our mother came with us three boys.

After a while Pandit (Nehru) came to us again and he told us to go to Rajasthan. So we went. Some went to Alwar, some to Bharatpur, and some to Hanumangarh. They gave us land.

Q: How much?

A: Eight bighas, ten bighas, sixteen bighas.

Q: How much land did you get?

A: I got sixteen bighas.

Q: Just for you or all of you together (the three brothers)?

A: No, just for me. They told us to make our names separate since we were all adults and would have our own families.

Q: Was the land barani (dry) or was it irrigated?

A: Some of it was irrigated. Some of these were lands which had been left behind by the Muslims who had gone away. We farmed our land and we lived comfortably. After some time the families grew. Then it was not enough for everyone. Some began to weave charpais, some did carpentry. They left the villages and went to Alwar, then to Delhi. As they did well and earned well, more of us came to Delhi. I also went, my brother also came. We lived in Kasturba Nagar first. Then during the Emergency Pandit said, 'Go to Trilokpuri.'

Q: Pandit? Which Pandit?

A: Indiraji, Pandit's daughter told us to go to Trilokpuri. She gave us plots, we built houses and we lived there. We always gave the vote to Congress because Pandit brought us here and then Indira gave us plots. Why did they kill us? We always gave the vote to Congress—even when there was Janata. Indiraji gave everybody shelter, not just the Hindus. Why should they kill us? Those who killed Indira are still alive whereas we have been destroyed.

Who did this? It should be found out who did this. Do they want the Sikh seed (beej) to be destroyed? It is not so easy to destroy the Sikh (beej). They will grow again—Aurangzeb could not destroy the Sikhs even though the Guru's son was killed. Still the Sikhs raised their heads again. If it was not for the Sikhs there would have been no Hindustan today. Do you know the Meos? They are Muslims now but they were Hindus before. Even now they wear the langot (i.e. dhoti) like Hindus. Like that everyone would have become Muslims if it had not been for the Sikhs.

Q: What happened on that day? When did you hear about Mrs Gandhi's assassination?

A: We heard in the afternoon or in the evening. We felt bad.

Q: Did you feel scared when you knew that Sikhs had killed her?

A: Why should we feel scared? We didn't do anything. Two security guards had killed her.

Q: Did you distribute sweets? It is said that people got angry because sardars distributed sweets and attacked them.

A: *Nahi, hamne aisa kuch nahi kiya* (We did not do anything like that.)

Q: Even Rajivji says that only where Sikhs celebrated by distributing sweets the killing was very bad.*

A: Tell Rajiv to come here. We will tell him everything ourselves.

Q: Did you hear of anyone who distributed sweets?

A: Some say that a Sikh in Block 28 distributed sweets. We did not see it but some people say so. But the people around ate the sweets. (*Kha liya. Sab ne kha liya, kisine mana nahi kiya.*) Why did they eat it if they did not like it?

Q: What happened next day?

A: In the morning, some people were preparing to go to work. But I was not going anywhere. There is a TV in the neighbourhood. They said come and watch. I went to see there were many people watching.

Q: What did you see?

A: Many people came, *do-teen sardar bhi the*. (There were one or two sardars also.)

Q: What else did you see?

A: We saw Amitabh Bachchan. He came with Sanjay's son. Then he went away.

Q: When did you first hear that there was trouble in the area?

A: There is a Sikh who has a chakki (flourmill) opposite our house. He closed his chakki and started to go to home. But at about 10 or so. He took a bus and was going home. But at Patparganj some people stopped the bus and said *koi sardar hai—sardaron ko mar rahe hain, unko utaardo* (Any sardar here? They are attacking sardars, let them get off). So, he got off and returned back to our mohalla. We told him don't be scared, just stay quietly here. Still we were not worried. Then after some time we heard that big crowd had burnt the gurdwara of Block 36.

Q: Did you have your own gurdwara in your block also?

---

* Interview with M.J. Akbar in *Sunday*, 10-16 March 1985.

A: *Aalishaan gurdwara tha hamara, sab jaladiya.* (We had a grand gurdwara. Everything was burnt). When we heard about Block 36 then we started getting worried. Some people hid. There was the house of Muslims who went away after giving the key to Pandit who told me to hide. I hid there and he locked it from outside and went off. The other men took their kirpans and stood outside in the gali to prevent the mob from coming. I did not see anything after I hid until I came out later.

Q: Did you see anyone among the people whom you recognized before you hid?

A: There were Sukhpal and Rampal who live in our neighbourhood.

Q: Were yours neighbours, people from the blocks, in the mob?

A: Yes, there were some of our block people. Some of the Gujars from Chilla village were there. They were leading the mob. The mob was saying *maro, kato sardaron ko* (kill the sardars). There was lot of noise—people crying, running up and down the lanes. The crowd hit the men with iron rods and then put kerosene on them and set them on fire. I kept on hiding—I didn't know where others were. My two sons, grandchildren, daughters-in-law, wife, I didn't know anything about them. After about a few hours Pandit (a brahman of the neighbourhood) came and opened the door. Some women came in to hide and they said— 'Baba, *tumhara Labh Singh khatam ho gaya* (Baba your Labh Singh is dead)'. They told me how he lay in the gali burning for a long time. He asked for water, for his mother and father. When the mob went off the women gave him water. He was a brave and courageous man, big and strong, so he did not give up easily. He kept struggling. After a time, the mob came back and beat him with the rods again. Only then he died. Even then I did not know about my other son. He was still alive, hiding somewhere. Only next morning they found him at 4 a.m. They pulled him out and they killed him.

Now both my adult sons are no longer there, see this girl. She is the first one's widow—she is ill. Because she is ill and had to have a child they came to stay with me in Block 32. They lived in Block 36. If they had not come my son might still have been alive. I am old, my eyes are weak but for the sake of these helpless people I have to be strong. If a man has sons and nothing else, he still has everything. A man without sons is without his arms. He can do nothing. He is like cripple.

Q: Many of your people say that there were chudas and chamars in the mob who did the killing and looting?

A: There were all sorts of people—*Muslim bhi the, Pandit bhi the, baniye bhi the* (There were Muslims, there were brahmans, there were banias also).

Q: *Baniye bhi the* (There were banias also?)

A: *Baniye bhi the—jisne kabhi billi nahin mari ho wo aadmi maar rahe the* (Yes, people who had never attacked even a cat were now killing men).

Q: How did you managed to escape?

A: In the night the Pandit came back. He opened the door and he told us to run away. But where could we go? There was danger everywhere. I went to my house—everything was looted and burnt. Opposite my house there was a jhuggi with a charpai. I went and hid under the charpai and remained there. In the morning again the mobs came. They were searching for any Sikhs still left alive. They came to the jhuggi. Some people said—*yahan koi nahi hai, sab bhag gaye hain* (there is no one here, everyone has run away). But some of the people insisted on searching. They dragged me out and were going to attack me but some boys of our locality said, is *baba ko nahin maarne denge* (we won't let you kill this baba). Then the crowd pushed me and went away. I tried to run away. I went in the direction of Patparganj. Many women and children were also escaping. After a while I met this daughter-in-law and my younger boys. We all tried to escape with some other women. I was the only man among them. They told me to walk like a blind man with my hand on the shoulder of one of the women. But there was still a danger to me and my youngest son who looked like an adolescent. Then someone said, 'Put on girls' clothes for him.' So he dressed in a salwar kameez. Mobs were roaming all the time. When we reached Patparganj we met a chamaar who was a farmer. He gave us some water to drink and he saved us. I told him, 'See my daughter-in-law is ill. She cannot walk'. So he gave us a cart to go in. His wife came with us. On both sides, he put his jawan sons with dandas who walked beside the cart. The old chamar had been a *sarkari karmchari* (government employee). Now he had some land which he farms. He was from Kasturba Nagar and he knew that we were all from there originally. They walked with us for a while. Then we came down the bridge and there he left us. We walked some more distance and reached near Chilla gaon (village) and stopped there, some young men saw us and they said amongst themselves, 'We will take some these girls in the night. This one is nice and also this one.' We were frightened and helpless. But then some old people from Chilla gaon came. They gave us channa and roti to eat. They told us to sleep in the temple and they did not let anything happen to us. But next morning there was still trouble since more mobs came. The villagers could not save us anymore. They told us to go. We didn't know what to do and where to go. So we thought, 'Let us go to our homes, let us die in our homes', and so we went back to Trilokpuri. Then we saw some policemen. For three days there was no police to help us. Now there were two or three. They told us to go to the thana. We were taken there. Then the army came and we were safe. SHO of the Kalyanpuri thana was good. He saved us.

Q: How did all this *maar kaat* (killings) take place?

A: This is the work of Sukhpal, Rampal and Ashok doctor. (We only gave him votes. See how he treated us afterwards!) and H.K.L. Bhagat. Bhagat is behind it. If he had said anything, nothing could have happened to us. Who elected him? We—but how did he treat us?

Q: How did Bhagat do anything?

A. *Uske ishare ke bina kuch nahin ho sakta tha* (Without a sign from him nothing could have happened). Can anything happen to anyone in my house in my presence without my knowing or doing anything? He knew everything, he gave the order. Later he got bail for some of the arrested people. Why did he do that? He came to see us in the camp. Everyone was angry. The women drove him away after abusing him. He never showed himself to us again.

Bring a tape recorder.* I will tell you everything and you tell the others what happened.

Q: What happened to all of you after the riots?

A: My daughter-in-law got these flats here in Tilak Vihar. We came here. I have opened a small tea shop here. The Sis Ganj Gurdwara gives them a pension of two hundred and fifty rupees each. Last month someone stole all the money in the gurdwara itself. I don't know how it happened. Somehow we are all managing. This one is ill. She has fits—the bhoot (spirit) has got into her. When it gets inside she says that a Muslim man is wanting to take her away.

Q: Did this start after the riots?

A: No, she has been ill for the last three or four years. She always says this. She also cannot walk properly.†

---

* The electricity had broken down, so we could not record the interview on the tape recorder.

† The daughter-in-law is a pleasant looking-person who smiles often although her eyes look sad. She appears to have a good equation with people around her. There is some controversy between the NEM volunteers and Phanda Singh about her treatment. Phanda Singh took her to the hospital where bone TB appears to have been diagnosed. But he is now trying a Sikh doctor who will cure her through a combination of medicine and faith. NEM volunteers are trying to persuade him to continue the hospital treatment which will require her to be put into a plaster. Phanda Singh cannot quite accept this because a male doctor will put the cast on.

Q: Were you here when Longowal* came?

A: Yes, I was here. He spoke well. He told us we must be united and we must make aman (peace). I heard him in the gurdwara also.

Q: What did he say there?

A: *Wahan bhi acha bola* (He talked well there also). *Yahi bola ke auraton keliye kuch karna hoga* (He said we must do something for the women).

Q: *Suna hai wahan kuch aur bola* (It is said that he had a different tone there?)

A: *Yahi bola, theek bola* (He said this only, it was alright). *Patiala main bhi raja ne acha bola* (The Raja [Capt. Amrinder Singh] also spoke well in Patiala).

Q: How did you go to Patiala?

A: We went to Amritsar to Harmandir Sahib and then to Patiala. I took my daughter-in-law.

Q: Did you go for the first time?

A: Yes, we went for the first time. On our way back, we returned via Patiala.†

Q: Was it wrong for Beant Singh and Satwant Singh to kill Mrs Gandhi?

A: Yes, it was wrong. Very wrong. They should be punished. Why are they alive and so many of us dead?

Q: There have been many bomb explosions recently.‡ What do you think about them?

A: They are bad. Very bad.

---

* The President of the Akali Dal.

† The Sindhi Sikhs had participated in a tradition which they had not been a part of before, for the first time.

‡ This is in reference to a spate of terrorist bombings across the country, which were widely associated in public perception at the time with the agitation for a separate Khalistan for the Sikhs.

Q: It is said that some Sikhs were taking revenge for the November killing of the Sikhs. What do you feel about revenge?

A: How do we know that it was the Sikhs? No names have been mentioned in the newspapers. Full enquiry should be done about who is doing these things.

Q: A few names have come. It appears that they are Sikhs.

A: If it was Sikhs doing it why should they use bombs? Anyone can get killed by bombs—even Sikhs. In buses and trains all travel, not just non-Sikhs. Also if it was done by Sikhs would they not have done so in Block 32? Trilokpuri, where the maximum number of Sikhs have been killed, where the neighbours themselves killed and where no Sikhs are now left? The bombs would have been put there if it was the work of Sikhs. It was even thrown into the house of Sikhs in Tilak Nagar and injured two small Sikh girls in the house. This is not the work of Sikhs.

Q: Even if you don't agree that it was Sikhs, just suppose (*kahne keliye*) it was Sikhs seeking revenge. What do you say?

A: It was wrong, innocent people were killed. Things get worse not better with acts like this. It goes on getting worse and poor people like us only suffer. The others who do it are safe.

Q: You were angry with Bhagat, Sukhpal and others. Suppose the Sikhs had taken revenge against them and not against innocent people would it have been alright then?

A: No, people should not do these things. There should be *kanooni karwahi* (judicial proceedings). Only after doing that should those who are found guilty be punished. *Ham to kahte hain jaanch hona chahiye—uske baad koyi bhi uske khilaaf kanoon ke adhar pe karwahi chalani chahiye. Nahin to koi kisi ko maarega aur uske badle mein koi phir maarega, isse aman nahi ban sakta* (I say that there should be an enquiry. After that the guilty should be punished according to the law, otherwise someone will kill someone else and they will in their turn kill others ... we cannot have peace like that.

'Badshah...Maintain Our Honour'
BALWANT SINGH GRANTHI

Interviewed by
KULBIR and ANIL

During the carnage, many gurdwaras were burnt. This interview in May 1985 with Granthi Balwant Singh, touches on sentiments towards religion, and particularly the desecration of the Guru Granth Sahib. It also discusses Sikh political issues, the role played by Bhindranwala and the issue of Khalistan. The granthi had a narrow escape during the pogrom; he discusses the sympathetic responses of the Sikhs themselves to the assassination of Indira Gandhi, contrary to the rumours that Sikhs had celebrated her death. The interview was originally published in Delhi Riots: Three Days in the Life of a Nation *by Uma Chakravarti and Nandita Haksar (1987).*

Balwant Singh is the granthi at the gurdwara of BC Block in Shalimar Bagh. He has very little formal learning but can quote from the scriptures finding examples for his contemporary experiences. He has been trying to get compensation for the loss of his personal property which was lying within the precincts of the gurdwara when it was attacked, but has met with little success. Kulbir got to know him while Balwant Singh was trying to file his compensation claims.

Q: Let us start the interview with your recounting of events from the 31st of October. At what time did you come to know of the assassination of Indira Gandhi?

A: I came to know the news at about two o'clock on the 31st. Behind our place there was a children's function and one of the children came up to me and said, 'Uncleji, the Prime Minister of the country, Indiraji, is dead.'

Q: What did you feel at the time when you first heard the news?

A: I felt very shocked when I heard the news…she was doing good things for the country and I felt the support of the nation had gone… I felt all this very deeply but I could not say anything or do anything… I felt constrained (*main majboor tha*).

Q: What did you feel about what might happen?

A: What could I feel? What had to happen had happened (*jo honasi ho gayasi*). What was going to happen, no one could say. Only parmatma knew what was going to happen.

Q: Did you come to know immediately that the killers of Indira Gandhi were two Sikhs?

A: No, I didn't know that, I didn't know anything…

Q: What exactly was the news you got?

A: I just got the news that someone had shot her and that she was in the Medical Institute.

Q: When did you come to know that she had been assassinated by her guards who were Sikhs?

A: I got to know this at about eight o'clock in the evening when I came out of the gurdwara after doing the kirtan. When I came out, the sant said that the assassins of Indira Gandhi are Sikhs. At the same time, I also heard that the Sikhs were being attacked around the Medical Institute, that they were being pulled out of vehicles and beaten up and the vehicles were being destroyed. The thought occurred in my mind that in the heat of the moment there could be violence. If in return (for the assassination) Sikhs are being attacked it is wrong. Because if one Sikh has killed, it doesn't mean that any passing Sikh should be attacked, that their vehicles be destroyed or that they should be burnt or killed.

We slept that night without any clear idea about what was or was not happening. Next morning, we had to take out the *prabhat-pheri* (procession) for Guru Purab (festival of Guru Nanak's birthday). Our secretary said that the prabhat-pheri must be absolutely calm (shaant). We should not have the usual band-baja and there should be no celebration. He said, '*Afsos karna hai, afsosnal chup karke chalo*' (we must grieve and show our grief by being silent). After returning we should read the Shabad (holy verses) and perform the ardas (prayer). There should be no gana-bajana (singing or using the band) on the way.

We went on the prabhat-pheri and returned quietly and did the ardas. After that I said to the sewadar, 'Let us make some tea and have it.' We made the tea and had just drunk it and put the cups down without knowing anything much, but in the meanwhile the gurdwara had been encircled. We were just sitting there and thinking sorrowfully about the death of Prime Minister of the country (*desh de pradhan mantra poore ho gaye ne*), it is not right, whoever has killed her has done wrong. We also thought we don't know what, nuks (wrong) there was. It is possible that they had some dukh in their hearts that as a result of that dukh they killed her. We had just put down our cups when we discovered that the gurdwara had been encircled. They were saying, 'Burn the gurdwara, kill them they have killed our mother.' We closed the doors and bolted them and took shelter behind it.

Q: Was this the room?

A: It was the sewadar's room. It was good that I was not in my room at that time because that faces the street. My children had gone to the pind (village). I was alone and had gone to the sewadar's room and just put down the teacup when we were encircled. Abuses were being shouted, no one's mother or sister was spared (by the abusers) and they were saying, 'Burn the gurdwara, kill the Sikhs; the Sikhs have killed our mother.' We closed the doors and the windows. The window panes were broken with stones, there was a makeshift wall at the back which was also broken and the stones started coming in our direction. The doors were broken. After that I tried to show courage and thought that I should come out—maybe I could request some of them—who knows somebody might feel compassion in their hearts…

Q: You hadn't been attacked till then?

A: No, we were inside till then. We (two other sewadars and I) came out. We came out and I folded my hands and pleaded, 'But what is our fault? Why are we being attacked? If Beant Singh and Satwant Singh have killed, take revenge against them. Why are you attacking the whole community (quam) and burning the gurdwara?' But they continued to shout abuses and said, 'Maro, maro!' Stones started falling on me. Then I ran out... There is nursing home called Saraswati Nursing Home nearby. I ran towards it thinking that I might get treated there and get my head wound stitched as my head was bleeding...

Q: So, you had been attacked by them?

A: Yes, but I didn't fall down...

Q: What were you attacked with?

A: Someone had an iron rod in his hand, the kind that is used as support to lay the roof. They used that to hit me. Initially I didn't know that I was bleeding but then I realized that my whole head was wet with the blood from my wound. I ran to the nursing home hoping that I'd get some help and that they'd stitch up the wound. The nursing home is nearby and is run by a lady. The doors were closed. I knocked on the door repeatedly and called out, 'Doctor Sahib, open the door, my head is wounded I have been attacked by these people (*mera sar phat gaya hai mujhe logo ne mara hai*). I tried to get into the house when one person said 'sala, run off otherwise we will kill you.' I then ran into the gali behind this gurdwara. I didn't know which direction to go, everywhere there seemed to be attacking people, death seemed to be everywhere.

Q: How many people were there?

A: About five to six hundred people. The entire compound of the gurdwara and the streets around it were filled with people. This gali was also full of people. I ran straight, away from this gali. As I was running straight, a bania from the gali picked up a stone, even though I knew him as someone to exchange greetings with. Behind me were other attackers. I didn't know what to do but there was a gap in the wall and I ran past it to a sardarji's kothi (house).

When I got there, I was seen by Hindu tenants who live upstairs. The sardar was the owner and lived downstairs and on the second floor also there were sardars. The Hindus from the upstairs had come down and he opened the gate. They know me. He saw me bleeding and said, 'Go upstairs quickly.' I went upstairs and took shelter with them. In the meanwhile the sewadar who was hurt also reached there on his own. And there was one other person who was also bleeding and he too came running to his house. They didn't know that I was already there.

After that the Hindu gentleman, Shri Dharamweer, sent his son to get medicines from the chemist. He got some capsules, which they gave us. There were lots of wounds, on the head, on the legs, feet and back. Haldi (turmeric) was applied on the wounds and warm milk with haldi was given to us to drink. We had the tablets too. We stayed there on the 1st. We could not go out at all and we could not even look outside. The curtains were drawn and the inside of the house was completely blotted out. Not even any indication of light was allowed to show.

Q: Wasn't the sardarji's house attacked?

A: Yes, it had been attacked but the Hindu tenant Shri Dharamveer had gone down. They have a very large family. There are two brothers who live with their families and they had all gone down. The name plate of the sardar had been broken by them earlier and when the mob came to attack the house they quickly said that the house was theirs. The attackers said that if that was so they should say, 'Indira Gandhi ki jai'. So he said, 'Indira Gandhi ki jai'. Then they taunted him, 'Have you worn bangles that you are saying that the sardar's house is yours?' The tenant said, 'No no. This house is mine.' Again attackers said, 'Have you worn bangles?' The tenant said, 'Baba, think that I have worn bangles. You are forcing me to say that the house is not mine, but it is my house.' So then the attackers went off.

On the night of the 2nd, I was awake thinking what bad times had fallen on us. People are laughing at us; the Hindus in the gali were ridiculing us. They were saying that attacks are taking place on the sardars because the sardars had killed Indira. See how their gurdwaras have been burnt, their factories and houses are burnt and so many of them have been killed. I thought to myself about what times we had been led into by the parmatma. Did this mean that if we lived it would have to be as Hindus? That we could not take the name of Sikhism? Lying there I did an ardas to the Guru, saying 'Badsha (lord), you have given us the Sikh form (swaroop), you have given us the beard. Uphold the honour of this beard. Maintain our honour for us. I don't think I can exist as a mona, cutting my hair and walking about in trousers. I hated the pant and shirt.' (There was a time when I used to wear it but for a long time I had not used such clothes.) I thought 'parmatma if you have to make me into a mona it is better that you call me to your-self'. The wise men of old had said 'If man lives he should live well, with dignity.' So I thought to myself that it doesn't mean that because all this has happened one should give up. If one were to cut the hair and be kicked around what kind of existence would that be? It would be useless.

I had been thinking thoughts like this. I dropped off to sleep. I had just dropped off when the people I was staying with woke me and said, 'These people are saying that you have a transmitter. They say "We have found a transmitter at the gurdwara and we have found out from it that you have one here too."'

Q: When did his happen?

A: On the 2nd night.

Q: Who were they?

A: The people who were keeping guard in the area, the ones who went around shouting 'jagte raho'. So, the gentleman [asking about the] transmitter. I said, 'If I had a transmitter it means that while you sleep comfortably I would be keeping awake at night using it. What salary do we get? If I had a transmitter I would be doing something big. We do sewa (service) sweeping the floors twice a day. We clean the gurdwara and by this service we are bringing up our children.'

Our host said, 'What can I do? The people in the gali are saying that you have a transmitter.' Then he went downstairs and said that we had no transmitter, and that he had just verified from us that we did not have it. They said, 'Whatever it is, you had better get rid of them. Today the police came, they have gone through the area. Tomorrow if the police comes and raids your house, they will arrest these people but you will also be arrested. You have given them refuge.'

Our protector had a discussion with some others about what he should do. They had to find a way. They were naturally afraid, so they thought they could send us to someone in Block BA whom they knew. They went there to find out but no one opened the door as they were afraid. Fear had entered everyone's hearts so they did not open the doors.

When the messenger returned to the house there was another discussion. Then they thought that the gurdwaras could be explored. They had heard that camps had been set up in some of the gurdwaras and so one of them said, 'We should find out about them.' One had been set up at Singarpur where some of the sardars had got together. So someone was sent to find out about it. He found that a camp had actually been set up over there. The pradhan of that place, Niranjan Singh, sent a vehicle and a driver to rescue us. We were taken out from Shalimar Bagh that night and so we went to Singarpur. This was the night of the 2nd.

On the 3rd morning we got there. There were about 500 people there: taxi drivers, mechanics and others. One of the mechanics had been burnt. We stayed at Singarpur on the 3rd and on the 4th. The wound on my head was still raw, the hair was just coming out by itself. I thought, 'For the sake of this hair, people have been burnt. The hair that I had protected so far, that hair is just coming out by itself today. The same hair which would not break off easily even when it was pulled was now falling off by itself.' I was so upset just thinking about my condition. So, I went to the camp president's wife and I said to her, 'Behenji' (sister) you are my mother, sister, and every-one for me. Please think of me as your chotapra (younger brother) and wash my hair so that I might be able to comb it. It is the fourth day now since I used the kanga (comb) on my hair even though Guru Gobind Singh Maharaj has said that one must use the comb twice a day on the hair. But it is four days since I combed it.' She heated some water, put Dettol in it and washed my hair for me.

In the meanwhile, one of my brothers, who lives in Rajinder Nagar, was told by someone that our gurdwara had been attacked and that I was wounded. He wanted to come immediately but one lady stopped him by saying, 'No my boy, you must not go. The sardars are in trouble, death is stalking them (*sardaron de sir maut mandra raha hai*). You must not go. I'll go and find out.' Although she was a sardarni who could know whether she was a woman of the sardars or woman of the monas? She came to this gurdwara looking for me, and did not find me there. Her brother lives somewhere at the back so she went to him. They knew that I had taken shelter in Singarpur so they brought her here on a scooter on the 5th. She told me how anxious my younger brother was and that he had sent her there to look for me. I got ready to leave with her. But there was no turban for my head. I just had the two clothes that I was wearing. I started to leave nanga-sir (bareheaded) but the pradhan stopped me and said, 'Bhai Sahab ji don't go without a turban. You are the wazir (representative) of Guru Gobind Singh. It does not behoove you to go out like this. Even though you are leaving us and going, it is not good that you are going nanga-sir.'

I said, 'We must be grateful to the parmatma for everything. When Guru Gobind Singh had to go the jang (battle) he had only the pana (small cloth under the turban). He had no footwear, his clothes were torn, and he had only the stones to rest his head on. But through all this he had no complaints. Even after losing all his four sons while he was going to the battle he said:

> Mitterpyare nu halmuridan da kehna
> yarde da sanusatthar change*

Whatever the beloved guru has ordered for his followers is acceptable; I would not want to give him up. Even the worst distress which is better than the greatest material benefit without him. You know even though Guru Gobind Singh suffered greatly he had no complaints and he gave thanks to the parmatma. He said, 'If we are to receive satthar (beatings) we'll receive them.' So, also, if it is ordained by the parmatma that I should go nanga-sir then I'll go nanga-sir; if not, if there is a dastar (turban), then I'll put on a dastar.

The pradhan sahib said, 'The dastars are here, please take one.' I covered my head with a dastar and went to Rajinder Nagar. I stayed for about a week in Rajinder Nagar but I came to the gurdwara on the 6th and the 7th to make preparations for Gurpurab which fell on the 8th. The pradhan said we will merely perform ardas and have no other ceremony. So, we sants sat down together and did ardas and read the Granth Sahib at the feet of the Guru, we asked for strength so that we could go through these difficult days and accept our hardships. Because, you see, a man can get derailed (*dol sakda hai*) and so he needs strength. When Guru Gobind Singh saw his sons becoming martyred in front of his own eyes he had still showed his gratitude (*shukar kita si*). He said, 'Parmatma I had a great debt towards you, I could not redeem the debt all together in one lot. I am doing it little by little. I have given you my sons, I sent them to the battle, then mother was martyred, father had already become a shaheed earlier.' Thus, we also requested the

---

* Let the Beloved know my condition/Deathbed with my Beloved is better than body burning without Him.

parmatma to give us strength and courage, so that we could go according to their precepts (updesh). We quietly prayed without any sound…

Q: In this gurdwara?

A: Yes, in the gurdwara.

Q: Had it been burnt?

A: It had been completely burnt. Everything had been destroyed. The Granth Sahib had been defiled by someone urinating on it. All the pages had been torn off each one of them. We tried to gather all the scattered pieces of whatever was around, of whatever was left of the Granth Sahib.

Q: Where are the remnants?

A: It was burnt … (at this point the Granthiji broke down and wept inconsolably. After a while he collected himself and said). The Maharaj was insulted. We don't mind so much for ourselves. I could have been martyred (*main shaheed ho janda*). I don't mind the fact that my house was looted. After all it was the parmatma who gave it to me. But what I could not bear was that he who had given everything to me should be insulted and defiled with urine. We were shocked (asimahfoossi) to think that the whole world honoured the Granth Sahib but that right here it had been treated so badly. Which bhagat, fakir, pir, or guru has not been mentioned in it? It is the words (bani) of all of them. Is there no mention of Ram Chandraji, Hanuman, Sita, Kabir, Raidas the Charmar, and DhannaJat? They have not just burnt and defiled the Granth Sahib. In their stupidity, they forgot that they were burning their own pirs and fakirs along with it.

The sants picked up each piece. Some had fallen here, some had fallen there. It was scattered everywhere. We collected every single remnant together and performed the sanskaras (rituals). After doing the sanskaras we put flowers on the Maharaj just as when a person reaches his end we collect his remains after the cremation. A few days later we took the remains which we had tied together and kept in a bundle to the Jamuna and immersed them there. For some people, it might have just been ashes. But for us the words of the gurus were in it and so we went and immersed the remains of the Granth Sahib in the Jamuna.

 After that we filed our claims but got no reply. When we went to find out what had happened we were told that there would be no compensation but that they would rebuild our gurdwara for us. We thought, 'Nevermind in what way it is going to be rebuilt. At least we will be able to install the Maharaj and so we gave thanks to the parmatma.'

Q: Who built the gurdwara?

A: The DDA. (Delhi Development Authority)

Q: Was it rebuilt completely?

A: Yes, the whole thing was redone. Its face is completely new. Half the walls we rebuilt and then a cement roof was laid. Then the sants requested help and slowly things began to come in. Slowly the gurdwara began to function again and we could tell the parmatma what we had suffered.

Q: Can you tell us whether you have an idea about where the 300 or 400 people who attacked you came from?

A: They came from the neighbouring villages—there is a village called Saidpur nearby. They came from this direction (gives an indication). They came along this gali and this road.

Q: Did you recognize any of them?

A: They were all strangers.

Q: But what about the bania who ran after you with a stone?

A: We don't have much to do with the banias. I can't say anything about whether it was definitely a bania or not, or whether he was from the neighbourhood or from elsewhere. I was too frightened to take proper notion of anything. (It appeared to the interviewers that the granthi had spontaneously and unwittingly described the bania's threatening gesture but had had second thoughts in passing on this information. He diverted the question to save his embarrassment.)

Q: How did the people in the neighbourhood react to you when you returned? Did anyone pass comments against you or anything like that?

A: There are some people who respect Guru Gobind Singh, like the family which gave us shelter. But there are others who didn't revere the gurus like the people who came and said that we had transmitters. They wanted us to be thrown out, right then in the night from the house where we had taken shelter. There are always people like them who pass comments...

Q: Anil: I am also a Punjabi although I'm not a Sikh and in my family whenever there is any occasion for joy and sorrow we have a path (reading of the Granth Sahib) in our house. All the members of my household respect the gurus. Aren't there people like them in your neighbourhood who come and pay their respect to the Granth Sahib? Weren't there people like that when you were being accused of keeping a transmitter?

A: They were all banias.

Q: All of them were banias?

A: Yes, the person who alleged that we had a transmitter was a bania. But those who respected the gurus treated us as their own brothers. They looked after us as their own people. They brought us the capsules for treating our wounds. The sardars could not go out at all. They were all in hiding and they had to go about under cover even to ease themselves.

Q: When you returned to the gurdwara how did you feel? Did you feel that you could return to your normal routine? Did you feel that everything would become all right again?

A: Now it feels that maybe the gurdwara will be able to function again, that the sangat (community of devotees) will be able to reassemble. But before this everything was very uncertain. I thought that if we all have to live as monas we can't have gurdwaras, because the monas would not make gurdwaras. If the monas were to allow the making of gurdwaras, they would not have burnt the Sikhs. They would certainly not have destroyed the gurdwaras would they?

Q: Kulbir: You had said that there was a bania who ran after you with a stone. You had also said that occasionally you had exchanged greetings with him in the past, but that you did not know him beyond that. Despite this, you don't know his name?

A: No, I don't know his name. As I said earlier, banias don't come to the gurdwaras.

Q: But do you think you can remember any of the faces of the people who attacked you?

A: There was man who used to sell sabzi (vegetables) in these galis. He was one of the people who attacked me with the iron rod when my head was injured. Afterwards I tried to look for him. Sometimes I went out specially thinking, 'Who knows, I might see him somewhere.' But he was nowhere to be seen.

Q: Do you know his name?

A: No, who knows the names of the sabziwalas? I just knew that he was a sabziwala. He was definitely here in the gali when my head was attacked. I asked people here as well as in Shalimar Bagh B Block about the sabziwala but nobody knew what had happened to him. They all said he had completely stopped coming to this area. I don't know if he is around or where he is.

Q: At that time, when you were being attacked, or when you were hiding did you see the police at all?

A: Not at the time when we were attacked. But later when we were in hiding and the gurdwara was being burnt, the police van came. Some of the people in the sangat (and there are so many people in the sangat, Sikhs as well as others who respect the gurus) so we don't know everyone's names. The rioters ran away but the police shouted, 'Sala—this is the time that you have got to do whatever you want. Why are you running off? Do whatever you like. We will return in ten hours.'

Q: This was actually said by the police?

A: This is what the police said. 'Do whatever you like, we'll come back in ten hours.' Some of the scared ones in the mob had run off but others called them back and they regrouped. They broke into the gurdwara, broke the lock of my room, removed the fan and everything else—absolutely everything they could lay their hands on. They did not even leave a spoon in place. They left nothing.

Q: Do you know which area these policemen belonged to?

A: I didn't see the police since I was hiding.

Q: Those who saw the police—what did they say about where the police had come from? From the Shalimar thana, or elsewhere?

A: They didn't say anything about that. They just said that the police came and said that the rioters could do what they liked, and that they would return in ten hours, 'Have no fear, do as you please' they said. The mob had begun to disperse but after this they started looting and destroying again.

Q: Later on, you must have got to know that the army had taken charge of the area. Did you see them?

A: Yes, at that time I was with my younger brother in the Rajinder Nagar gurdwara. The army was in position there. There was a military vehicle which was posted there on duty throughout the day and night.

Q: You didn't see the military in this area?

A: No, there was no military in this area.

Q: Tell us how you feel these days. Do you feel that people are treating you with suspicion or show that they are angry with you? Do they treat you as different from them, as other (paraya) than themselves?

A: It is like this: they seem to view me not only as an outsider but also as representing danger. Day before yesterday I was returning from Ghanta Ghar in a bus. Just ahead of me was a sardar woman and her child who were getting ready to get off the bus. We all had to get down here on the Ring Road. The child was right ahead, behind it was the woman, and I was behind her. The child indicated that the bus should stop but the driver didn't pay attention. So, I said, 'Bhai sahib (brother), this is a bus stop, you should stop the bus as indicated to you. Why didn't you stop?' The driver said, 'You are talking rubbish, you didn't tell me to stop. Am I your servant to stop the bus wherever you want it to stop?' I got off quietly and didn't say anything to him. What could I say? If he had any sympathy for us, he would have noticed that we had got ready to get off at the stand and would have stopped the bus. Even when I spoke politely to him saying, 'Driver sahib you should have stopped the bus here, you know it's a stand,' he retorted rudely saying, 'Don't talk nonsense, I'm not your servant.' We got off quietly and went home.

Q: But the drivers of the DTC buses behave like this with everyone, with you, with us and everyone else. So, isn't it possible that after the November attacks we may all have just become more sensitive to what people are saying or doing these days?

A: Yes, it's possible, but some people who had earlier exchanged greetings with us, shown affection and respect for us, now they avoid us and just pass me by on the street.

Q: How do you think we can go back to the relationships and to the brotherly feelings between people that existed in the past?

A: Only if one can consider each other as brothers, if one can respect the differences of others whether they are Hindus, Muslims or Sikhs, if there are no difference between castes, between high and low, then people can live like brothers. You just said that the Granth Sahib was respected in your family, that the path was recited on all occasions, if things remain like this then there will be no ladai or jhagda (fights or quarrels). But if the thought occurs in the mind that, 'We only respect the Geeta, that Guru Gobind Singh is nothing', then difference and feelings of us and them will come. This will lead to a darar (crack) between people. Guru Nanak made no distinctions. Right in the beginning of the gurbani he said, *'Aval allah noor upaya, kudrat ke sabh bande, ek noor te sabh jag upjaya, kaun bhae kyo mande...'* [One God is the creator of this light in creation, everyone belongs to this creation. One light has given birth to the entire creation, then how can one be good or other bad...] You must have heard this saying. Elsewhere he has said 'Hari ka basa' the location of Hari, is treated as being in the South, the Muslims do sijda (pay obeisance) in the direction of the West, but you haven't thought of who is in the East? Rab (God) is there also, he is everywhere only everyone needs to understand in his heart that God is one; it is only the names by which he is worshipped which are different. If everyone forgets the distinction of this is a Hindu, this is a Sikh, this is a Muslim, this is a Christian, this is a nai, this is a chamar, but that everyone is equal then we are like brothers.

Q: As you are a granthi of a gurdwara you must be aware that the work of the Akali Dal is carried on from the Golden Temple at Amritsar. What is your view about what was happening in the Golden Temple before Operation Blue Star took place? What do you think about the Akali Dal and the SGPC [Shiromani Gurudwara Prabandhak Committee], and do you think what was happening in the Golden Temple was correct?

A: What is good for the quam (community), what is good for the country, that is correct. If it is not good then I repeat that those activities are not correct.

Q: What do you think about Bhindranwale?

A: What do you mean?

Q: What do you think about whatever he was doing before Operation Blue Star, about the markat (killings) in Punjab which took place in his name.

A: It is wrong to say that this was being done in his name. Bhindranwale was not concerned with siysat (power, administration). He was a sant. He had sacrificed everything. He did not even have tea. I have heard from other sants and people that he did not even eat onions, far less, did he have meat or fish. When he heard the mention of meat or fish he said that if one could eat these things then one might as well eat the flesh of a child. It is not just a question of eating flesh, it is the question of the taking of life. If he did not even eat meat what could he have had to do with killings? It is only a sazish (conspiracy) to malign him. If you go on maligning a person he will become infamous (badnam). How can one know the truth? Bhindranwale did not do anything wrong. He did everything for the Sikh community and the community of the gurus.

Q: How do you view the Akali Dal and what is your understanding of the Anandpur sahib resolution?

A: As far as the Anandpur Sahib resolution is concerned, it is only demanding the implementation of promises made by the government earlier. If today the Sikh qaum is asking for those things then we are behind the demands, we support them. It is like this, if sitting here in front of you I am promised this book I can ask for it anytime. It becomes my right to do so. But if instead of the book that you had promised me, I demand the shirt that you are wearing that would not be legitimate (najaiz).

Q: What in your opinion, are the things that were promised not being given?

A: The government had said that there are many parts of Punjab, like Chandigarh which they would give to Punjab. They also said that Punjab has a right to the river waters. Whatever they had said they must give. Now Chandigarh falls in Punjab, Punjabi is the language spoken there, that should come to Punjab. We feel that this should be so.

Q: What are the things that you think are rightfully yours and so you should fight for them? Do you think that for what should rightfully belong to Punjab you can, and you should, fight?

A: Not fight...

Q: By fighting (ladna) I mean a movement, (andolan) or something like having demonstrations, etc.

A: Everyone fights for one's rights. Suppose there are two brothers, and both have equal rights to the inheritance, it is their haq (right) to get it. If the father thinks that one is more able than the other, he may in his lifetime divide the property unequally. The one who gets less may still think, 'Well it's all right, I'll manage with this much only.' But if he is promised something and does not get it and the father says you don't have any rights, that creates bitterness.

Q: Do you feel that whatever is in Punjab it is meant only for the Sikhs?

A: There are others in Punjab apart from the Sikhs. There are the Hindus and other sects too. If the Sikhs have made certain demands it is not merely for the Sikhs. There are lots of monas in Chandigarh. They are also Punjabis. Where will they go? They'll also gain. The demand for water is also similar, Hindus will also get it. It is not as if it will be given selectively.

Q: Then why is it that only Sikhs participate in all the agitations? Why don't the Hindus or Muslims participate? Is it a shortcoming of the Akali Dal that they have not been able to get their support; to convince them that the demands are for everyone; that everyone will gain. If it is not just for Sikhs, it is for all the Punjabis. Then why are the Sikhs only agitated about these demands?

A: If there was someone to tell them...

Q: There were any number of sants and leaders who could communicate this to all the people. After all there is Longowal, Tohra, Dharamvir and there was Bhindranwale—there were all these people who could have done something. People do listen to the words of the netas (leaders).

A: The leaders did say so just as I am saying these things to you now. It is my understanding that if Chandigarh goes to Punjab all Punjabis will gain from it; that if they are asking for something for Punjab it is not only for the Sikhs, it is for everyone.

Q: The non-Sikhs should of course try and understand but the Sikh leaders must also attempt to convince the others on this issue.

A: Yes, they must certainly try and do so. They are all brothers. In the Punjab, many daughters of the Hindus are married to the Sikhs and the Sikhs are married into the non-Sikhs. If a Hindu did not have a son, he often vowed to make his first child a Sikh if he had a son. The second child may have remained a mona. Now you tell me how can they be different? This is a conspiracy to separate the Punjabis and break their unity.

Q: What were your reactions to the news of Rajiv Gandhi having been made Prime Minister on the evening of the 31st October immediately after Mrs Gandhi had been assassinated?

A: I thought it was not right…

Q: Why did you think so?

A: There were many senior leaders who were already experienced who could have been prime minister. Someone who does not have enough knowledge about running the government, someone who was so new, should not have been made prime minister. They should have chosen a person who was older and had more experience.

But even so if Rajiv had wanted he could have successfully controlled the situation and this (carnage) would not have happened in the country. When the attack on Amritsar took place, we were all sitting here and discussing the events and we said, 'Whatever happens outside, nothing will happen in Delhi—this is the capital after all.' But what happened has probably never happened anywhere before. This is what we felt afterwards.

Rajiv Gandhi should have thought more carefully. He should have realized what he was doing, that this is how he was starting his career. If the elders are strong the children are under control. If they weaken, the children take advantage of the situation and do whatever they like.

Q: Do you feel that when the carnage was taking place they knew what was happening and still did not stop it?

A: Now suppose any calamity takes place, some big neta dies unexpectedly of a heart attack or is shot, or anything it comes immediately in the news and TV. All over India there were mobs attacking the Sikhs, and arson and looting took place. Would they (i.e. those in power) have not got to know? No police came, no fire brigade came. Was everyone sitting there and crying? Was there no one to think that the situation should be controlled? It could have been controlled. What happened to the telephones, to the transmitters at that time when this killing, arson and looting was taking place?

Q: Do you think that had some senior neta been there instead of Rajiv Gandhi he would have controlled the situation?

A: Yes, he could have. Maybe, Rajiv felt that my mother has been killed, she has been killed by a sardar. Maybe with the feeling of revenge he said one should take 'badla'—*khoon ka badla khoon* (blood for blood). Because when people came to attack, they said the same thing. They said '*Khoon ka badla khoon, tumme humari ma ko mara* (You killed our mother), *hum sardaron ko marenge, sardaron ko jaladenge*' (we'll kill the sardars, we'll burn them). So, Rajiv may have said *khoon ka badla khoon*. But the others should have thought that 'Well, the assassination has taken place. We don't know with what feeling this was done. But was this the fault of the Sikhs?' The case against Satwant and Beant could have taken its course later on. But what happened should not have happened.

Q: Do you think that the Blue Star Operation was justified?

A: It was wrong.

Q: If you think that it was incorrect, who do you think was responsible for this event?

A: Suppose it is conceded that Bhindranwale was at fault...

Q: Tell us your views.

A: I'm telling you my views. If I agree that Bhindranwale was at fault even then he should have been caught, he should have been arrested. At the time that the Bangladesh war took place the Indian Army had succeeded in making the Pakistan Army surrender (hands up karaditasi). A force of one lakh Muslims were made to do hands up. But in the case of one Bhindranwale they had to go in with tanks… Why? If he was guilty, he could have been caught. He could have been arrested. Where was the need to go in with tanks? When the Indian army has the power to challenge and defeat a different nation (quam) why did they have to use the army and tanks against Bhindranwale who was after all an Indian? Was capturing or arresting him beyond their capabilities?

Q: So, then what do we understand about whom you consider to be at fault?

A: At this point of time it appears that the government is to be blamed.

Q: Within the government itself do you consider any particular person to be responsible?

A: Which particular person can we point out? It was decided by the sarkar (government) to send tanks and canon. At that time, at the time of Blue Star, Indira was in power. She should have thought about why she was sending in the army, why she sent the tanks into the Darbar Sahib whose angan (courtyard) had been laid by the mussalmans.

Q: If in your understanding Indira Gandhi was responsible for all this, how do you view what happened on the 31st? Do you think it was something sudden, or that it had to happen? Was it wrong?

A: It was sudden, and it should not have happened. We have heard that when Satwant and Beant went to Punjab they saw that many people had been martyred but that did not affect them. But when they went to the Darbar Sahib and saw the condition there, the evidence of what had happened, the marks of the canon, the marks of destruction—that affected them. People say that they were full of anguish when they saw what had happened at the Darbar Sahib (just as I was telling you a little while earlier about the desecration of the Maharaj I had wept). They then took a vow, standing right there, that they would take revenge.

Q: This means that Beant and Satwant Singh thought that Indira Gandhi was responsible (for the attack on the Golden Temple and therefore its desecration) and that was the reason for the assassination?

A: Yes, that's why they killed her.

Q: Now after discussing all this, what is your reaction to what is now constantly coming up in the newspapers and that is the issue of Khalistan? Do you think that Khalistan should be created?

A: I don't want a Khalistan...

Q: Why?

A: Because this would mean a separation of the Sikhs. All the Sikhs would have to go off there. Just as when Pakistan was made... Aren't there Muslims in Hindustan now? Which corner (of India) is there where mussalmans do not live? Look at Delhi, aren't there mussalmans here? Aren't there mussalmans in Punjab? Even if a Khalistan is made the Sikhs of Delhi will remain in Delhi—I live in Delhi, I'll continue to live here.

Q: That's as far as if and when Khalistan is made. But do you think the demand for it is all right?

A: See it's like this. Khalistan is not a demand of the Akalis. It's not the Akalis who are saying 'We want Khalistan.' There's only one person—Jagjit Singh Chauhan who is sitting in a foreign country and saying, 'I want Khalistan; I've made the map of Khalistan; I've made the currency; everything is done.' What's the use of that? That's not going to have any effect.

Q: So, you think it's wrong?

A: Yes, I think it's wrong. There should be no Khalistan.

Q: What do you think about the people who helped others at the time of the attacks on Sikhs in Delhi? What do you think about the future? Do you think that the fact that there were those who helped the sardars is a good indication for the future?

A: We often think of those who helped us with gratitude. It makes us feel that we have brothers who don't treat us as different from them, those who don't have feelings of 'they are different, I am different.' We will never forget, as long as we live, those who helped us; that we were in the jaws of death and they saved us from it. When I meet the people who helped us, I do sijda to them, my head bows to them and with reverence I say, 'Sat Sri Akal Babuji.' And I cannot help repeating how grateful I am for what they did; that they risked themselves for us and that if they hadn't done so we wouldn't be here now.

Q: The last thing we'd like to ask you is about the relief work after the carnage: What do you think about the relief that you got? What do you feel about the relief committees that were set up, about the publication of the PUCL-PUDR book on Who Are the Guilty? Do you think that the work they did was right and if it was right was it enough?

A: I think that the aid committees were very good. But the compensation that people got was too little and it was not given in full. What the government has given us is nothing...

Q: For loss of life or loss of property?

A: Both, to give Rs 10,000 for a person who was killed is nothing. You don't get a person for Rs 10,000.

Q: But you don't get back a person even with Rs 1 lakh.

A: No, of course not. But still Rs 10,000 is too little. If a woman is widowed what will she do with just 10,000? How far will it go? If a person has lost everything in the arson, property worth lakhs, what is Rs 10,000 or 8,000 as compensation? It is nothing.

Q: But what about the committees? Did they do good work? Was their work satisfactory? Could they have done more?

A: What was done was very good. If there were more people to help it would have also been good. But whatever they did we are grateful. It is like the offering that you put for the Maharaj. Whatever is put is accepted. One does not think you put only 25 paise, you should have put more. But the compensation from the government was too little. And here in my case they rebuilt the skeleton of the gurdwara and thought that it was everything. All my household goods, everything I had was lost. How can I do justice to my children? They have lost everything I had collected for them.

    My brother was to buy a scooter and he had left the money for it with me. That too got looted. The government just said 'We've made your gurdwara for you. The room that you lived in is also rebuilt. Now you will get nothing more.' But I say, I should also get compensation. I am not a businessman, I have two children and I do a service at the gurdwara. I should also be compensated for my losses. I had collected things over the years but now my house is bereft of everything—*bilkul ujda paya hai.* (It has been uprooted).

31 October 1984

JARNAIL SINGH

Translated from the Hindi by
VAISHALI MATHUR

This excerpt from 'I Accuse... The Anti-Sikh Violence of 1984' depicts the autobiographical experience of Jarnail Singh, a journalist and later a politician with the Aam Admi Party. Having witnessed the anti-Sikh massacre first-hand, Singh expresses his outrage about the state's indifference towards the victims of the massacre and the subsequent years of injustice. In 2009. Singh, hurled a shoe at P. Chidambaram who was then the Home Minister of India. In his book, written later the same year, Singh attempts to give reasons for his action. In this excerpt, he suggests how the events of 1984 had a permanent impression on his childhood self's memory, and how his relationships with his neighbours and friends were transformed forever.

Before Partition, my grandfather used to live in a village close to Lahore. When he came to India, he came empty-handed and was allotted a house in Lajpat Nagar that had a tin roof, which made it very cold in winter and very hot in summer. But my parents felt that at least it was a home. The roof abutted the neighbouring house and it was possible to reach every house nearby by simply climbing on to it.

My father got a job as a carpenter, and with that, a regular income started to come in. As time went by, we improved the house and it felt like a home. Our family was a large one—I have five brothers and three sisters. When we were growing up, we would roam around Lajpat Nagar the whole day and it never worried my mother.

Lajpat Nagar was a refugee colony for the Hindus and Sikhs who had come from Pakistan after Partition. They all shared the same experiences of pain and separation which gave a sense of common purpose—no one felt alienated here. One of our neighbours was an elderly lady called Bhabhiji by everyone. She was from Multan and was especially close to my mother. In fact, after Bhabhiji died, her daughter-in-law treated my mother like her mother-in-law, as that is what Bhabhiji would have wanted. Some years ago, when Bhabhiji's grandchildren got married, my mother took on the role of the grandmother-in law, though Bhabhiji had been a Hindu and my mother was a Sikh.

It had never mattered. But on this day, 31 October 1984, there were those who wanted all such relationships to be severed. Bhabhiji came to the house several times that day. 'Don't worry,' she said in Multani, but she clearly didn't believe her own words. Rumours were rife in the neighbourhood that after Mrs Gandhi's assassination at the hands of her Sikh bodyguards, mobs were attacking Sikhs in several areas of the city. But in quiet Lajpat Nagar on the afternoon of 31 October, that seemed distant, even if worrying. Nonetheless, Mother removed our father's nameplate from outside the house and warned Bhabhiji not to come too often for her own safety. Ours was the only Sikh house in the entire lane, though there were others across the nallah.

At home, the worry lines on Papa's face were apparent. In the evening, my aunt, who lived in Arjun Nagar near Safdarjung Enclave, called and related an incident about her Sikh neighbour. He had been crossing the road at the All India Institute of Medical Science (AIIMS) when he saw an angry mob pulling Sikhs out of their vehicles and beating them up; their pagris were being torn off. He himself had escaped by a whisker. We heard that President Giani Zail Singh had gone to AIIMS to pay his respects to the slain prime minister and the mob threw stones at his cavalcade. When Mother came back after taking my aunt's call in the neighbouring house of Kabul Singh (we did not have a telephone), she looked very uneasy. However, no one could imagine then what was to take place the next day. Since Indira Gandhi was the prime minister, national mourning had been declared. Radio and television (only AIR and Doordarshan in those days) were only broadcasting mournful veena music. We kids were not happy with this at all. Mourning was for grown-ups; as far as we children were concerned, it was a holiday and we wanted to see the normal programmes on television.

On 1 November, early in the morning, we went out to play cricket in the nearby Shiv Vatika park with our friends from the neighbourhood. This park was to one side of the colony and we would play for hours—unchecked and unaware. It was only when we got tired that we would remember we had homes. This was entirely usual—we would be so engrossed in the game that we would forgot that we had not eaten and would return only to be scolded by our mothers who would say, 'Why! You didn't find a mother in the park to feed you? Stay there!' We knew they weren't really angry. But today was different.

We had just reached the Sindhi school when we heard shouts and raised voices. A crowd was screaming. We looked at each other and decided that we would investigate further—I suppose all kids would have the same reaction. We were curious—and till then we'd had nothing to fear. However, just then my elder brother, who was thirteen years old at that time, said, 'Do you want to get scolded by Mother? Let's go straight home, we haven't even had breakfast this morning.' He was the strongest amongst us and generally no one opposed him. We had just reached our lane when we saw that Mother was standing outside the house, looking frantic with worry. I still remember the scolding that we got that day. She even slapped us once or twice. Mother was extremely worked up and the relief of seeing the three of us safe and sound somehow made her angrier. A neighbour's son, Raju, had actually been sent to look for us. He had searched the parks nearby but could not find us, as the Shiv Vatika park was a little distance away. When we could not be traced for a long time, Mother had became frantic. Even so, my brothers and I could not understand why she was so scared.

Before we could ask any questions, my two brothers and I were locked up in a room right at the back of the house. Its door had not been closed in a long time, so it was difficult to lock. Father used all his force and shut it tight. We could not understand was happening, but we realized that whatever it was, it was serious. Satvinder Kaur, my eldest sister, told us that there was some looting and Sikhs were being beaten up. This was the first time I had heard the word 'loot'. Curious, I watched from the window: Mother was now washing clothes but clearly also keeping a watch on events in the street.

When the noise of the mob began to get louder, Mother told us to climb up to the 'oltee', the small space at the head of the staircase, and hide there. Usually we only went up there while playing hide-and-seek—and we were always scolded for it; but today we were actually being told to do so. For a long time, my two brothers and I—we were then thirteen, eleven and ten years old—crouched in that dark, cramped place. My elder brother, Jasbir Singh, had been sent off to a neighbour's house—Mother had heard that adolescent boys were being especially targeted and she felt he'd be safer out of our house. It was suffocating up in the attic. Mother had been too distracted to give us any food and we had not even had our breakfast that morning—we'd run off to play cricket without eating anything. We were famished till we found a large tin box full of wheat flour biscuits from Chander Bakery. Mother had got them made, planning to give us a couple every day on winter mornings as atta was said to keep you warm. This tin was stored in the oltee. We finished almost the whole box—I can still remember how good they tasted. We were so young, so unscarred then. It never occurred to us to wonder why we had to hide like criminals in our own house inside a colony we had lived in all our lives, surrounded by neighbours with whom we'd always had good relations. How could this have happened? Even today, I don't know. While we were still locked up there, Bhabhiji had turned up again. She told Mother that the gurdwara had been set on fire and Sikh shops in the nearby Krishna Market were being looted and set ablaze. Bhabhiji had just seen a neighbour's son carrying boxes of shoes out of the looted shops. He had picked up twenty pairs for himself from the Central Market shop, Volga, which belonged to a sardar. It is a different thing that he found he had stolen twenty pairs of the same type of shoe. He was an exception. Most of our neighbours in the colony did not participate in the mob frenzy; but they did not do anything to stop it. Nor did they actively get together with the looters and plunderers, though some boys seized the opportunity to pick up things.

We were taken out of the room late in the night. Then our eldest brother, Gurcharan, who had a bad leg due to a childhood attack of polio, decided to go to Niwaspuri. Our father had recently been allotted a government quarter in Niwaspuri as he was in the Central Public Works Department (CPWD) and Gurcharan was staying there, as it was near his college. Despite being plagued by polio, he had been studying hard and after completing his B.Com. he was planning to study further to become a company secretary. People at home told him not to leave the house because the situation was not good. He dismissed their warnings: 'I am disabled and going on a tricycle, who will say anything to me?' His confidence in the kindness of strangers was misplaced that day: 1 November 1984. He was attacked a short distance from the house. His three-wheeled cycle was overturned. His pagri was pulled off and the mob started beating him, heedless of his cries of pain. His disability made it impossible for him to run. He was lying in the dust, while the blows rained down on him. The mob left him bleeding and shaken on the road. A few shopkeepers, who knew him but hadn't intervened when he was actually being beaten up, came forward once the mob had left. They put the cycle straight and helped him back on it. He came home somehow, but for a long time he was in a state of shock. He had always been treated with consideration. That day he learnt that the only thing that mattered was that he was a Sikh.

We spent the entire day taking God's name. The next day, 2 November, Mother looked even more worried. Our aunt had called up with some shocking news. Mother's younger brother, our uncle Gulzar Singh, and other Sikh drivers had been attacked by the mob at the Hyatt Regency hotel's taxi stand. Mama, our uncle, used to run his taxi there, a taxi bought with the money saved by our maternal grandfather when he had worked in Baluchistan before Partition. The mob had beaten up all the Sikh taxi drivers at the rank very badly, leaving them bleeding and bruised, their clothes covered with blood.

They had been left for dead. Uncle was a strapping young man. If there had been only five or even ten against him, he could have tackled them alone. But the attackers ran into hundreds.

Despite his severe injuries, we had learnt that it was useless to take him to a government hospital. AIIMS was the nearest hospital, but news had spread that President Zail Singh's motor cavalcade had been attacked by angry mobs when he had come to the hospital to pay his respects to the slain prime minister. If that was the treatment meted out to the head of state, what hope did ordinary Sikhs have? Government hospitals were not admitting injured Sikhs; we heard that such hospitals had actually closed their burns unit—so that the many Sikhs who had been set ablaze by the mobs were unable to get the treatment that they so desperately needed.

One of the most inhuman acts of the mobs was to fit car tyres over their victims' heads and then set the tyres alight. There were many Sikhs with burn injuries, but even if a victim managed to reach a government hospital, he would have been turned back. In fact, several Sikhs who were turned away from hospitals fell victim to mobs on their way home. My uncle, despite his injuries, had to be kept at home. My aunt could not find a doctor to treat him—many were too scared to go to the house of a Sikh, fearing retribution from the mobs. A private nurse—a Christian—who lived nearby, agreed to come every day and dress the wounds. It was such gestures—the courage and compassion of strangers—that no one who has been through those days can forget.

That day, 2 November, a police jeep went around the colony announcing that a curfew would be imposed within half an hour. They advised everyone to stay home. Mother was relieved. 'Everything will be okay now,' she said; after all, the mobs could not gather to attack during a curfew. But the curfew was not implemented. Anyone who breaks a curfew is liable to be shot at sight, or at least apprehended. But from what I saw on 2 November, no sooner had the jeep announcing curfew passed by than more and more people would spill out of their homes. People told me later that local Congressmen were responsible for the attacks on the Sikhs of Lajpat Nagar. Some even alleged that the two sons of a local leader were seen brandishing the voters' list, so that the mobs could be directed to Sikh houses. The Hindus in our neighbourhood decided to set up patrols at night so that they could protect their lives and property.

This patrol was set up close to our house and all the people on it were from our neighbourhood, so I knew them all. Escaping from my mother, I reached the spot where they had gathered. That is when I came to know that our non-Sikh neighbours were also scared. Rumours were rife that, to avenge Sikh killings, a train-load of Sikhs were coming from Punjab ready to attack innocent Hindus and that many Hindus were being killed in Punjab. Another rumour, also widespread, was that the Sikhs had mixed poison in the city's drinking water supply. I actually asked someone how he thought this was possible and he pointed to the reservoir which supplied water to Lajpat Nagar. But even I, a child at the time, knew immediately this was ridiculous. In the first place, who could climb such a huge tank? And if they had managed to poison the water, wouldn't the water flow to Sikh houses too? But it was such a strong rumour that I half-believed it too. I had just drunk some water at home and I was scared—this is how the disinformation was working. The purpose of the rumour was to make everyone believe that the Sikhs were on a rampage, to incite public opinion against them, to quell any sympathy that might be developing for them because of the mobs' killing spree.

We didn't know then the extent of the horror that had taken place. Reports in the newspapers were few; but our family and friends would hear about the violence from their families and friends. The stories we heard were unbelievable—but we had to believe them. We had seen the spires of black smoke from burning taxi stands from our roof; we had heard about innocent Sikhs being brutally beaten; accounts of the massacres in Kalyanpuri and Trilokpuri were beginning to come out. All this was frightening, because no one knew why this had happened; who was behind it. Shock and worry had gripped my parents; my brothers and I were scared as well, but we were children and we did not really understand the full extent of the violence.

After ten days, when life began returning to normal we were

allowed to go and play in the park again. We were tired of staying home. The park was our life. All three of us went to play and we found the other kids in the park were in the middle of a game of touchball—where you have to hit the other players with the ball. The ball used to cost just fifty paise but the hits really hurt. The three of us took a while to realize that we were being hit the hardest and most often. It dawned on us that the other boys were making us targets. It was not a game; it was a form of making us scapegoats. None of the other children were being treated that way. The balls thrown at them were ones they could catch easily; the ball wasn't being thrown at them with the intention to hurt. Perhaps we should have just stopped playing—but we were children too. We were not in the habit of running away. Swiftly, the three of us targeted the others, one by one. It was a war, not a game. The hits were painful, but we three pretended they didn't hurt. We didn't stop playing with the kids in the park—we had played with them all our lives. But that day we all realized that the question of being a Hindu or a Sikh had entered even children's games.

We were all in the same age group and went to the same school. We spent our free time together and plucked Ramchandra Aunty's and Roshini Aunty's guavas together. We used to fight earlier too but now we became the objects of taunts, '*sardaron ke barah baj gaye*,' they would shout. They'd said this to us before, but this was different; this was not a joke, but a taunt. One of the boys, Titu we called him, said, 'If you fight too much, I will call the same people who killed Sikhs on 31 October and 1 November. Your house got saved in the riots but this time I will tell them the correct address.' Titu was in my class, his mother and my mother were friends. Children have fights, it's natural; but it was also natural that we started reacting aggressively too. Today, I am still friends with many of those boys; we don't speak of that time. When I was younger, I thought I would forget. I know now that things will never be the same again.

Now the Tears Have Dried Up

DHIREN BHAGAT

This was first published as an article in the Sunday Observer *on 25 November 1984. Dhiren Bhagat, a journalist, witnessed the massacres of 1984. His article throws light on how politicians of all parties used the events of 1984 as a vote-game. He also critically describes the issues involved in the resettlement of the survivors. In a way, he points out the lacunae in the administration and institutions, as well as the failure of the idea that every individual is entitled to the right to live with dignity and freedom irrespective of his or her religion.*

On 9 November when a senior minister's wife turned up with two hundred blankets at the refugee relief camp set up by Sardar Mehtab Singh by his house in Karol Bagh's Ajmal Khan Park, things weren't quite as smooth as she would have liked. 'We accorded her whatever reception was required,' Jaspal Singh, the organizer's son, recalled, with what I took to be a faint touch of irony, 'but the volunteers who had been working here since the camp was started, they were all agreed that no government assistance should be accepted.' This seems to have been a fairly standard response: all over Delhi volunteers and residents of camps have reacted this way to what they perceive to be the government's callousness in delaying aid. One volunteer made a similar point about the Congress party: 'The Congress says we haven't organized the riots. Okay. But then tell me, when a calamity like this occurs, all workers of all parties come to help. Where have the Congress party men gone?' The minister's wife, it appears, 'felt a bit bad and small'. Understanding the reaction of the volunteers, she asked the organizers if she could do anything. Would they like to meet her husband? Could he be of help? They went to see him the next day. To their surprise, perhaps, she confirmed their stories of Congress involvement. She had been visiting various camps and had picked up enough information. 'If we had one name, the minister's wife and PA confirmed many others.' The minister seemed convinced.

Later, at the same meeting, the camp organizers asked the minister to do something to restore Sikh confidence in the government and the ruling party. It was important, they said, that those who had incited and led the mobs be punished, both in the courts and with expulsion from the party. Now it was the minister's turn to plead his woes. 'Confidentially,' he is reported to have said, 'in this government my own position is not clear. Till I get close enough to Rajiv, how can I put your case to him?'

For political Delhi, the riots might never have occurred. As speculation over who would be favoured with Congress tickets grew this past week, no other concern was manifest. I dined at the home of one such Congress hopeful and the chatter of party district presidents and city presidents graced the table. At one point, a guest who had nothing to do with the Congress Party mentioned the riots. The host rose to the occasion, '*Haan, woh jo Jan Sanghiyon ne kiya, haan* (Yes, that which the Jan Sanghis did)' and the sentence trailed off. I protested and my protest was carried—but only because a joint secretary of the party who was present came up with the most guilty, hangdog expression I have ever seen. I may be naïve, but I am convinced that this was the first time since 31 October that our host had begun to understand the complicity of his party in the riots. (If you read only the *Times of India*, the *National Herald* and the *Patriot*, and mix with the right people, such blessed ignorance is only to be expected.) After dinner, and after the assistant inspector of police who had read the party hopeful's hand had left, we asked what predictions the palmist had made. '*Kehta hai ke chance bees per cent badh gaya hai* (He says chances have increased twenty per cent).' '*Pehle kya kehta tha, kya chance tha* (What did he say your chances were earlier)?' the district president inquired. And the serious reply: '*Pehle kehta tha sau per cent chance tha ticket ka, ab kehta hai savasau per cent chance hai* (He said first that I had a 100 per cent chance of winning a ticket, now he says I have a 125 per cent chance).'

Earlier that day, I had spoken to a friend of mine in the Opposition, a fairly important party aide. I had sympathized with him about the new situation and then (in my innocence) said that at least they now had a proper issue to fight the election on: who had started the Delhi riots? His reply made perfect sense: 'Fight the election on this issue?' he said.'Are you crazy? Go to the villages and they are saying *aur kyoon nahin maara Sikhon ko* (Why didn't they kill more Sikhs)? In Bombay and Delhi, if we are lucky, this will count; in the press, amongst the intellectuals. In the rest of India, no way. It will backfire and people will say *achha kiya Congress ne* (the Congress did well). What can we do in such a country?' So, at last I knew why the Congress party hopeful didn't need to know about the riots.

'The tears have dried up,' Jaspal Singh said to me at his father's camp at Ajmal Khan Park. After 12 November, the government representatives who used to come by regularly stopped coming. Even the response of the Indian press they had found disappointing. With very few exceptions, most of the reporting had been slanted and had tried to play down the impact of the riots. 'Many reporters used to come here and take down details of cases, but after a few days when the people in the camp saw that none of their stories were appearing in the papers they stopped talking to the press."What's the use?" they said.'

The administration, however, has begun to throw its weight. Class I officers from all public sector undertakings have been deputed to report on what can be done. There are many suggestions in the air. Since the residents of colonies like Trilokpuri do not wish to go back ('Do you want us to go back and live among those who killed our fathers and raped our sisters?'), it was suggested to the government that it exchange those plots for others of the same size in other colonies, preferably colonies where several Sikhs could live together in comparative safety. The government's first response to this suggestion was: 'Right, surrender your land first'. The residents of the camps were willing to do so, but the organizers intervened and said they would only countenance exchange of plots, not immediate surrender. Another suggestion that has been made is that the government allocate alternative plots and free cement to those whose houses have been damaged and get the able-bodied among the refugees to start building their own dwellings. 'That will keep the men busy,' said a Sikh camp organizer to me. 'When the men are idle who can say what their minds will turn to? So far, we have forbidden them from any slogan-shouting, not even Bole so nihaal within the camp, but if they are unemployed for long who can say?'

Young Sikhs have begun comparing the position of their co-religionists with that of the Jews and have begun thinking in terms of kibbutz-style dwellings. But kibbutz-style protection works both ways. Certainly, those within the kibbutzes will be more protected in the event of another such carnage, but those who choose to live apart will be even more vulnerable.

Several Sikhs have begun contemplating building a new colony to resettle the refugees. Tilaknagar and Fatehnagar have been discussed as possible sites. But it is not enough to build houses; many of the people who have fled from their homes have lost their means of survival as well. So, there is talk of setting up small-scale industries in the new colonies, knitting and papad-making. But for any such industry to succeed, marketing institutions are required.

The horrors of the riots remain, a permanent legacy. Resettlement can only be a partial reparation. Those who are involved in the resettlement are constantly reminded of this. 'Yesterday Mr Seth, an assistant labour commissioner who has been attached to us,' Jaspal Singh recalled, 'came with us to the Trans-Yamuna area for a survey to identify loss of life and loss of dwelling units. He had three colonies to visit. He could only go to three houses and then he broke down and cried. He said, "It is not possible, I can't go on. Just fill in the forms, you confirm them and I'll sign them." We were in a house where the women were going about their work and there were ashes and bones all around. You see, the men had not yet returned and there was no one to clear the phul.'

'I COULD SEE HOUSES BURNING, TAXI STANDS BURNING':
MANMOHAN SINGH AND GURSHARAN KAUR

Interviewed by
DAMAN SINGH

In Strictly Personal: Manmohan and Gursharan *(HarperCollins, 2014), her book about her parents, Manmohan Singh and Gursharan Kaur, Daman Singh has a chapter on the events following Indira Gandhi's assassination in 1984. It charts former Prime Minister Manmohan Singh's experiences as the Governor of the Reserve Bank of India in Bombay at the time. It also touches on the experiences of his relatives and the impact of the time on their personal lives. Excerpts from this chapter have been included here as they exemplify how identity surfaces at times of communal conflict, no matter how privileged a person's position. If the movements of a person of the stature of Dr Manmohan Singh were restricted due to his religious identity, one can only imagine the plight of ordinary people in the same situation. The conversations in this excerpt are between Daman Singh and her parents.*

By the late 1970s, religion and politics in Punjab were hopelessly entangled with each other. The resultant turmoil would last close to a decade and a half. Armed groups sought to settle questions of faith as well as contests of power by force. A section of Sikhs demanded a separate state that they called Khalistan. Targeted by militants, Hindus started leaving Punjab in large numbers. Sikhs who did not support the militant cause were threatened or killed. Police action was inadequate and ineffectual. Outside Punjab, planes were hijacked and bombs were detonated. Talks between the Akali Dal and the central government started and stopped, only to start and stop again. By the end of 1983, the Golden Temple at Amritsar had become the command centre of militant activities.

In April 1984, violence reached its peak. In June, the Indian Army entered the Golden Temple. Hundreds of people lost their lives. The temple complex was devastated by artillery fire. Prime Minister Indira Gandhi was assassinated by two Sikh security guards in her own home in October. And that November, thousands of Sikhs living in Delhi and other cities were massacred.

~

My father was a student at Amritsar and at Hoshiarpur during the 1950s. He began his academic career in Hoshiarpur and taught in Chandigarh till 1966. Once he joined the central government, he saw the official view of the Punjab situation. For the unofficial view, he relied on friends and relatives from Punjab. I wonder whether he realized the havoc that it was heading for.

'There was unrest in the '80s when terrorist groups came into existence, but until that time life in Punjab was, I think, peaceful. In the '50s and '60s there were several agitations by the Akali Dal for setting up a Punjabi-speaking state. That demand was conceded in 1966. Then there were elections in Punjab and an Akali Dal government came into office. This satisfied them because it was essentially a struggle for power. But that government didn't last very long. And then, in 1972, a Congress government led by Giani Zail Singh came into being. The atmosphere was quite peaceful, but in the late '70s the phenomenon of Sant Bhindranwale came on the scene. His followers terrorized a lot of people and they also killed some prominent Hindus.'

'Some analysts say that the Punjab agitation was essentially a struggle for greater autonomy for states vis-a-vis the centre...'

'That was what the Akalis claimed, but they were never able to explain exactly what they wanted.'

'Greater religious freedom, perhaps?'

'No, it was not a struggle for religious freedom. Under the Constitution of India, everyone is free to practice the religion of his choice. All citizens have freedom of worship.'

'But wasn't there a sense of discrimination—'

'There was no—'

'A perceived sense of discrimination—'

'Yes, a perceived sense of discrimination. But in fact, the Sikhs had done quite well in India. They were a small minority but their percentage in the armed forces and in the central forces were quite impressive. And Punjab's progress in terms of economic development was also quite impressive. Punjab was until very recently, the number one state in India in terms of standard of living indicators.'

'Then what do you think fed this perception?'

'Objectively speaking, the Sikhs had no reason to feel aggrieved. But people got carried away. There was a considerable amount of unemployment among young people. They were attracted to terrorism as an ideology, fed by religious fanaticism.'

'When the situation took a communal turn, was that unexpected?'

'Communal issues had always been there. The Akalis created a sense of perceived grievance among the Sikhs all the time. But when it came to sharing power, the Akalis combined with the Jan Sangh in forming a government. Every time there was a chance, the Akalis and the Jan Sangh got together.'

'How do you explain that?'

'Well, I think sharing power unites people.'

Five years of Congress rule ended in April 1977. For the next decade no government would be able to complete its term in office. Punctuated by periods of president's rule, the Congress and the Akali Dal-Jan Sangh combine took turns to rule Punjab. The longest-ever stretch of president's rule lasted from 1987 to 1992. This would be followed by a Congress government and then an Akali Dal one, each of which was finally able to govern for five years.

'When the supporters of Bhindranwale moved into various gurdwaras, did the Sikh community react?'

'They had the support of the Akali Dal, they had the support of the Shiromani Gurdwara Prabandhak Committee. I think that is what resulted in the Sikh religious places becoming centres of terrorist activity. The Akal Takht became the seat of Sant Bhindranwale. It was a violation of everything that Sikhism stood for.'

'So, voices against this—'

'The voices against them were pretty weak at one time.'

'Do you remember what you thought then?'

'I was very worried about the consequences of all this. I could sense a feeling in the air which was not very healthy.'

Elements of the Sikh diaspora provided both moral and material support to separatist activity in Punjab. I ask whether he was aware of this when he lived in England and in America.

'I kept away from them.'

'Deliberately?'

'No, but I didn't do anything to associate myself with them. There were some people among them who believed in Khalistan.'

Ajit Singh's name comes up at this point. He is a former student of my father, and a friend of long standing. As an academic, he made a name for himself at Cambridge University. Ajit had been approached by a group of Sikhs who wanted to open a bank in England. They asked for his support as a prominent Sikh intellectual.

'And you told him to stay away—'

'Yes, at that time I was the Governor of the Reserve Bank.'

'What was your apprehension?'

'That it would become a bank that financed separatist activities.'

As the situation deteriorated, my parents worried about our relatives, most of whom lived in Punjab. But the unrest was not restricted to Punjab alone. It also spread to Delhi and to Haryana.

'How did this affect you, say, as an official?'

'Well, I was worried as an individual. I was worried as a Sikh.'

'Why?'

'Because people started looking upon Sikhs as undesirable characters.'

'In what way?'

'Because the association of Sikhs with terrorism had affected the attitude of people towards the Sikhs.'

'But how was that visible, this attitude?'

'It was quite visible.'

'How?'

'When it came to giving jobs, when it came to giving houses on rent, when it came to employment—there was a certain fear, distrust.'

I can see that he does not like being badgered like this.

In those days he was required to travel a great deal, in India and abroad, whether alone or with an official delegation. On many occasions he was made to step aside for intrusive questioning and stringent security checks. But, as he points out, ordinary people had to put up with far worse.

~

Operation Blue Star was launched on 5 June—after Punjab was stilled by imposition of curfew in major towns, suspension of transport and communications, interruption of electricity supply, and censorship of press. The outer defences and fortifications built by militants around the temple complex were destroyed. Buildings within the complex, including the Akal Takht, were stormed. The main shrine itself remained untouched. According to the official count, eighty-three military personnel and 493 civilians were killed. Of the 1,592 people apprehended during the operation, 379 were detained. A large amount of arms and ammunition was recovered. According to unofficial estimates, the casualties were in thousands. And various sources alleged the excessive use of force, torture and summary executions.

My parents were in Bombay when this happened. They had heard the prime minister address the nation on television the night of 2 June.

'Yes. I did listen to that. I felt very sad that the holiest places of the Sikh religion had to be rescued from terrorists by armed intervention by the Indian armed forces. I felt very sad.'

'At that time very little information was given out about the operation. But slowly as more and more information came out—'

'It was a big shock that so much blood was shed.'

'And the spontaneous reaction of Sikhs against the central government—did you share that?'

'I didn't share that.'

'No? Not at any level?'

'No. I felt sad as a Sikh that the Golden Temple had to witness these events. But I thought that these people had forced the situation. I think no country can turn a blind eye to secessionist activities.'

'Sikh soldiers deserted the army, various officers and Members of Parliament resigned, some returned awards that had been given to them by the central government…'

'That was an emotional reaction on some people's part. But I didn't feel that way. It was a period of general confusion, of distrust.'

What I remember most from that time is the awful silence in the house.

~

My mother prefers not to talk about Operation Blue Star. I ask her several questions. She either says she does not know, or that she does not remember. If I were to read her mind, it would probably tell me that Sikh gurus never preached hatred towards anyone. People like Bhindranwale interpreted Sikhism in their own way—that was not the popular view. The Congress used him for its own political gain. There were a lot of extremists who extorted money from people. There were killings of Hindus as well as Sikhs. When the police were given a free hand, they pulled out young Sikhs from their homes and killed them in fake encounters. Why were militants allowed to stay in the Akal Takht? If they were not, there would have been no guns, no bombs, no tanks.

She is willing to talk about the specific case of her cousin who was one of the 1,592 people apprehended from the Golden Temple, as well as one of the 379 detained.

'She was missing for quite some time, then we found out that she had been taken prisoner. They charged her with firing from an M-something. She had actually come to visit the Golden Temple. She did not live far from there, maybe just five minutes away. Maybe she had decided to offer certain prayers for a certain number of days—I'm not sure. There were army and police patrols around the Darbar Sahib. They stopped her on the way and told her to go back, not to go inside. She said, no, I have to go. If she had listened, nothing would have happened. She went in, and then there was a lot of firing. She lost an eye. A lot of people died. Some jumped into the sarovar, or some were dumped into the sarovar, I don't know much about it. But a lot of people were killed.'

'How was she rescued?'

'She wasn't rescued. She was in jail for four or five years.'

'Years!'

'Yes. She was sent to Jodhpur jail. I remember talking to so many people. I probably spoke to Buta Singh—he was the home minister—telling him that this is what happened. She had a small child, about a year old. Nothing happened. In the end I don't know when exactly she was released.'

~

Mrs Gandhi was assassinated on 31 October 1984. My father remembers that day clearly.

'I was in the office, in the Reserve Bank, and suddenly the news came. And I felt very sad. I was very close to Indiraji. It was a shock. We arranged a condolence meeting. There was tension in Bombay city, but nothing happened against the Sikh population.'

'Do you think there was a reason for that?'

'I think the administration was strong. Where the administration was weak, a lot of atrocities took place against innocent Sikhs. In Delhi itself many were killed.'

According to my mother, there were rumours that Sikhs in Bombay had asked—and perhaps paid—the Shiv Sena for protection.

'You came to Delhi for Mrs Gandhi's funeral, didn't you?'

'I couldn't go for it.'

'But I thought you did—'

'I came to lay a wreath when she was lying in state at Teen Murti Bhavan. But I couldn't attend the funeral.'

'Why not?'

'At that time I was advised that the communal atmosphere was too charged. And I could see houses burning, taxi stands burning.'

'So what did you do?'

'I stayed in the Reserve Bank guest house.'

'You just stayed in the guest house?'

'Yes. I just stayed there. Kiki and Vijay were in Ashok Vihar.* In all localities where there were Sikh houses, the Sikhs were attacked.'

My father's uncle, Gopal Singh, owned a petrol pump in Dehradun. It was burned down. Mohni bhenji's daughter, Neetu, lived in Kanpur. Her home was burned down too. Gobind bhenji's daughter, Veena, lived in Sagar. Their house and shop were also burned down. My mother's cousin, Harbhajan, had just been transferred to Delhi. He and his wife were stranded at the Delhi airport for over twenty-four hours. Taking along a Hindu friend, their son Guddu went to pick them up. Their car was stoned on the way. They reached the airport with great difficulty and did not think it was possible to return with two Sikhs in the car. So, the friend left with their luggage. Guddu stayed with his parents at the airport until a Reserve Bank official arrived and took them to Harbans bhapaji's house under police escort. To escape a similar experience, our friend Vindu stayed with my parents in Bombay for several days until it was considered safe for him to return to Delhi.

Kiki and Vijay were living in the house that my parents built. Ashok Vihar was hit by rioting. I was then studying at Anand, in Gujarat. On 5 November my mother wrote to tell me what was going on:

> What a terrible tragedy has hit our country! Delhi has been badly damaged. Your Daddy wanted to go to Delhi on Thursday but was advised not to. Then he went on Saturday morning by the Air India flight at 3.30 a.m., and came back on Sunday (yesterday) by the 6.30 a.m. flight and reached here at 8.30. He could only go to Teen Murti Bhavan straight from the airport and the rest of the day he spent at the flat. He sent the car for Kiki and Vijay to come to the flat to meet him there because it was too dangerous for him to go anywhere.
>
> A gang came to burn our house in Ashok Vihar, but Vijay

---

* Daman Singh's elder sister and brother-in-law, respectively.

saved it. Some people said that actually this house belongs to a Sikh, but Vijay told them that he had bought the house and he was the owner. Even Panditji [the priest at the temple opposite the house] joined those people. At some places Hindu neighbours came forward and protected their Sikh neighbours, but [not everywhere]... The whole thing is so sickening. Mrs Gandhi's assassination was bad enough but what has happened afterwards is absolutely disgusting.

~

The events of 1984 would fuel the next phase of the Punjab agitation. Violence stepped up. Militants acquired assault rifles and sophisticated explosives. Elections were held in 1985. The Akali Dal came to power. President's rule followed less than two years later. The centre resumed talks with various groups and factions. Police action intensified. Militants were evacuated from the Golden Temple again in 1986, and yet again in 1988. Arbitrary detention, torture, and killing of innocent people were widely alleged.

Almost as many civilians were killed during 1990 and 1991 as in the preceding twelve years. In February 1992, assembly elections were held amidst huge deployment of security forces. They were boycotted by the Akalis and voter turnout was minimal. Though it won less than ten per cent of the popular vote, the Congress formed a government. Casualties were down by the end of that year. And in panchayat elections held in January 1993 the turnout was a reassuring 82 per cent.

By the end of 1993, the days of militancy were officially over. A total of 21,469 people had lost their lives since the early 1980s. A majority of them were Sikhs. And the sense of anger persisted.

'Yes it did. But I realized that anger was not the answer. Anger I could understand, but I didn't think it could yield any results. The Sikhs have been—and will always be—an integral part of the Indian polity. Our gurus sacrificed all their being in order to protect Indian culture and civilization. To separate Sikhism or Sikhs from the rest of the Indian polity is something I never appreciated.'

'Do you think such episodes are now in the past?'

'No, I don't think so. I think there are a lot of tensions built into the body politic of a poor country trying to modernize itself. And because the process of modernization is not free of risk, some people go forward, others are left out. Those who are left out feel hurt, and they believe that it is because of the system.'

'So the state—'

'The state has to preserve law and order, and people have to realize that violence has no role in a democratic polity. Fortunately, we have a democracy. People can change their government, people can express their dissent, there are opportunities for people to express their feelings. We have to ensure that violence is not resorted to for the redressal of grievances. At the same time it is the obligation of the governing elite to ensure that in the process of governance—in the process of social and economic change—the interests of the weaker sections are protected, that they can truly become partners in progress. So that they also get a share—an equitable share—in development.'

'But over the past twenty years—'

'Well, efforts have been made. We have programmes and plan schemes for scheduled castes, scheduled tribes, minorities. I think there are problems in their implementation, but the intent is certainly there to take everybody along, particularly the weaker sections of society. We are the only country where there is affirmative action for scheduled castes, scheduled tribes, backward classes.'

'What about the use of force?'

'Force is used only against those who take up arms against the state. No state can allow that.'

'In your experience have the victims of riots ever found justice?'

'I think there are weaknesses in our system. But it would be wrong to say that there is no effort to ameliorate the suffering of the people who are at the receiving end of this violence.'

'Yes, but can our legal system actually deliver justice?'

'There are defects in our legal system. Several people who committed crimes against the Sikhs have taken advantage of the court system to escape punishment. These are problems of growing up. All developed countries have gone through these stages. And hopefully the march of democracy, plus greater educational facilities, will provide opportunities to deal with these issues more purposefully.'

'Punjab is also a case where the mingling of religion and politics—'

'Yes. That tells us that mingling of religion and politics can lead to dangerous results.'

'What about relations between the Centre and the states?'

'The Constitution of India provides us a system where there is ample opportunity for the development of states. At the same time the Constitution ensures that the Union is strong enough to protect the country against external and internal emergency situations. That—we need. I think our Consitution has—on the whole—proved to be a very effective instrument.'

'But while the Constitution may draw the lines, isn't there always scope for interpretation?'

'Yes, I think those who operate the Constitution leave much to be desired.'

~

When my parents returned from Bombay, they spent the first few weeks in Ashok Vihar. Several houses in the area still bore signs of the riots. It was hard to forget what had happened. And it was hard to imagine what would happen in the future. Kiki and Vijay did not want our parents to live there, ever. They advised them to sell the house.

The house belonged more to my mother than anyone else. In 1986 it was sold.

Had Sardarji Lived...

HARSH MANDER

The following extract is by Harsh Mander, from Fatal Accidents of Birth: Stories of Suffering, Oppression and Resistance *(Speaking Tiger, 2016). Lachmi, from a Labana Sikh community, lost her husband and many members of her family in 1984 and now lives in Tilak Vihar Widow's Colony. Her struggle to keep her children untouched by drugs has been her greatest success.*

It would be hard to find a building more burdened with suffering and memory in all of Delhi. And yet, if you walked past it, you would hardly turn your head to look at it again. There was nothing that distinguished it from the tens of thousands of other urban cages anywhere in the country. Floor after floor was crowded with one-room tenements, of the kind that governments occasionally build as homes for people of very meagre means. The customary signs of neglect were visible everywhere: peeling paint, crumbling plaster, exposed electric wires, stale unlit rooms. Also, the forced intimacy and vibrancy of community living—clothes and underwear hung out to dry on small verandahs; boys playing cricket in narrow corridors; girls in uniforms rushing from school to housework; women gathered in knots chatting, snatching some brief moments of leisure from the chores of cooking and cleaning.

It would be difficult to know, from the outside, that it was in this unsightly apartment building in Tilak Vihar that the government had settled 450 widows and their children who survived the terrible massacre of Sikh men and boys in 1984 on the streets of Delhi. It was official fiat which conjured within its walls a community of suffering, one in which several hundred boys and girls grew up with no fathers. These children initially assumed that this is how life is for all children. But each was destined to gradually and separately learn and struggle agonizingly to come to terms with the dreadful truths of how they lost their fathers and brothers: to tyres flung around their necks and set on fire, to daggers and guns, to sticks and iron rods, to the betrayal of neighbours, to the sudden eruption of a volcano of mindless, deadly hate.

My engagement with Tilak Vihar had begun with a small research project in which I and a couple of young colleagues, Navjot Singh and Manisha Sobhrajani, tried to assess the conditions of the widows and their children. But the pervasiveness, depth and hopelessness of the suffering that we encountered in the tenements of Tilak Vihar was so stunning that I felt I had to reach out to friends with an appeal to start a small initiative of solidarity and healing with the widows and their families. Some wonderful caring friends came forward and a modest enterprise took shape, and is ongoing.

It was on one of my visits to Tilak Vihar that I met Lachmi Kaur in a dank, airless third-floor apartment. An unlettered matriarch, she had lived there half her life. It was within the cramped confines of this home that she raised her children and grandchildren with fierce love and resolve. She stood resolutely between them, the survivors of the slaughter in 1984, and all that had disfigured her own life: want, illiteracy and hate.

Lachmi Kaur looked much older than her age. She often sobbed, alternating between rage, heartache and defeat as she summoned her memories and shared them with me. I observed in her a woman who had been severely battered, but who remained proud and unbroken. One of her sons, in his thirties, unendingly paced the small apartment like a caged animal, muttering under his breath. Her younger son, in his late twenties, slept all day, refusing to work. She toiled to feed them both, as well as their wives and children.

Nine years before Lachmi was born, her parents were uprooted from their village in the Sukkur-Rohri area of Sindh in what is now Pakistan. The violence of Partition drove them first to the twin cities of Sukkur-Rohri. But they were eventually forced to flee from there too. They migrated from city to city in what was then the Bombay Province, unsuccessfully searching for work and a homestead. They were finally allotted a plot of agricultural land in a village, Tes Ki Buli, near Alwar in Rajasthan, almost a decade after they had left Pakistan as refugees. Lachmi was born in 1956, soon after their arrival in the village. She joined her parents in the fields as a young child, planting saplings, harvesting paddy, picking weeds and cutting sugarcane. She never went to school.

Her family belonged to a subaltern sect of the Sikhs, the Labanas, who are more comfortable speaking Sindhi (and now Hindi) than Punjabi. They worship in separate gurdwaras, and follow many unusual religious practices, such as the worship of the graves of prominent individuals of their community, similar to Sufi dargahs, which other orthodox Sikhs would find sacrilegious. When she was thirteen, her parents found her a Labana Sikh groom, Sundar Singh, from a neighbouring village. Soon after they were wed, Sundar Singh moved alone to Delhi to seek better prospects and managed to build a hut in the slum resettlement colony of Mangolpuri. He initially sold vegetables on a handcart and gradually saved enough to bring over his young teenaged bride, Lachmi. Together, they set up a successful meat shop. One by one, all her seven brothers followed them to the metropolis and settled in the same neighbourhood. Some pulled rickshaws, others wove charpoys. Her husband, whom she called Sardarji, would buy goats from the wholesale market in Paharganj and skin them himself, after ritually killing them in the jhatka manner—slaughtering the animal with a single strike of the knife to sever the head from the body—in conformity with Sikh religious tenets. He would hang the carcasses in his kiosk in the small market adjacent to the Hanuman statue near the cinema hall in Mangolpuri, and would dress, weigh and sell the meat through the day.

In time, as their business grew, Lachmi also learned to assist her husband. She would herself slaughter the goats, and that too with a single jhatka strike. She recalled that it was perhaps this practice which helped her keep a level head during the slaughter of 1984, as she hid and tried to rescue seven men even after her husband and brothers had been killed. She was accustomed to the sight of flowing blood, she said.

She bore three children, two boys and a girl, and insisted on sending them all to school. She was content with her life.

This life changed irrevocably one afternoon when people came to their colony, lamenting, 'Indira Gandhi has been killed.' The day was 31 October 1984. Lachmi's immediate response was that of grief. Many in their settlement credited Prime Minister Indira Gandhi with settling poor people like them—many of whom had been uprooted from slums—in Mangolpuri, with house-sites in their own name. There were very few Sikhs in the colony, perhaps twenty families, all of whom were Labanas. Most of the residents of the locality belonged to the scheduled and the backward castes. These included members of the denotified tribe, Sansi, in large numbers, who now mainly make a living from selling alcohol. Lachmi's neighbours on all sides were Sansi, except the house right opposite, in which lived a eunuch.

Lachmi did not light the fire in her kitchen that evening, in mourning for the departed leader. Sardarji, her husband, was confused about how he should respond to her assassination; after all, he knew that it was on Indira Gandhi's orders that troops had stormed the Golden Temple in Amritsar and ravaged the sacred structure. In revenge, two of her Sikh bodyguards gunned her down in the garden of her official residence. But Lachmi recalled asking him, in tears, to shut his shop down for a day, in tribute and gratitude to the woman who had given them their home. Hearing Lachmi say this, she recalled, even Sardarji broke down and exclaimed affectionately: 'Look how this illiterate woman is trying to make sense of all of this for me!'

It was because they were in mourning that the entire family was home when the mobs arrived.

The rioters were armed strangers from outside Magolpuri, but were joined by many residents from within the colony. They began to pull out Sikh men and youths from every home. They soon lit fires on all the exit routes to prevent the Sikhs from escaping. Lachmi desperately pleaded with their only neighbour who had not joined the mobs, the eunuch, to hide her husband in her home, but she refused. 'This is beyond me. They are killing all Sikhs. Do you want me to get killed?' she asked agitatedly.

Sardarji did not want to endanger his entire family and as the waves of rioters moved closer to their house, resolved to make a run for the Mangolpuri Police Station. What happened next was related to Lachmi by other Sikh men who survived because they had shaved their beards and chopped off their long hair.

He was waylaid by the mob and felled with two or three blows to the head with heavy sticks. He still tried to escape by pelting bricks at the horde, when policemen from that very same police station surrounded him, flung a tyre around his neck and set it afire. The survivors told Lachmi that even with a flaming tyre around his neck, Sardarji kept fending off the throng with bricks and kept running until he was finally shot dead by a uniformed policeman. He collapsed close to his meat shop, and right opposite the police station. Five of Lachmi's seven brothers were also slaughtered in the massacre, which was to continue unabated for three days and three nights.

Some rioters then reached their home and fell upon Lachmi's older son, at that time around twelve years old, with sticks. When they struck blows upon his head, Lachmi tried to shield him with her own body and begged the attackers to let him go. The boy fell unconscious and the attackers left him for dead. Lachmi quickly hid him in the toilet. When she later went to feed him, he started crying and complained that his head ached. By the time they reached the relief camp in Punjabi Bagh four days later, he was seized with a high fever and one of his arms was paralyzed. She got him treated, even taking him to doctors in private practice, but his arm remains crippled and he walks with a pronounced limp. His mind is restless and in torment, unceasingly battling the demons of that day.

Even though she had lost her husband and brothers, Lachmi held herself together, looking desperately for ways to save the seven Sikh men in her neighbourhood who still survived. She pleaded with all the people she knew but no one came forward. Their eunuch neighbour was the only one who agreed, finally, to help hide them in a loft in her home.

Meanwhile, a neighbour tried to take advantage of the situation and grabbed Lachmi. She slapped him fiercely and asked how he could molest someone who was like his sister. Enraged, the man went out and led a mob to the eunuch's house, from where they mercilessly chased out and lynched the hiding Sikh men. Of those seven, only one survived. He was Lachmi's teenaged brother, whom she managed to save by disguising him as a girl. The killings continued.

There were six Labana Sikh households on their street. Out of the menfolk, only four ultimately survived.

Apart from the eunuch, none of their neighbours helped, except for one Dalit jamadar, a stranger who came to their ravaged home at night with cooked rice for the children. She was initially frightened that he may try to rape her, like their neighbour had attempted that afternoon. But he reassured her, saying, 'Don't worry, Lachmiji, you are like my sister.' Lachmi recalled: 'He appeared like an angel out of nowhere and disappeared after giving us food and succour that night. He neither told us his name nor gave us his address ... nothing.'

For three days as the rioting continued, they hid in Mangolpuri. On the morning of 3 November 1984, the military finally moved in. They pulled in all the survivors—mostly women and children—into their olive-green trucks and transported them out of the colony to a civilian camp in Punjabi Bagh. Lachmi remembered, 'The soldiers and officers were kind to us, but the civil authorities to whom they handed us over were callous and did not even care to give us water to drink.' From Punjabi Bagh, they were moved to another camp in Rani Bagh. After that, Sikh organizations came forward with aid and shifted them to a gurdwara in Greater Kailash. There they were looked after for a month and a half, at the end of which—humiliated and tired of living on charity—most people vacated the camps. Lachmi went back to her village in Alwar with her children, to the home of her birth.

While in Alwar she heard that compensation as well as jobs were being offered to victims of the 1984 riots. She not did want to burden her indigent parents, so after a month or two of mourning she came back to Delhi. After living for a few more months in various camps, she was allotted the apartment in Tilak Vihar in early 1985, about four months after the riots. The building had been constructed before the 1984 carnage to rehabilitate people who had been uprooted from slums because of demolitions carried out by the government. But after the massacre, officials decided to allot the building and its apartments to some of the many Sikh widows whose husbands had been slaughtered on Delhi's streets. Incidentally, Lachmi had to struggle with officials of the Delhi Development Authority even for this accommodation, for it had been assigned to another woman named Lachmi Kaur, whose dead husband was also named Sundar Singh.

To start with, the compensation of ten thousand rupees which she got from the government helped her feed and clothe her family. Then a Sikh organization, Nishkam, started a centre for the rehabilitation of the widows, where she was paid two hundred and fifty rupees a month to pound and pack red chilli powder, salt and spices. Eventually, in 1986, she was given a government job. Being unlettered, she only qualified as a peon at a local school. Her salary from this school remained the principal income for her entire extended family even two decades later.

Each of the women in Tilak Vihar relate similar stories of toil, struggle and courage in raising their children and siblings. Nothing had prepared these mostly unlettered working-class women to face the world alone. But they fought valiantly, often heroically, to raise their children and grandchildren, battling profound loss, memory and penury. Nearly thirty years later, Gauri Gill, a photographer, brought together a little book containing numerous testimonies of the widows and their children.[*] In the book, Darshan Kaur recounts, 'I have seen nothing of life. I have only cried. But still, you may have noticed, none of us is a beggar. I trekked 35 kilometres to work every day (to save money), but I have not begged.' Gopi Kaur was given a job as a water woman in Kailash Nagar. But 'I never knew how to take a bus, had never stepped out of the house...I would first be dropped by my brother, then my son. In the bus I would go crazy, crying right up until Darya Ganj.' Pappi Kaur was only fifteen when eleven members of

---

[*] Gauri Gill, *1984*, Kafila. www.gaurigill.com

her family were killed, and she hid under a pile of corpses to escape the rampaging mobs. Today she makes a living by making electrical sockets.

Some of the sons also grew up to support their mothers in their struggles. Manjit was just a month old when his father, grandfather and three uncles were all burnt to death. His mother died of cancer, and he dropped out of school to work as a driver. Autorickshaw-driver Gurdayal says, 'My father and two brothers were both killed in the '1984 riots, and here I am, uneducated, trying my best to make ends meet.' But many of their children, especially sons and younger brothers, like Lachmi's, now middle-aged men, could not cope with gruesome memories of the brutal ways their fathers were killed, and fell prey to mental illness and drug addiction. Bhaggi Kaur, who lost her husband in 1984, now mourns her son who took an overdose of painkillers eight years ago. The widows lamented, 'Our lives lie in ruins, as do those of our children. If we can see any hope in the far distance, it is that maybe our grandchildren will one day be able to see a little happiness.'

There was no question of Lachmi ever returning to their home in Mangolpuri. It would have meant stepping willfully into a life of fear in a neighbourhood peopled by non-Sikhs, and of gruesome memories. Lachmi therefore sold her house for merely twenty thousand rupees—a distress sale—to a local resident who had been an acquaintance of her husband. The man coerced her into selling the house, saying that if she refused, she would lose the twenty thousand rupees and might even wash her hands off the property. Lachmi later learnt that soon after, the man sold the same house for a huge profit and moved back to Kanpur. For her, in those early days, every rupee counted. She could not have waited for better times.

Lachmi filed a police complaint after her husband's death. She was given a death certificate but no action was taken on her complaint. There were some Sikh organizations which helped her pursue her claims for compensation, but no one came forward to help her fight the criminal cases and bring to book the policeman who had killed Sardarji in cold blood, or even her neighbours who had joined the rampaging mobs. She said to me, 'I believe the perpetrators should be punished, and something should be done to alter the sad state of affairs where only innocent victims like us are being punished with hardship and despair. The Sikhs who killed Indira Gandhi have been punished with death, so why should poor innocent Sikhs like us continue to suffer? Our worlds were uprooted and our breadwinners killed and we were left to fend for ourselves. We have somehow struggled to survive...'

But Lachmi harboured no bitterness. 'I am just an illiterate woman. But I believe it is the same blood which flows in everyone's veins. I do not have the energy to hate anyone, although I do wonder how the perpetrators did not feel ashamed about killing innocents. That they still do not.' She had heard about the Gujarat massacre of 2002. 'I don't think targeting any one religious community is right, whether Sikhs or Muslims. Why should anyone be attacked and why should any poor person get killed? In my heart, I feel the pain of anyone who suffers misfortune, including people killed in riots or by bombs; I feel their shock and their fears.' She broke down. 'We have been through such tragedy and have had to endure it all; we know how it feels.'

She recalled the quarter century that she had lived until then in her home in Tilak Vihar, devoted to one single uncompromising mission: of trying to raise her children—and grandchildren—as good human beings. She was convinced that they should not be unlettered like her. Her elder son could never study—saddled as he had become with disability and painful memories—but she sent her younger boy and girl to a government school nearby. She worried obsessively that they would stumble and fall without a father to guide them. And so, she became both father and mother to them. She was vigilant for the slightest misdemeanour, and would punish them even if she suspected that they had strayed from the straight and the narrow. One day, her son brought home from school a pencil which did not belong to him. She thrashed him roundly, and it was a furious Lachmi who stormed into school the following morning to berate his bemused teacher for failing to teach her son right from wrong. She tried to insulate all of them from what she felt was bad company and the evil influence of their environment.

Over time, an unfortunate vocation—born of desperation—came to haunt this colony of widows. It was hard for the single women, many of them without education, unaccustomed to negotiating with the world alone, to raise their children single-handedly. Some got government jobs, others looked for work as domestic helps, but money was always in short supply. And so it was that gradually, over the years, the colony evolved as a centre of drug peddling. No one knows when and how it started. As the young boys grew older, this was the vocation into which many were inexorably drawn. What the women had not understood was that the same drugs which they traded would drag their own children into their lethal illusory comforts. Today, many women of the colony despair, most of all, about their sons who have drifted away from them, dealing in and themselves using drugs, sometimes dying of overdoses even while in their teens.

This was Lachmi's worst nightmare, that she would lose her sons and grandsons to drugs. Her only success in this quarter century of penury and struggle, she said, is that none of her boys have fallen to drugs. They may have stumbled or been defeated in many other ways, but not by drugs.

Her elder son initially recovered from the blows to his head, although he would still fall prey to frequent bouts of extreme rage and depression. But these did not last long, and he would soon return to normal. Lachmi married him off to a young woman, Asha. He even found employment in a factory and would bring home nine hundred rupees a month, and bonuses. But his younger son met with a road accident in 2002 which crushed one of his legs. The sight of his injured son completely collapsed his already unsteady mental balance. That same day, he rampaged through the house, breaking everything in sight. He hasn't recovered since, said Lachmi. He confined himself in the one-bedroom house, limping without halt from kitchen to living room and back, speaking incoherently. Lachmi took him to doctors in Delhi and even Jaipur, but none could find a cure.

Her younger son was moody and irresponsible. He did stay away from drugs and drug-peddlers but that was his only achievement. He would mostly mope around the house. He would not take work seriously, and hawked vegetables from a cart when it pleased him, which was not very often. On our visit, too, we found him stretched out in bed, which was where he spent much of his days. It was only Lachmi's grown daughter, Vidya, and her daughters-in-law who, working as domestic help, brought in some money to supplement Lachmi's income. Some of Lachmi's grandchildren were in a boarding school in Punjab, set up especially for survivors of the killings of 1984; one was mentally challenged and lived with the family; and another boy, Gurdeep, she was training in music so that he could grow to become a granthi and sing from the scriptures.

As she narrated them to us, her troubles seemed unending. Of her brothers who survived the massacres, one died of drug abuse, leaving behind a family of seven sons. The remaining brother, too, had turned to drugs and would beat up their mother and father when intoxicated. Since Lachmi's father was paralyzed, her mother was forced to beg at gurdwaras to somehow support the family.

Most of all, Lachmi desperately missed Sardarji. 'Had he been around I would not have been the way I am today…I would not have to struggle at this age with failing eyesight and children whose lives lie ruined. Had Sardarji lived…'

Affidavits Filed with the Nanavati Commission

The following affidavits were filed to the Nanavati Commission, a one-man commission headed by a senior retired judge of the Supreme Court of India, Justice G.T. Nanavati, which was constituted by the National Democratic Alliance (NDA) government in 2000. The purpose of this commission was to investigate the killings of Sikhs during the 1984 anti-Sikh riots. The survivors re-filed their affidavits, and some of the victims who couldn't file their pleas in 1984–85 filed them to this commission. The report details accusations against three senior Congress leaders, Jagdish Tytler, H.K.L. Bhagat and Sajjan Kumar. Following this report, Tytler was forced to resign from the Union Cabinet. Congress Prime Minister Dr Manmohan Singh also made an apology to the Sikhs. Recently, Sajjan Kumar has been convicted and given life imprisonment.

The affidavits primarily state the truth from the witnesses' perspectives as closely as possible. Many of these affidavits were written following a template, measuring the loss in terms of material costs and the number of people killed or otherwise affected. It is evident that some people were offered ready-made narratives. Such affidavits are eye-openers to the apathy of the official procedures. However, some of these affidavits were self-written. Care has been taken to mainly reproduce these, written by the survivors themselves or narrated in detail to their lawyers. Some of these affidavits clearly describe how senior Congress leaders had openly instigated violence against the Sikhs. One of the accounts describes the manner in which the Sikh bodyguard of Giani Zail Singh, the President of India at the time, was attacked and was about to be lynched when the police saved him. Despite this instance, the police did not generally stop mobs from attacking Sikhs. Another account by a Sikh policeman suggests how Sikhs were treated within the police force itself.

These affidavits have been reproduced as written. Since they are testimonies, spelling mistakes and the grammatical errors need to be overlooked. These affidavits have been reproduced from a CD titled Carnage 84: Massacre of 4000 Sikhs in Delhi, and described as 'A Delhi Sikh Gurudwara Managing Committee (DSGMC) presentation'. The material was put together by Senior Advocate H.S. Phoolka; Prof. N.S. Bawa; Wing Commander R.S. Chhatwal and Commodore J.M.S. Sood. The consultant editor was Manoj Mitta, and it was designed and programmed by Simran Kaur and Hitesh Wadhwa in 2001. Legal and technical research was conducted by Satinder Singh.

I

I, Gurmeet Singh, S/o S. Mohan Singh, R/o H. No. H-579, Phase-I, Mohali, Tehsil Mohali, Distt. Ropar, do hereby solemnly affirm and declare as under:

1. That during October/November'84, I was residing at H. No. 8-B, Vishvakarma Park, Laxmi Nagar, Delhi. I was owner of a Taxi Stand at ISBT, Kashmiri Gate, Delhi. I also worked as Taxi Driver.
2. That on 31-10-84, when I took some passengers in the taxi from ISBT to Vasant Vihar, I came to know there that vehicles of Sikhs were being burnt and Sikhs were being persecuted and killed. I was highly scared. I took my taxi to Malai Mandir, R.K. Puram, New Delhi Taxi Stand and parked the taxi there. It was about 9:00 p.m. by then and 7–8 Sikh taxi drivers were at the said Taxi Stand.
3. That when I was standing at R.K. Puram Taxi Stand, a mob of about 150–200 persons armed with kerosene oil, powder etc. came there and started burning the taxis parked there. In no time the said mob ran after to kill us. All of us fled from that place to save our lives and hid here and there.
4. That when it was completely dark I somehow managed to reach my house at Vishvakarma Park, Delhi-92. At Vishvakarma Park

there were about 40 houses of Sikhs, all of whom belong to our 'Saini' Biradari and belong to Distt. Ropar, Punjab.

5. That on 1-11-84, at about 10:00 a.m., a mob of about 100 persons came towards our houses to attack us. There is a gurdwara situated near Yamuna Pushta (near our house). We, all Sikhs numbering about 100 came out our houses and assembled around the gurdwara. We had our traditional kirpans with us. Some of us had lathis & sticks to defend ourselves. We all collectively resisted the attack of the mob and kept them at bay. Some of our men guarded the streets leading to our houses. The mob did not dare to attack us and kept standing at the distance shouting slogans. Six armed policemen were also there but they were not taking any action to stop the mob but instead they incited the mob to attack us.

6. That at about 11:00–11:30 a.m., a white coloured Ambassador car stopped at Yamuna Pushta. About 150–200 persons riding on scooters, motorcycles and tempos were also following the car. These persons were raising anti-Sikh slogans and were carrying lathis, sariyas etc. Shri H.K.L. Bhagat alighted from the said Ambassador car. I know Shri H.K.L. Bhagat closely and personally as I had been a strong supporter of Congress (I). Shri Bhagat had engaged my vehicle during elections and I took rallies during the election of Shri H.K.L. Bhagat. On seeing Shri H.K.L. Bhagat the abovesaid six policemen came towards Shri Bhagat and saluted him. Shri Bhagat pointed towards us and asked the policemen and the mob as to how these Sikhs have not been killed so far. He incited the mob to kill all of us (Sikhs). After saying this, Shri H.K.L. Bhagat went away. Some of his followers on scooter remained there and others followed Shri Bhagat.

7. That immediately thereafter, the police came towards the gurdwara and asked us to surrender our kirpans and ordered us to go inside otherwise the police will open fire. We did not surrender our kirpans but went inside the gurdwara. The police then left.

8. That after some time, the mob attacked us. But all of us came out of the gurdwara and challenged the mob. On seeing us, the mob ran away.

9. That the mob attack continued throughout 1-11-84 and on 2-11-84 as well. But due to our vigilance & determination to defend ourselves, we repulsed all the attacks by the mob.
10. That on 3-11-84, I learnt that my uncle S. Rattan Singh and his partner were burnt alive along with their taxi No.DLT-4788 while proceeding towards Khureji, Delhi, which is situated about 3–4 kms. from our place. On 4-11-84, I along with some other persons went towards Khureji and in the way I saw badly burnt said taxi of my uncle. Burnt dead bodies of my uncle and his partner were still in the taxi.
11. That later on, when I went to Malai Mandir, R.K. Puram, New Delhi Taxi Stand, I found that all four taxis including my taxi No. DLT-4118 had been burnt to ashes. The burnt taxi shell was sold to a junk dealer for Rs 3,000/-. FIR No. 417, dated 1-11-84, was filed with the Police Station R.K. Puram by S. Balbir Singh, owner of the Taxi Stand who belonged to my village.
12. That after the riots our family sold our valuable house for peanuts and moved to village. Later on, we moved to Mohali.

II

I, Satu Singh, S/o S. Sunder Singh, aged about 60 yrs., R/o C-19A, Sangam Park, Rana Pratap Bagh, Delhi, do hereby solemnly affirm and declare as under:

1. That in November 1984, I was residing at E-583, Jagjeet Nagar, Near New Usmanpur, Gawari, New Delhi.
2. That on 1-11-84, at about 9–9:30 a.m., I went to the local gurdwara situated at Jagjeet Nagar where I found two more Sikh persons who were sitting in the gurdwara. I told them that why they are sitting here as 144 Cr. P.C. has already been imposed in the area.
3. That consequently I along with all other persons left the gurdwara and went to the house of S. Sunder Singh, which is situated just near to the gurdwara. From there I saw that mob

came and attacked the gurdwara and set on fire the gurdwara along with holy book Shri Guru Granth Sahib by the rioters.

4. That somehow all the other attacked to my house and cut my hair myself and left the house along with my brother S. Shital Singh aged about thirty-two years. My brother then started running towards Gownda Chowk. As soon as my brother reached at Gownda Chowk, he was surrounded by the rioters from all sides.

5. That someone from the mob hit one piece of brick on the head of my brother S. Shital Singh; consequently he fell down on the road.

6. That when my brother fell down on the road immediately thereafter H.K.L. Bhagat, who was already standing in the mob with black goggles and the people standing there were calling him as Bhagat Ji, Bhagat Ji, uttered the words to the rioters that *'Yeh Saap Ka Bacha Hai, Isko Maro, Mat Choro, Agar Choroge To Bada Dukh Dega.'*

7. That someone from the mob threw some chemical on the face of my brother consequently his face started burning and thereafter few persons from the mob put kerosene oil on a truck tyre and then threw it on my brother. Someone from the mob then set on fire the said tyre so body of my brother started burning.

8. That when the body of my brother was burning then H.K.L. Bhagat again uttered that call your Guru Gobind Singh, I want to see him where is he. My brother then replied that Guru Gobind Singh is with me and you do whatever you want to do.

9. That after some time the body of my brother was burning, I left the place and came back to my house. Where I found that my house was already burnt and left arm of my father was fractured. My mother aged about 80 yrs. was also died due to shock.

10. That I went to the house of Mr Palaa Singh opposite my house and the other family members took shelter in another neighbouring house of one Pandit. At 10 p.m. on 1-11-84, I went to the house of Mr Chatis Gujjar and took shelter in his house. In his house there were other Sikh children inside the house.

11. That the mob of about 3000 came to the house of Mr Chatis Gujjar and enquired about the Sikhs if they took shelter in his

house. He refused and said that there were only Sikh children are there in his house. He protected them from the rioters.

12. That on 2-11-84, mob again came and enquired that whether is any Sikh is staying in his house then Mr Chatis Gujjar again replied the same.
13. That on 4-11-84, at about 10 a.m., military came and took me along with other children who took shelter in his house to Nanaksar Camp. I remained there up to May 1985 and thereafter shifted to Tilak Vihar.
14. That I lodged a police report on 10th or 11th November 1984, with the Police Station Seelampur, New Delhi and suffered a loss of Rs 20–25,000/.

III

I, Wazir Singh, S/o S. Dharam Singh, aged about 32 yrs., R/o A2-D, Tilak Vihar, Delhi, do hereby solemnly affirm and declare as under:

1. That in 1984, I was living with my grandmother Late Peari Bai in Block No-32/30, Himmatpuri, Delhi.
2. That on 31 October 1984, I was working in the factory of Mr Puppy under the name and style of Harjeet Mechanicals, Lal Quarters, Krishna Nagar, Jheel. At about 12:30 noon, Mr Puppy told his employees/workers that our Prime Minister Smt. Indira Gandhi has been assassinated and the markets are being closed. I came back to my grandmother's house.
3. That at about 9 or 9:30 p.m., I heard the noise from outside that Mr H.K.L. Bhagat (MP) has come to the house of Rampal Saroj. I came out of my house and when I enquired about Mr H.K.L. Bhagat (MP) I was told that all the local leaders of Congress (I) and Mr H.K.L. Bhagat (MP) are attending a meeting in the house of Rampal Saroj.
4. That after about half an hour the meeting ended and I saw Mr H.K.L. Bhagat (MP) and other local leaders coming out of the house of Rampal Saroj and Mr H.K.L. Bhagat (MP) left in his

cream colour car. I know Mr H.K.L. Bhagat (MP) as he used to come in our colony at the time of elections for votes. All the local leaders were shouting anti-Sikh slogans.

5. That no incident took place on 31st October, 1984.
6. That on 1-11-84, at about 10–10:30 a.m., I saw a mob of about 40-50 persons shouting slogans, 'Khoon Ka Badla Khoon' and armed with weapons like iron rods, knives etc. setting the jhuggis on fire. Many Sikhs had came out of their houses for self-defence but policemen numbering about 4-5 asked us to go back to our houses.
7. That Rampal Saroj at whose house the meeting was held by H.K.L. Bhagat was leading the mob and other leaders were also in the mob. H.K.L. Bhagat had given instructions in the meeting to kill the Sikhs.
8. That after some time the mob attacked and burnt the gurdwara. Thereafter, the mob attacked the houses of Sikhs.
9. That my parents were living in Jawahar Park. I took a cycle and left from the backside to go to my parents' house. I escaped alongside a nallah and nobody noticed.
10. That at my parents' house, our neighbour Sharma gave shelter to us where we stayed for two days and thereafter we went to police chowki Jawahar Park. From there we came to Shyam Lal College Relief Camp where we stayed for 7–8 days.

IV

I, Surinder Singh, S/o S. Ajit Singh, aged about 52 yrs., R/o A-4, Staff Qtrs., Gurdwara Rakab Ganj, New Delhi, presently Head Granthi of Gurdwara Moti Bagh, New Delhi, do hereby solemnly affirm and declare as under:

1. That during October/November 1984, I was the Head Granthi of Gurdwara Pulbangash, near Azad Market, Delhi-7.
2. That on 31-10-84, at about 8 p.m., some miscreants set a car of one Gurcharan Singh Grover, the proprietor of B-Tex (firm

manufacturing undergarments at Bahadurgarh Road) who along with his family had come to the gurdwara to offer prayers. We came out on seeing the fire but by that time the miscreants had run away from the scene. Within 10–15 minutes, there was huge fire and smoke on the Bahadurgarh roadside. Some people came running and shouting that the house of Gurcharan Singh Grover had been set on fire. Gurcharan Singh's family got scarred [scared] and remained in the gurdwara till 5:00 in the morning.

3. That on 1-11-84, at about 9 a.m., a big mob carrying lathis, iron rods, kerosene oil etc. attacked. The mob was being led by Jagdish Tytler, the Congress(I) MP of our area. He incited the mob to burn and kill the Sikhs. Some people in the mob were carrying flags of Congress. They were raising slogans like '*Khoon Ka Badla Khoon Se Lenge; Sardar Gaddar Hain; Mar Do, Jala Do*' etc. 5–6 policemen were also with the mob. On being incited by Jagdish Tytler the mob attacked and burnt the gurdwara. Thakur Singh, who was a retired Delhi Police Inspector and an employee of the Gurdwara Management Committee was killed by the mob. Badal Singh, a Sewadar of the gurdwara was also killed and burnt alive by putting burning tyre around his neck. I was watching the entire incident helplessly from the top floor of the gurdwara. The gurdwara was also set on fire but the fire did not reach the top floor of the gurdwara.

4. That in the night the Muslim neighbours rescued us. When I returned on 8 November 1984, I found that all my household goods had been looted.

5. That on 10-11-84, Shri Jagdish Tytler came to the gurdwara and asked me to sign on two sheets of paper, which I refused to sign.

V

I, Smt. Joginder Kaur W/o Late S. Amrik Singh, aged 35 yrs., R/o RZ-58, Kailash Puri, Palam Colony, Delhi, do hereby solemnly affirm and declare as under:

1. That my husband S. Amrik Singh came to house at about 2:30 a.m. on November 1st, 1984, and told me that the police

had taken him to Police Station, Sadar, Delhi Cantt. The police damaged his three wheeler scooter and beat him with lathis. The police beated him in a police jeep and said that they will loot the Sikhs. They gave him a gun and asked him to shoot and kill Sikhs. But at that time somebody said that it will be a mistake to give gun to a sardar. Thereupon they snatched the gun from him and ordered him to go away from their sight.

2. That we used to give this three wheeler scooter to the driver but on that day my husband himself drove it. My husband is a driver foreman in Delhi Electric Supply Undertaking. On 1st, about 6 a.m. when I climbed [to] the roof I heard lot of noise. All the neighbours had climbed on their roof top. I immediately came down and woke up Sardarji (my husband) and my children. My neighbour Srivastava assured us that there is nothing to worry and that we can come to their house. Myself, my husband and my three sons came to Srivastava's house at RZ-58.

3. That our house was looted after 8 a.m. and it was set on fire after looting. The persons who set the house on fire included one Vijay Khan, Puran and his accomplices who set on fire our scooter and other household effects. The same mob came again at about 6 p.m. in the evening. They wanted to search Srivastava's house. Thereupon Srivastava asked all of us to hide in the house of Mr Gopal, resident of RZ-54.

4. That from the evening of November 1st, 1984, till November 2nd, 1984, (upto 6 p.m.) we remained at the house of Mr Gopal aforesaid. My husband to save the life of my children, and at the insistence of Mr Gopal cut his hair. After this, Mr Gopal forcibly led us out of his house. Mr Gopal was well aware that there was no way for us outside and there was great danger. However, hiding ourselves, all the family members sought refuge in a house nearby which was under construction. But there was no doors in this house and the mob also arrived at that time. We tried to save ourselves. My husband Amrik Singh and my elder son Gurnam Singh got separated from us. I, along with the two younger sons, came out on the street. Even though one or two persons

tried to catch us but eventually I succeeded to come out along with two sons.

5. That when we were crossing through the Indra Park, some people came to kill us but on my folded hand requests we were spared. One or two persons told us that if we want to save our lives we should reach gurdwara after crossing the line near the culvert.

6. That when after crossing the line we were approaching near the gurdwara, we met a policeman. I begged him for help. He said, 'Do not talk with us. We will shoot you.' I again begged him but he gave the same reply. We spent that night by hiding ourselves in the bushes.

7. That on 3 November 1984, when we were hiding in the bushes that the mob came towards that side. They had torches and lights with them. They spotted us in the bushes and caught hold of us. I told them that we were Hindus but they saw the turban marks on the foreheads of my sons. They said, 'You are sardars. You have got your hair cut just now.' The mob started beating both my sons. At this I said in Hindi, 'We are Hindus. Do not beat us.' Thereupon one person out of the mob came out and said, 'Listen to them carefully. Do not say them anything.' He asked the other men to take us to the mandir and keep us there. When we were being taken to the mandir some people tried to hit my son with sword and iron rods but I came forward and thus rescued my sons. The sword hit on my leg which started bleeding profusely. In the mandir to save us, the pujari sent us inside the mandir and locked the gate from outside. The pujari asked us to sit there and that he will send us to gurdwara when the curfew is lifted. This was the Shivmandir of Sagarpur. Outside the mandir the mob was shouting at pujari and threatened to break open the lock. They also tried to break open the lock. This continued for a long time and in the meantime many more persons joined the mob. Then somebody shouted that the mandir be set on fire if the pujari did not open the lock. When they poured kerosene oil from the grill of the mandir and tried to set it on fire, I dashed my forehead at the feet of Devi and prayed her to appear and save us. My sons started

weeping loudly along with me. At that time one person who had wrapped a blanket around himself came forward and asked the mob not to set the mandir on fire. That man asked me, 'Sister, where have you to go?' I told him that we had to go to Maharani Bagh. He said that he is also from that side and he would save us. When I asked him as to how he single-handed can save us from so many men he said that, as already said, he will save us. But I did not believe him. He told me that he has the key of the back door and when he would give a signal we should escape from the back door. When I hesitated, he said that he is police inspector and also has a revolver with him. He removed his blanket and showed me the revolver. He was wearing a police uniform. He showed me his identity card also and upon this I believed him. Then he made an announcement at the loud speaker of the mandir, 'Extremists have arrived towards the railway line. Run for your lives.' Many from the mob ran towards the lines and he made us come out from the back gate. He called 5–6 more persons and instructed them that we have to be saved. Hardly had he taken us for some distance that the mob returned and surrounded us. Some people in the mob enquired the police inspector that why he was taking the two sardar children and thereby putting them to a loss of Rs 500 each. The mob told the Inspector that they would not allow the sardar children to go. At this the inspector drew out his revolver and one more man drew out his revolver and threatened the mob to shoot anybody who will come forward. The mob retreated and they took us out from that place. In the way, other persons accompanying the inspector, also removed their blanket. Two of them were in police uniform. One of them was a police inspector. In the way they told us that they do not know how they got pity on us, otherwise they were apprehending and killing sardars. They accompanied us up to and left us at Gurdwara Sadar Cantt.

8. That on reaching the Relief Camp at gurdwara, on 5 November 1985, I came to know that my husband and my eldest son who had hid themselves in the house of Chakkiwala were dragged out from his house and killed and burnt.

9. That on 5 November 1985, we were brought to Gurdwara Bala Sahib.
10. That our house has been totally burnt to ashes and all the household effects have been either burnt or looted. I have suffered a loss of about three lakhs of rupees.

VI

I, Piara Singh, S/o S. Ajit Singh, aged 42 yrs., R/o RZ-20/H, Main Sagarpur, Gali No. 5/1, New Delhi, do hereby solemnly affirm and declare as under:

1. That I am staying at RZ-20/H, Main Sagarpur, Gali No. 5/1, New Delhi, since my marriage in 1981.
2. That I am staying in the house since 1977. I was working as Motor Machenic [mechanic] in a workshop at Rajouri Garden.
3. That in November 1984, I was staying at above address along with my family.
4. That on 31 October 1984, I started hearing loud noise in our area from 6 p.m. At about 9 p.m. I saw many people running across the road in front of my house carrying utensils. Later, I learnt that a shop of Sikh has been looted.
5. That at about 10 p.m. on 31 October 1984, a mob of 250–300 persons came to our house. Immediately they started beating me and my brother S. Nachhatar Singh with iron rods and lathis which they were carrying with them. They beat us till we fell down unconscious. 3–4 persons from the crowd came forward and said 'They have died, let us move forward', before leaving.
6. That they put our house on fire. They threw some powder on my brother and upon me. My brother and myself being unconscious could not protect ourselves from fire.
7. That after the mob went away, my family members along with my mother and wife, dragged the unconscious bodies of my brother and myself to our neighbour house of Mrs Bala. Mrs Bala is still

living there. We stayed in the house of Mrs Bala till 1 November 1984, afternoon.

8. That on 1 November 1984, by noon, mob again came and threatened Mrs Bala and her husband to bring out the Sikhs, otherwise they will burn their house. But Mrs Bala very bravely told them to come inside and search their house knowing fully well that Sikhs were hiding inside the home. The crowd after hearing this went away.
9. That on 1 November 1984, at about 2 p.m. I regained some consciousness, but my brother continued to be unconscious.
10. That when I became little conscious my mother and I left Mrs Bala's house and went to army unit gurdwara across railway line.
11. That little later, my bhabi and my wife, dressed ourselves in saris and we two along with children left for Army gurdwara, leaving my brother still unconscious in the house of Mrs Bala.
12. That on 2-11-84, at about 3 p.m. my husband regained consciousness. Then about 3–4 neighbours escorted my husband to Army unit gurdwara and the whole family was together again.
13. That on 4-11-84, we shifted to Delhi Cantt. gurdwara where a camp was established—we stayed in the camp for next two months till 31 December 1984.
14. That we came to our house on 31 December 1984, and found it was completely looted and burnt. With financial help from relatives and friends, we partially repaired it and tried to restart the life.
15. That on 10-11-84, an FIR was lodged by my chachaji, uncle—who was staying in our adjoining house and was also taking shelter at Delhi Cantt. Gurdwara. (copy enclosed)
16. That my brother and I suffered severe injury during the beating on 31 October 1984, in our bodies. This got worsened with some white powder thrown on him by mob and later when my brother was partially burnt while he was unconscious on 31 October 1984.
17. That my brother is continuously under treatment at various hospitals. Safdarjung hospital, AIIMS, Jeewan hospital and other private practitioners.

18. That his condition is continuously getting worsened and now he is unable to even walk.
19. That my brother is unable to walk and as such is unable to work. He was the only source of income in the family. (Medical reports 11 in No. are enclosed)
20. That the house expenses are being met by me doing tailoring work at my house.
21. That my brother is suffering from 100% disability due to the heavy beating and burning on the night of 31 October 1984.
22. That we suffered household loss of Rs1,20,000. (FIR enclosed)
23. That I received a total compensation of Rs 2,000 only.

VII

I, Jitender Kaur, W/o S. Gurcharan Singh, R/o FU-34, Vishakha Enclave, Pitampura, Delhi, do hereby solemnly affirm and declare as under:

1. That I had been allotted DSIDC (Delhi State Infrastructure Development Corporation Ltd.) shed in February, 1977 during International Women's Year 1977 in the Brain Drain Scheme for unemployed graduates.
2. That I had started work in various food products under the name and style of 'Oriental Food Products' and was dealing in Food items like jams, ketchup, vinegars, syrups, pickles, cocktails etc. and was also exporting the goods to Hong Kong.
3. That in 1984 riots, my unit was looted and burnt. I suffered a heavy loss, mental depression and left for Jallandhar with my family and returned in January, 1985. I could not file the FIR as the date was over, but I did send a few letters to the Lt. Governor, Delhi State without any response. Due to great mental shock, heavy financial loss, due to unit remaining closed. The semi-finished products like pulps, puries [purees] having been spoiled were thrown away and the finished products like jam bottles were damaged in bulk, which became unfit for sale. [E]specially

window paws [panes], and damages to the building etc. during the period were beyond recovery. All these losses/damages upset my mental/physical structure to such an extent that became afraid to visit my unit for which I had spent my all sources.

4. That though mental depression was beyond my control and till date am not free from it, even after continued medical treatment and under compelling circumstances.

5. That I applied to DSIDC to give me rebate as per Central Interest Subsidy Act, 1992, but the DSIDC has refused to give me interest subsidy and I am also ready to pay all the dues of the DSIDC after deducting the interest as per the Act under the RBI directions to the financial institutions.

6. That instead of taking steps to rehabilitate my sick unit, DSIDC refused to give me benefit under the Central Interest Subsidy Act, 1992, which are applicable for the 1984 riots victims. I after deducting the interest offered DSIDC to take the loan amount of Rs 2,40,000 from the Riot Hit Unit. DSIDC vide their letter dated 19-2-96, after keeping the 2 cheques for about 3 months returned the said cheques. I arranged the said loan amount from my relatives and friends to repay the DSIDC.

7. That I had treated the DSIDC as my parent organization even after suffering so much heavy loss, but their refusal to accept my payment for Rs 2,40,000 when they accepted such payments from other Riot hit units has put me in compelling circumstances to fight to my fundamental rights.

8. That I humbly pray before the Hon'ble Commission to do justice to me by getting me my legal rights for the shed treating the payments already made as full and final payments towards the cost of the shed & providing me loan facilities at reasonable interest to be paid in instalments, because I am not able even to get any loan, what to speak of Rs 2,40,000, which was refused by DSIDC in 1996. Because if a decision regarding final cost of the shed had been taken at a proper time the accumulated dues payable by my unit could be arranged/managed when unit was functioning. A sick unit cannot be granted loan etc.

VIII

I, Sharanjit Singh, S/o S. Mohinder Singh, aged about 40 yrs., R/o Staff Qtr.103, Guru Harkrishan Public School, Purvi Marg, Vasant Vihar, New Delhi, do hereby on solemn affirmation state as under:

1. That I am working as Lab. Incharge in Shri Guru Harkrishan Public School, Vasant Vihar and residing in the same school premises since 1980.
2. That in November 1984, I was present in my house bearing Qtr. No. 103, Staff Building, Shri Guru Harkrishan Public School, Vasant Vihar, New Delhi.
3. That on 1-11-84, at about 8:30 a.m., Mr Balwan Singh, peon of head master of the school informed me that mob is building up near the Munirka village and they are going to attack to school at any moment, then took the said Balwan Singh, peon to head master Mr R.S. Garewal, where he had narrated the entire story to him. Immediately, thereafter, Head Master Mr R.S. Garewal called a meeting all persons available in the school building in staff quarters. While we were discussing this issue by that time, we saw a mob of about 100 men approaching the school from Munirka village side who were carrying cans of petrol/kerosene and bundles of rags. They broke the boundary fence and approached to us the ground where three buses and three matadors were parked.
4. That when the miscreants was setting the vehicles on fire and they were pelting stones upon us where we were standing and we were throwing the same on them. Mr Labh Singh, the then state officer of the school telephoned to our school transporter and teacher to inform the students that the school would remain close on 1st–3rd November 1984, these days were declared as holidays by the government. Mr Labh Singh also requested the miscreants not to set the vehicles on fire as they belong to the school but they threatened to kill him if he didn't run away, rather they attacked him with iron bar, which they carried. I was

present there along with Mr Labh Singh at that time.

5. That the mob went away after burning one matador [van] and thereafter we extinguished the same by pouring water on it.

6. That at about 10 a.m., on 1-11-84, a big mob came from the side of Purvi Marg and entered the school campus from both the main and domestic gates. They had come in about 6–8 DTC buses. This mob was led by one Mr Tokas, resident of Munirka village. I saw them coming out of these DTC buses and about five DTC buses were parked on the Palam Marg near the T-junction of Purvi Marg. I also saw some men directing three buses, which moved on to Purvi Marg towards Vasant Vihar Colony. The mob was raising slogans, 'Break and burn the school of sardars.' These rioters were also armed with lathis, long bars and big pipes.

7. That the rioters started pelting stones upon us as well as on the school building. Mr S.S. Bakshi was mercilessly beaten by the rioters and received grievous injuries in person. Mr G.S. Rathor, head of the music department also received injuries due to pelting stones upon them.

8. That these rioters had broken the glass panes of the doors and windows of the office and set fire to the office of the school as well as the basement. All the three laboratories were ransacked, broken and stores of Physics and Biology labs were set on fire. At that time I was standing near the staff residential quarters within the school building and saw all these incidents. At that time, I also saw some police person in uniform were moving outside the school boundary and they were not taking any action against the rioters.

9. That afterwards, the mob moved towards the domestic quarters and one portion of the mob, which had entered through the domestic gate had already set the principal's bungalow on fire. The other mob, which came from the main gate side had circled the residential quarters and started setting them on fire. The residence of the Head Master and one of the drivers' said residential quarters [was] set on fire by the rioters. They had broken the windowpanes of the staff quarters by pelting stones. The school principal Dr H.S. Singha was rescued by Mr Chadha—Additional

DCP, Hauz Khas and the Sikh families of the staff quarters were rescued by Ms. Nandita Haksar with the help of the volunteers, who belonged to Self-Financing Quarters, Munirka Enclave and some of the volunteers were students from JNU. For two night we stayed in Munirka Quarters along with our families and for two days we stayed in JNU Campus Quarters.

10. That the school had suffered a loss of Rs 35 to 40 lakh in total. An FIR was lodged with SHO Vasant Vihar P.S. but no action was taken on the said FIR by the police.

IX

I, Amar Singh, S/o Late S. Ram Singh, aged 58 yrs., R/o C-6/410, Yamna Vihar, Delhi, do hereby solemnly affirm and declare as under:

1. That in October/November 1984, I was residing with my family at the above mentioned address.
2. That on 31-10-84, no incident took place in our area.
3. That on 1-11-84, the Sikhs of our locality performed Prabhat Pheri (religious procession early in the morning). When we returned to the gurdwara after the Prabhat Pheri, the Sikh devotees decided to give a written information/representation to the SHO of the area about the situation prevailing in our locality stating that there was apprehension of riots taking place and that appropriate steps should be taken by the police to protect the life and property of the residents of our area.
4. That on 1-11-84, at about 9–10 a.m., when I was standing on the terrace of my house, I saw a white-coloured car standing near the park. One person sitting in the car was pointing towards my house and giving some directions to a group of persons carrying lathis, iron rods, sticks etc. standing near the car. After some time, the car went away after giving the directions and the people who got the instructions/directions from persons inside the car, attacked my house. They were about 500–600 persons. The mob caught hold of me and beat me mercilessly. Two Hindu

boys saved me by dragging me towards the gallery and advised me to lie down quietly and pretend like a dead body. I followed their advice. Then those boys started shouting to the mob that the sardar was dead and that the mob should proceed further. On hearing this, the mob went away presuming me to be dead.

5. That after some time, about 15–16 persons came to my street and started inquiring about my dead body from the neighbours. I could hear this conversation from the bathroom where I was concealed by the neighbours. The neighbours told those persons that the dead body of Amar Singh has been taken away by some unknown persons. But the persons who came to inquire about my dead body showed a list to my neighbours and said, 'Look Amar Singh's name has not been struck off from the list so his dead body has not been taken away.' These persons then searched the house of our neighbours but could not locate me. Then these persons gave threat to my neighbours of dire consequences if the information regarding Amar Singh proved to be false and thereafter, they went away.

6. That I was saved by my neighbours and was rescued on 4-11-84, by the army and taken to Nanaksar Camp.

X

I, D.P. Gulati, S/o M.D. Gulati, aged about 56 yrs., R/o ED-43 A, Pitampura, Delhi-34, do hereby solemnly affirm and declare as under:

1. In October/November 1984 I was working as an Engineer with the Delhi Development Authority. The head office is situated at Vikas Sadan, INA, New Delhi. I was posted at Rajindra Place.
2. On 31.10.1984 I went to Vikas Sadan INA, on official work. At about 5-6 p.m. I went to AIIMS side as I had come to know that Shrimati Indira Gandhi had been injured and taken to AIIMS. When I reached the crossing of AIIMS from INA market side, I saw about 500-600 persons coming from the road between Safdarjang and AIIMS towards INA. These persons were

raising anti-Sikh slogans like 'Sikhon Ko Maar Do, Khattam Kar Do' and were being led by Shri Arjan Dass who was an elected Congress(I) leader of Kidwai Nagar. He was initiating the mob to attack the Sikhs. Some persons (about 20-25) caught hold of one Sikh photographer. His camera was snatched. His turban was removed and set on fire and he was badly beaten. The sardar ran and boarded a DTC bus and saved himself. At that time normal traffic was running on the roads. Thereafter those 20-25 persons of the mob forcibly stopped a Sikh couple coming from South Extension side on a motorcycle. The sardar was beaten badly and his motorcycle was burnt by taking out petrol from the motorcycle. One sardar cyclist was also beaten badly. 3-4 scooterists who were sardar were also beaten in similar manner. Some persons in the mob also manhandled the Sikh traffic policeman who was manning the traffic at the crossing of AIIMS. Then I saw that this mob pelted stones on the car of President Giani Zail Singh. His one Sikh bodyguard who was riding on motorcycle was manhandled by the mob. His turban was removed and he was about to be lynched by the mob that in the meantime the police saved him. This sardar bodyguard took shelter in the police control room van parked near AIIMS. At that time two police control room vans were standing at the crossing of AIIMS towards the corner of the boundary wall but the mob continued to attack the sikhs.

3. Then the mob scattered in various directions, some persons went towards Bhikaji Cama Place, some towards South Extension, some towards Yusuf Sarai side and some came towards INA market.
4. I remember that in that mob only 25-30 persons were including in attacks on sardars while others were spectators.
5. I remained there for about an hour or so and somehow reached Central Sectt. from there I took DTC bus and reached home at Patel Nagar. All my vehicles including a postal van were burning on the Tughlak Road.

XI

I, Harbans Singh, S/o Late Niranjan Singh, aged 66 yrs., R/o H.No.61, Block-A, Gali No.8, Bhajanpura, Delhi-53, do hereby solemnly affirm and declare as under:

1. That during October/November 1984, I along with my family was residing at Govt. Quarter No. T-44, Bara Mor Sarai, Railway Colony, Koriyapul, Delhi-6.
2. That during October/November 1984, I was posted at Police Station Yamuna Puri as a Sub Inspector of Delhi Police. I have retired in 1992.
3. That on 31-10-84, at about 5 p.m., the then SHO of P.S. Yamuna Puri instructed all officers present in the police station to get arms and ammunition from the Malkhana Incharge, Head Constable Ram Sidhi. All the officers present in the police station were given arms and ammunition. I requested Head Constable Ram Sidhi to provide me with arms and ammunition but he refused to give me arms and ammunition. Even my Junior Officers like ASI Chander Pal was given arms and ammunition by the Malkhana Incharge Head Constable Ram Sidhi but I was not given.
4. That when I did not get the arms and ammunition, I complained about this fact to the then SHO Inspector Ramesh Pal Singh. But the SHO neither gave any reply nor instructed the Malkhana Incharge to provide me arms and ammunition.
5. That on 31-10-84, at night I remained and slept at the police station as the SHO ordered that all police personnel shall remain at the police station because of situation prevailing at that time.
6. That on 1-11-84, I was put on emergency duty from 8 a.m.–8 p.m. At about 8:30 a.m. a group of 6–7 non-Sikhs of Yamuna Vihar came to the Police Station and asked the SHO to arrest the sardars who are carrying on Parbhat Pheri (early morning religious congregation moving on foot in the area and chanting prayers), since Section 144 Cr. P.C. was enforced. Prabhat Pheris were being taken out by Sikhs in the early mornings since Guru

Nanak Dev Ji's birthday anniversary was falling on 8 November 1984. They also handed over a written complaint to the SHO. The SHO asked me to take his vehicle and go to Gurdwara Singh Sabha, Yamuna Vihar, which is about 2 furlongs away. I went to the gurdwara but I found that only one sewadar was there who told me that the Prabhat Pheri was over and the devotees had gone their respective homes. I came back and reported the same to SHO at the police station. The SHO asked me not to go out and to remain at the police station.

7. That on 1-11-84 around noon time, I went to the Wireless Room of the P.S. There I heard a message that 'Sikhs carrying kirpans are moving in Angad Nagar area.' From the other side the instructions came, 'Send force to arrest them immediately.' I heard numerous other messages where the information was given about the attack on the gurdwaras and the houses of the Sikhs but in response to those messages no instructions were given to take any action. I was totally disillusioned over this approach and I went back to my room and remained there only.

8. That on 1-11-84 at about 5 p.m., I saw about 10–15 dead bodies in a private tempo parked just in front of the police station Yamuna Puri.

9. That I remained in the police station throughout on 1-11-84 and 2-11-84 and till 6 p.m., of 3-11-84 and I did not go to the area at all.

10. That on 3-11-84, army officers came in the police station at about 12 noon or 1:00 p.m.. At about 6 p.m., the SHO instructed ASI Banwari Lal to escort me to my house. ASI Banwari Lal first went to Karol Bagh to fetch the tiffin from SHO's house and later dropped me at my house. En route I saw that many shops in the Tyre market opposite Filmistan Cinema were burning and there were no fire brigade to extinguish the raging fire.

11. That 1-11-84, 2-11-84 and 3-11-84 the police of P.S. Yamuna Puri did not arrest any rioter.

12. That in December 1984, I was handed over the investigation in FIR No. 277—P.S. Yamuna Puri. Nobody had been arrested

by the police in this FIR. I made arrest of the accused after the investigation was handed over to me in December 1984. I arrested more than twenty accused in this case. I found that there were many lapses in the police investigation. No site plan had been prepared by the previous I.O. Jai Singh. No recoveries had been made and only very brief and incomplete statements had been recorded. I tried my best to make recoveries but as lot of time had elapsed therefore I could not do much. The previous I.O. had made no efforts to establish the identity of the culprits and apprehend the culprits, even though the victims in their statements had revealed their names.

XII

I, Bhagwani Bai, W/o Shri Sewa Singh, aged 65 yrs., R/o Sector 16, Rohini, New Delhi, do hereby solemnly affirm and declare as under:

1. That I was residing at C-3/245, Sultanpuri, Delhi.
2. That on 1 November 1984, Sajjan Kumar then Member of Parliament of our area, whom I know for past few [years] came to my house with a mob and ordered them to kill the inmates and burn the house. My two sons were dragged out and Sajjan Kumar got my sons Hoshiar Singh, 21 yrs. and Mohan Singh 18 yrs. burnt before my eyes.
3. That on 3 November 1984 military rescued us and took us to Rani Bagh Camp from where we were forcibly turned out on 12-11-84 to fend for ourselves, the camp having been declared closed.
4. That my statement was not recorded by police and instead they just handed over a paper purported to be a copy of the police report. This was merely a statement of loss suffered. Despite my repeated requests to the police to apprehend the culprits nothing was done.
5. That I pointed out the grave lapses in not correctly recording the statement and narration of events but was curtly turned away by the police.

6. That no investigation whatsoever has been made in the murder of my sons and burning of my house and those who committed the heinous crimes are freely roaming about in the area.
7. That my above stated deposition has been recorded as per my instructions the same has been translated and read out to me in vernacular. I understand the same fully and is correct.

XIII

I, Manbhari Kaur, W/o Late S. Kuldeep Singh, aged about 32 yrs., R/o E-6/191, Sultanpuri, New Delhi, do hereby solemnly affirm and declare as under:

1. That in November 1984, I was living in a joint family along with my husband and in-laws at A-4/175, Sultanpuri, New Delhi.
2. That on 1 November 1984, the mob of about 2000–3000 people attacked the houses and properties of Sikh families of our locality. The mob was being led by Sajjan Kumar, Gupta and Nathu, who owns a kerosene oil depot. I can recognize the said persons in case they are brought before me.
3. That the mob had burnt our house and looted our property at Sultan Puri, Delhi and they also killed my husband Shri Kuldip Singh by dragging him out of the house. He was taking on the road and then after beating him mercilessly by lathis, he was then burnt alive.
4. That by dragging him out, the mob had thrown some powder on our faces due to which there was some smoke.
5. That I had lodged the complaint with the S.H.O., P.S. Sultan Puri, Delhi which is being attached with this affidavit.
6. That no investigation whatsoever has been made in the murder of my son and burning of my house and those who committed the heinous crimes are freely roaming about in the area.
7. That my above stated deposition has been recorded as per my instruction, the same has been translated and read out to me in vernacular. I understand the same fully and is correct.

XIV

I, Phota Singh, S/o S. Doonger Singh, aged 70 yrs., R/o C-45C, Tilak Vihar, New Delhi, do hereby solemnly affirm and declare as under:

1. That I was residing at A-4/124-126, Sultanpuri, New Delhi prior to November 1984.
2. That on 1 November 1984, a mob of 500–600 persons carrying cans of oil, rods and tyres, led by Sajjan Kumar, then Member of Parliament of our constituency, Gupta of kerosene depot, Jai Bhagwan, Islam, Peerea, Hanuman Prasad of ration depot, Nathu Pradhan, Udal Jat, Gauri Shankar, Jai Kishan, P.A. to Sajjan Kumar along with S.H.O. with force arrived near my house. Sajjan Kumar made platform of his car. He exhorted the mob not loot but to kill Sikhs. A gun was fired and my son Dalgir Singh aged 22 yrs. was attacked and killed. Then he was burnt by putting tyre around his neck soaked in kerosene. I tried to intervene but a furious mob pushed me away.
3. That I fully know Nathu Pradhan, Gupta of kerosene depot, Jai Bhagwan, Islam, Peerea, Hanuman Prasad of ration depot, Udal Jat, Gauri Shankar, Jai Kishan, P.A. of Sajjan Kumar being known figures of the locality, who led the mob which committed violence, murdered my son and set my house on fire.
4. That on 3-11-84, military rescued us and took us to Rani Bagh Camp. But we were forcibly turned out of the camp on 12-11-84 to fond [fend] for ourselves, the camp having been declared closed.
5. That my statement was not recorded by police and instead they just handed over a paper purported to be a copy of the police report. This was merely a statement of loss suffered. Despite my repeated requests to the police to apprehend the culprits nothing was done.
6. That I pointed out that there were grave lapses in recording my statement and narration of events, but was curtly turned away by the police.

XV

Besides submitting an affidavit to the Nanavati Commission in September 2000, Khushwant Singh also deposed as a witness before the commission on 9 May 2001, along with a number of prominent citizens such as Jaya Jaitly, Madan Lal Khurana, Madhu Kishwar, Lt. Gen J.S. Aurora, Swami Agnivesh, and ex-Prime Minister I.K. Gujral. In the following transcription of his account, Khushwant Singh recounts how he witnessed a mob torch shops at Khan Market, a taxi stand and some cars in a neighbouring garage, while the police stood as mute spectators outside the gate of his apartment complex. When he called President Giani Zail Singh he was advised by his Secretary to take shelter in a Hindu friend's house.

KS: I have filed an affidavit dated 21.09.2000 before this Commission (the affidavit is taken on record and marked as exhibit No. W7/1). My affidavit may be treated as my examination-in-chief. I further say that, I was a member of the Rajya Sabha from 1980 to 1986. I was a nominated member. At that Mrs Gandhi was the Prime Minister. I did not have a close relationship with the family but the family was quite known to us. During the earlier part of the Emergency we were on visiting terms. With reference to the incident of the burning taxi stand, I further say that at that time I had seen about thirty policemen standing on the road in two rows. An Inspector and Sub-Inspector of Police were also there. The policemen had not tried to prevent the mob from burning the taxi stand, but they were simply watching the incident.

I knew President Zail Singh since many years. I was informed by my son-in-law, who was then informed by the officers monitoring the mob that a mob was on its way to my house. I rang up President Gaini Zail Singh. My son-in-law was informed by Shri Salman Haider, who later on became Foreign Secretary and High Commissioner in the UK. My son-in-law is not a Sikh. His name is Ravi Dayal. I rang up the

Secretary of the President and told him that I wanted to talk to the President, if I could get any help from him. After some time I was told by his Secretary that the President could not come to the phone and advised we to go to the house of a Hindu. The Secretary at that time was Shri Trilochan Singh, Vice-Chairman of the Minorities Commission. Having noticed the inaction of the police, I had thought it pointless to ask the police for help. I thought if I called the police, the mob would soon be upon me. I have written numerous articles about what is stated in my affidavit and what I had experienced during the time of 1984 anti-Sikh riots. In the first article, I wrote that I felt like a refugee in my own country and like a Jew in Nazi Germany. I was very pained as I had not seen any such riot earlier, where so many innocent Sikhs were killed only because of a crime committed by two or three Sikhs persons. I had felt that the violence which had taken place during those two or three days was quite organized and probably the government of the day had a hand in it.

Some cross-examination by Shri S.S. Gandhi, Senior Advocate on behalf of Delhi Police.

KS: My house is opposite the Ambassador Hotel. I am staying in a flat. From my flat I cannot see the road just outside our complex, but I could see the gate in front of which the road between our flats and the Ambassodor Hotel runs. Whatever I had seen had been seen by me after I had come to the gate on 31st October 1984 evening. Khan Market is on the left of my house. The distance between my gate and Khan Market is 50 yards. From near the gate I could see two sides of Khan Market. The shops which I have referred to in para 1 of my affidavit were situated on the front side of Khan Market. It is wrong to say that no shops were set on fire in Khan Market. It is wrong to say that shutters of only two or three shops were broken and were looted. I visited the shops after two or three days and I found charred remains of wooden shelves. The policemen who were standing there that evening were ten yards away from me and it being dark I could not identify them. It is unknown to me that the police immediately reached the place where the shops were looted and dispersed the crowd.

Q: I put up to you that the crowd which was indulging in looting the shops at Khan Market were dispersed by the policemen present there and while running, when they set the taxis on fire at the taxi stand, police followed them also.

KS: I do not accept this suggestion. I had seen the police doing nothing. The same mob was on rampage and it had burnt the taxi stand.

I had myself witnessed the incident referred by me in para 4 of my affidavit. From behind the hedge of our compound I had seen that incident. The crowd was burning three or four cars which were in the garage of Shri Sukhwant Singh. They had also attacked the Gurdwara. While I was watching all this, the Hindu residents of my complex had come to me and told me to get back into my flat, as there was danger to my life if I was seen by the mob. The crowd was shouting the slogan, 'Khoon ka badla khoon se lenge'.

I do not know the number of incidents that had taken place in my area on 31st October, 1984. I would not know if the police, after coming to know about the incident, had reached those places and tried to disperse the crowd from those places. I would not know if the crowd had run away from the police dispersing them and while receding they damaged what ever came their way, with the police following them.

No Cross examination by Shri K.K. Sud, ASG on behalf of Central Government.

SECTION II
SHORT STORIES

The Fiery Embrace

Parvinder Mehta

A story about true friendship in times of communal conflict, where the roles of the perpetrator and the victim are reversed. The story suggests that suffering is universal, as the differences between the two communities involved seem to have blurred towards the end.

'I do not know how to say this, Mr Joshi, but...your son Anil is alive against all odds. His body is burned everywhere, yet he lives... It has to be his good kismet that he is still breathing' said Dr Rao to Rajiv Joshi. The doctor continued with the details: Anil had suffered third-degree burns on his upper body; his neck was badly singed and melted where the chin should be. It would take months before he could see the outside world with his own eyes—if he survived. His parents, Rajiv and Savitri Joshi were grief-stricken. That their only son had risked his life for his best friend, Raja, trying to save him from the vicious anger of those good-for-nothing hoodlums was a painful thought for Savitri. Rajiv, on the other hand, was furious at his son for putting his own life at risk. That too for that Sikh boy, Raja, whom Rajiv never really cared much for!

Savitri was in tears, seeing her darling son's whole body wrapped in bandages and writhing in extreme pain. The stench of his burnt flesh was so overpowering. Seeing his burnt face where the flesh had simply melted, exposing the bare bone, was heart-wrenching shock for her. The nurse had scolded her for peeking in to look at her son's face. They had sedated him heavily as the pain was unbearable. The stench of burning flesh lingered everywhere in the room. Like a foul intrusion, human cries for help from similar pain could be heard from other nearby patients. A new bride in the next room had been transferred to the ICU for observation. Her doleful parents wailed and cursed the greedy in-laws who kept torturing her for more dowry. Savitri was overwhelmed and could not stand any longer. She came closer to the bed where Anil lay, covered with shrouding bandages. Would Anil die and leave them alone? Did Anil feel the same pain when Raja was dying? Savitri's tears could not be stopped, as she imagined Anil attempting to save Raja from those hateful flames. Raja, their next-door neighbour, always came inside to wish them and ask about their day. Why did they kill him? Savitri had heard from their maid, Chameli, that poor Raja had asked for help before the crowd pounced on him, kicking him mercilessly. Those men in white kurta-pajamas had shown no mercy at all. They were bloodthirsty hyenas, sniffing for Sikh blood. Savitri was not sure why she was haunted by Raja who was almost like another son to her. Oh how close the two of them were in school! She would snicker when they made fun of their South Indian teachers, mimicking their accents and angry responses. She thought of Rano, Raja's mother, who was more like a sister than her next-door neighbour. Where was she? Hai Ram! The poor woman! Savitri felt afraid for Rano now. Had Rano seen the charred, lifeless body of Raja, the apple of her eyes? What about Balkar Singh ji? Had he been burned too by the bloodthirsty mob?

Savitri had always considered Rano as her elder sister and called her Ranodidi. And Rano, a typical Punjabi woman, loved helping Savitri with those wonderful crochet designs for laces and woollen socks. Savitri even envied Rano's cooking and would eagerly wait for her share of the season's first gajar ka halwa—the carrot dessert simmering with sweetness and softness of khoya and golden raisins. Savitri actually waited for the time when Rano would bring the halwa. She'd even tried to make Rano's recipe once, but the results were not as mouth-watering as when Rano made it. 'Why do you bother, kudiye? I will make it for you,' Rano had laughed. Whenever Savitri was short of any spices, she would simply ask Rano for some, and they would end up gossiping about the spicy rumours that they had heard from their common maid, Chameli.

~

'Do you know that Duggal Sahib has a big gun in his house?' Chameli, a young girl of nineteen years old, washed the dishes faster than she talked. She would work in six houses, washing dishes and mopping the rooms. Chameli loved making tea for herself and sharing interesting gossip with the ladies of the houses after finishing her work. To clean and dust each corner, she had the freedom of walking through the whole house, even in the house of Ranjit Singh Duggal, the rich businessman, whose house was more like a castle, with a huge iron gate, and iron railings all over the walls. 'Yes, he has a gun and he does not let anybody in his room. I can only go when his new wife is there. But don't tell this to anyone that I told you, bibiji.' The Duggal family was a bit reclusive, living in that cage-like house. Duggal Sahib's new wife, Preeti, would only come out to pick the best tomatoes and other vegetables from Haria's vegetable cart. Preeti was indeed beautiful, with long hair touching her knees, fair skin, and light brown eyes that left you dazed. Her nimble, polished fingers were adept at picking the best onions, potatoes, peppers and string beans. She did not haggle with Haria like Savitri and Rano. Even Haria was shy whenever Preeti came out to buy the daily vegetables. Rano had met Preeti only a few times as the Duggal family had just moved to this house a month ago. She had seen Preeti with Duggal Sahib at the gurdwara, and had exchanged smiles with her then. She knew that Preeti was much younger to Duggal Sahib and had been married for a year or so now. Rano had been wondering if she should invite Preeti and Savitri for tea someday. She did not know that their meeting would come sooner than that.

After finishing her domestic chores, Rano was enjoying the sunny warmth in the verandah one day. It was October 31 and the days were beginning to get much colder. She was knitting a new burgundy sweater for Raja this winter. She had asked Savitri also to knit one for her son, and Chameli had already left after mopping and washing the dishes. When the doorbell rang, Rano went to see who was at the gate. It was Preeti in her lacy, yellow nightdress. She had never seen Preeti in her sleeping clothes. 'Didi, it is urgent! Can you please come with me? It is Balkar Singh ji on our phone.' Rano became alarmed, for Balkar never called for her on the phone unless someone died! Those were the days when Rano wished they could have a telephone connection installed in her home. She dropped her knitting needles, draped her chunni and rushed out to follow Preeti. Rano became self-conscious, realizing that she would be going inside Preeti's house for the very first time. As Preeti opened the gate, Rano could not help but notice the beautiful, white wickerwork hammock, dangling as if enjoying the cool breeze in the sunny afternoon by itself. The verandah floor was beautiful, with marble and granite tiles exquisitely arranged in a symmetrical design. Rano saw so many clay pots planted with roses, hyacinths, marigold, and even China rose, her favourite flower! It seemed as if Duggal Sahib was not at home, as his green Contessa was not there. Preeti opened the main door of the living room and Rano saw the deep blue velvet sofas, and the long silk curtains in the background, welcoming the sun rays from the French windows. The glass coffee table reflected the hidden colours of the room. The Beltek TV with the shuttered door was covered by a white crocheted tablecloth. She would ask Preeti to copy the lacy design and make one for her TV too. Rano saw oil paintings of Maharaja Ranjit Singh and Sohni-Mahiwal. She was struck by the beautiful painting of Guru Gobind Singh ji; another painting of Guru Nanak Dev ji seemed so life-like, his eyes consoling her with their magical warmth....

She came back to the moment with a start as Preeti handed her the black receiver of the phone. 'Hello,' said Rano with worry apparent on her face. 'Yes, haan hello, Rano!...are you and Raja ok?' Rano, surprised at hearing her husband's question, said 'Yes, why, what happened?' 'Didn't you hear? Indira Gandhi was shot! It is not right! They say that two Sikh bodyguards have shot her. I had to close the shop and am locked inside. Sharmaji came and told me that a mob is coming to our market and is looking for Sikhs for revenge. They just announced on the radio that Mrs Gandhi is dead! Lock the gates and do not open the door for anyone. Tell Raja not to go out today anywhere. It is getting bad here. I will come later when it is safe. Do not worry about me, Rano! Sharmaji is with me. Just make sure Raja is alright.'

Rano was shocked to hear all this! *They killed Indira Gandhi! Our Indira Gandhi! I must find Raja.* She thanked Preeti and hurriedly tried to rush out. 'Didi, is everything okay? Is Balkar Veer ji fine?' Rano looked at Preeti's worried face and told her, 'Indira Gandhi is dead! They are attacking Sikh shops. It is probably some angry goonday, who want to close his shop.' Rano never addressed Balkar by his name. 'Preeti, I think you should lock your gates too! Do not open the gate to anyone. And don't go out anywhere.' Rano repeated the advice that she got from Balkar. She quickly went out and crossed the street to enter her own house. Savitri was out hanging her washed clothes on the clothesline in the verandah. She saw the worried look on Rano's face and asked, 'Is everything okay?' Rano simply nodded and said, 'He had called! There is a problem. Indira Gandhi is dead and they have closed his shop in anger. He is with Sharmaji. Hey Waheguru! What is going to happen?' 'Oh no!' uttered Savitri in disbelief. 'I have to find Raja, it may not be safe,' Rano felt helpless suddenly. Savitri said, 'Don't worry, didi. I think Raja had gone with Anil an hour ago on the scooter.'

Anil and Raja had been friends for so long that people thought they were brothers. It almost seemed as if Raja was the first son, raised up as a Sikh in adherence to prayers for his birth answered, and Anil was his younger Hindu brother. Raja, with his curly black beard and colourful turban, always had a mesmerizing smile whenever he met Savitri. "Auntyji, your son is getting naughty now. Find a good girl for him before he falls in love with a South Indian girl! And then he will sing, *hum bane, tum bane, ik dujjay keliye!*" Savitri would always laugh with Raja when he joked about Anil. Anil would hide his smiles and be ready to retort: 'Saaley, wait till I tell your mother about what you were saying about Navjot Kaur!' Anil and Raja would secretly crack jokes about women's breasts and laugh with their eyes glimmering with naughtiness. Both Savitri and Rano would smile at their trivial jocularities.

~

As the flames caught him, his body, convulsing haphazardly, seemed like a giant mosquito sizzling when it blindly shatters against a burning candle. While the mosquito would die quietly, unseen with a kind of stupid dignity, Raja could not die so easily. The hiding spectators were utterly shocked and helpless, cowering so that none of the armed men could find them. The armed men, all dressed in white kurta-pyjamas, confidently holding heavy bamboo lathis in one hand and kerosene containers in the other, seemed hell-bent on the morning's mission. Faces covered with handkerchiefs, these men in white had resolved to kill and attack all Sikhs that they could find that day. Walking on foot, it was not difficult for this unknown mob to find out where Sikh families lived. Some of the people in the mob had, after all, visited these Sikhs in better times, some even had had tea and biscuits together, while others had smeared Holi colours in the spirit of brotherhood and shared Diwali sweets. Many had gone asking for donations to organize overnight jaagrans to appease the Mother Goddess.

Diwali, the festival of lights, and burning candles had just been celebrated... *There won't be much celebration from this year for these buggers. After all, these Sikhs needed to be taught a lesson! Their pride needed to be squashed like a bug. They had been too adamant with their better-than-everybody-else attitude and had been quite frankly bugging,* thought some of the men with their faces hidden behind their white kerchiefs. The blackness of their devious intentions was sheathed beneath those spotless triangular veils. It was easy for them to hide their faces, but not easy for Raja to hide his face. Some of the hairs of his beard were starting to singe and curl up like the tiny legs of the mosquito. Look at Raja now; he was always proud of his black beard and long hair, especially on Sundays, walking in the verandah of his house as his, silky hair covered his back and glimmered under the sun. Look at him now, screaming in pain but not uttering a single coherent word. The flames seem to be not doing their work. One of the men threw some more kerosene oil towards Raja, another put a rubber tire on Raja's neck. The fire seemed angry and provoked at its implied barrenness. Black smoke started smouldering on Raja's convulsing body, amidst ghastly shrieks. Penetrating him, the fire consumed him from all sides. Raja blindly ran towards the mob and managed to hold one man's shawl and snatch it from him. The man, shocked, let Raja have the shawl. How can a burning man not ask for sympathy? 'What have I done to you? I thought you were our friend, uncle!' Raja, with pain aggravating as the flames tormented him, knew that he would have no choice, no time to act. His eyes recognized Rajiv, Anil's father, face covered with a white embroidered handkerchief that he knew his mother had made for Anil's mother for Diwali. Rajiv tried to withdraw and hide behind others, lest people recognize him. He walked away from the turmoil.

'Stop, what are you all doing?' Anil, screamingly furious and visibly shaken, started punching some of the men. While returning from their college, Anil had found out about Mrs Gandhi's shooting. Anil drove the scooter while Raja sat behind him. They were two kilometres away from their homes when the mob had intercepted them. A few men dragged Raja away from the scooter and started beating him. Anil, mad with rage, tried to intervene but someone punched him on the face and he fell unconscious right there. The men then dragged Raja by his arms and brought him to the centre of the road. The mob became bigger as they unleashed a deluge of pent-up cruelty, kicking him, snatching his red turban off and throwing it far away.

When Anil regained consciousness, Raja was shrieking with unbearable pain. He ran towards Raja but did not know what to do to stop the fire. The heat of the fire and the tears from the foul-smelling smoke stinging his eyes were driving him crazy. He tried to take off Raja's clothes, but his arms were also on fire now. That human embrace between a burning man and his best friend brought them close enough to share the flames. Soon Raja's body found a mate in his suffering. The flames seemed happy at finding more to consume. 'Oh! No! Save Anil… Keep him away from this bastard.' *What was happening! They had only told us to crush the Sikhs wherever you find them. Why is this sardar hugging Anil!* The mob grew anxious and tried to separate the burning men. The fire that was consuming Raja now started devouring Anil too in this fiery embrace. What should they do? The fire was wild and excited, getting two victims for the price of one. Raja and Anil, glued to each other like Siamese twins, were like a big human torch in the middle of the road. This was no Olympics where proud men ran and displayed their patriotism while journalists took their pictures. This was the fire of religious hate. The mob believed that the Sikhs were all their enemies. *Yes, yes, they were our enemies indeed. Let him burn and die—but what do we do about Anil? What will we tell his poor parents?* Rajiv had already left for fear of being seen by someone.

By now, Anil knew what was happening to him in this painful ride. So, this is how it felt! The pain had become numb where it hurt him the most. Like waves, the pain bit him with hot, piercing pulses and then he felt icy pain all over. 'Help me, please!' screamed Anil in utter shock and despair. The mob, confused, tried to act but did not know what to do. They had thought only about assaulting Sikhs' pride and crushing their spirits, burning them in kerosene and leaving them to die. Raja fell on the ground lifelessly like a dead mosquito, the flames still trying to tag each other. Anil was still screaming, when finally one of the men in white came forward and tried to wrap him in a blanket and drag him away by force. Anil was shivering and convulsing; he could not forget Raja's last words as they resounded in his ears amidst the confusion and screaming of the other men in white around him. 'Forgive me brother, but you did not have to do this! Think about your father!' The pain was unbearable and delirious.

'Anil, are you able to listen to me? Do not worry; we are taking you to the hospital. We will take revenge for what he did to you! Chalo, let's go, bring the jeep around! You guys go on and find those cowards and drag them out. They killed our mother, now it is our turn! Don't leave a single Sikh!' There was now pandemonium everywhere. Anil, wrapped in a blanket, was carried away quickly and as the jeep came around, five men took Anil with them. You could see the steams of smoke fizzling out of the blanket as Anil was driven away. Raja's deeply charred body was still lying on the street. His eyes remained open with a deathly stare and haunted the onlookers as the mob moved on to find the next Sikh home.

~

One of the shocked onlookers was Chameli, going for her evening round of washing dishes. Rano bibiji's son, Raja, being pulled away violently and burned alive like that! Speechless, she recognized some of the men from her colony of slum-dwellers, and some of the sahibs whom she had seen living in the same neighborhood as Rano. Wasn't that Savitri bibiji's husband she had seen earlier? Some men were outsiders, holding canisters of kerosene oil and iron pipes and rods. She must warn Rano about them. Why are men so cruel? Chameli often thought about this. She was fed up of the abuse that her mother Shanti had to take because her drunk father always needed money for his liquor addiction. Girls have it hard in this life. A curse to be born as a girl, Chameli would hear Shanti confide to her often. Breathlessly running, Chameli took the shorter route to reach Rano's house. She knew the mob could reach Rano's house and she must save her. She went to the back door and started knocking loudly. Back doors were only accessible for maids, or close neighbours like Savitri who enjoyed backyard gossip with Rano most afternoons. 'Bibiji, please open the door. It is me Chameli! Bibiji! Please!' When Rano opened the door, she could not understand a word that Chameli was saying. Chameli was choking with tears and crying more than she could talk. 'What happened, Chameli?' At first Rano thought maybe Chameli's drunk father had beaten her or Shanti, but then she heard Raja's name mentioned. 'What happened to Raja? Tell me, kudiye!' 'Bibiji, those people burned Raja! I saw it with these cursed eyes! They burned him and Anil was also on fire!'

Raja ... burned? Rano could not understand what Chameli was blabbering about. Then she remembered Balkar's warning. Those people were out for revenge against Sikhs. Rano felt as if someone was sitting on her chest and strangling her. She felt a surge of emotions and tears filled her eyes. She wanted to scream yet not a sound came out because grief seemed to drown her in her own tears. *My Raja! I must get to him.* 'No, don't go there, bibiji! They know where you live. You should hide yourself!' 'Are you mad? I cannot leave Raja there. Tell me, where is he?' Chameli led the way as Rano, barefooted and with her head covered by her chunni, followed her swiftly. The roads were eerily quiet. Rano saw some people on their terraces looking around at the black smoke that was seen from afar. Rano became scared, gripped with a stifling fear. It was the shop of Mr Singh—Singh Electronics—robbed in daylight. The glass lay shattered, some TVs were shattered too. Rano suddenly stopped when she saw a red turban on the ground—its folds dishevelled carelessly, without any respect. To see a Sikh's turban on the street was an unimaginable idea. Rano knew that was Raja's turban. As the road turned, Rano's worst fears came true. There on the deserted road lay Raja, all black and smouldering, embraced by a fearful stench. 'Raja!' Rano tried calling, but for some reason her voice could not utter her son's name. Grief had gripped Rano's quivering body with a force so strong that she felt she was dying too. There lay her son, his eyes staring blankly as smoke fizzled out of his upper torso. His blistering scars complained to her of the ugly inhumanity of those demons. Raja's hair was all singed and had curled up in the fire as if withdrawn from the searing cruelty. Raja was dead, and there was nothing that Rano could do. Her voice refused to cooperate. Grief was strangling her from inside out. Suddenly there was a loud cacophony from the next alley: 'Khoon ka badla khoon se laingay! Blood for blood! They killed our mother! We will kill them!'

Chameli hissed, 'They are coming closer, bibiji! Let's go!' She pulled Rano up and tried to pull her along with her. Rano seemed to not care—yet with a ghastly resilience followed Chameli like a dazed, hypnotized woman. Chameli did not know what to do and whom to trust. She hurriedly hid her face with her chunni, and hid Rano's face with her chunni too. Rano seemed unaware of what was happening around her. Her chunni seemed to block the outside cruel world from her mind. She could not think, or utter, and felt a dried, parched heaviness as her voice struggled to come out. Out of nowhere she remembered Mata Gujri and her pain after the sacrifice of her four grandsons—the chaar sahibzaadeys, whose stories of bravery and courage had nourished Rano's childhood. Rano had always been mesmerized by the childhood stories of Guru Gobind Singh and his compassionate, warrior spirit. What will she do now? Raja is gone!

Was this a sacrifice? Or a demon's dance that snatched her son from her? She cannot leave Raja. No, she must hold him.

Rano tried to return but Chameli was forceful too. A bit ahead, they saw a green Contessa on fire with black smoke emanating from its shattered windows. A burnt arm hung out from the driver's window. Both Chameli and Rano knew whose arm it was. Chameli knew if Rano went back, then all horror would be unleashed. 'No, bibiji! You must listen to me. These demons are out for Sikh blood. They will kill you or worse, shame you in horrible ways! Please think about Sahibji.' Rano then remembered Balkar's injunctions and quietly followed Chameli back to her house, entering from the back door. Her body was tremulous and she could not speak. With an eerie sense of calm, Rano simply sat on her chair and, in a daze, resumed knitting the burgundy sweater. Her fingers magically knitted and purled the yarn as it slipped onto the needles in demure obedience. Suddenly, she saw no point in knitting. Raja was gone. She was utterly quiet, her eyes brimming with silent tears.

Chameli tried to shake Rano, as if bringing her senses back to the reality of the horror they had just undergone. When that didn't work, she went to the kitchen to make tea. She wondered where Preeti might be at this time. Should she try to find her or not? These questions were bothering her when the tea hissed in boiling rage and fizzled out of the hot pan as smoke came out of the gas stove. Chameli's fingers were numb and trembled when she tried to hold the pan to pour the tea, and she burned her hand. Her tears could not stop as she thought of Raja who would sometimes joke about her getting married to an old widower with four children; Rano would always scold Raja for teasing Chameli like a brother making his sister cry. Even then, Chameli would never cry because she knew Rano would scold Raja always. 'Raja, why do you make fun of the poor girl!' The more Chameli remembered Raja, the more she cried now. '*Why are men so cruel?*' Chameli knew she had to do something for Rano. She told her to not open the gate for anyone. Rano was eerily quiet, staring nowhere. 'He has not returned yet!' 'Don't worry bibiji, Sahib will come soon!'

It was almost an hour later when suddenly there was a soft knock on the back door. The sun was ready to set and the darkness was creeping up slowly. Chameli became fearful and urged Rano to not open the door. 'Rano! Rano! Are you there?' That was Balkar's voice! Chameli first looked through a hole in the door. It was a dishevelled man with hair cropped the way a cheap roadside barber would. 'That is not Sahib!' 'Rano, it's me Balkar. Please open the door!' Chameli and Rano were shocked for that was indeed his voice. Rano looked through the hole and saw Balkar's tearful eyes and suddenly opened the door. It was Balkar, but without his turban and beard! Rano could not believe her eyes and started crying. Balkar was crying too. He looked so different, Chameli thought to herself. A weak, frail man with a face robbed of his beautiful black beard and no turban on his head. There was a shame in his eyes: a shame that bothers you like prickly heat stings in June. Balkar, Chameli and Rano all felt this shame that robbed them of dignity, smearing them with the pain of grief and loss. 'Hey Waheguru! How did this all happen?'

Balkar then told them how Sharmaji suggested that Balkar must cut his hair if he wants to live. The mob was coming closer and it would be hard for them to hide any longer. At first Balkar refused, but then relented when Sharma insisted. 'Your hair can come back, but your life can't!' Sharmaji found scissors and cut Balkar's hair and shaved off his beard with a pocket knife. Balkar's pain at seeing his hair fall on the floor was quiet yet screamingly hurtful. To cut his birth hair was like a shameful disrobing. To un-Sikh him like that was a punch in his gut. The pain was not physical but emotional and unbearable. 'Where is Raja?' asked Balkar suddenly. Rano and Chameli both started crying. What a disgrace men can be, ready to kill any vestigial humanity for politics.

'Hey Waheguru, let me bring him home!' said Balkar. 'But...' Chameli interrupted, 'what if those goons are still there?' 'He is my son, even if dead!' 'Sahibji, wait...let me go and find Haria and we will find Raja.' Chameli left from the back door. The sun had simply vanished, gripping the neighbourhood with fearful darkness. Rano and Balkar sat on the blue cot and refused to turn any light on. They started reciting Kirtan Sohila, their daily evening prayer. *In the house that we praise and reflect on You, meditate and remember You, I am a sacrifice to you, my fearless lord, who bring eternal peace… I am meek and poor, but I am yours, save me, save me, O great Lord…*

Chameli came back after twenty minutes. She told them that police was patrolling the streets to prepare for overnight curfew. They had taken the charred bodies of the Sikh victims to the morgue and would release the bodies next day after identification. Chameli had to leave before curfew started and told Rano that she would come the next morning. 'Don't turn on any lights, pretend you are not here!' Rano was quietly thinking about Raja, and resumed reciting the Sohila.

~

Meanwhile, Savitri's worst fears had come true. Anil's body had stopped responding to the treatment and had developed sepsis. The doctors had told Savitri that Anil would not survive this ordeal. She waited painfully as Anil breathed his last breath. His son was gone, never to come back.

Savitri was horrified to later learn about the gruesome violence in their colony. Chameli had told her everything when she came to see her at the hospital. Her tears and sobbing had to be stopped when the nurse scolded her for causing a ruckus in the burns unit. Savitri came out with Chameli and could not believe that Raja had been burned alive. The realization that Anil and Raja were victims of the same violence was not missed on her. She wanted to hug Rano, but Chameli told her that they were not at their home. Ranjeet Singh Duggal had been killed and Preeti was nowhere to be found. Grief had crept in all of their lives like an unwanted weed: Rano, Savitri, Preeti and Chameli. Each in her own way was mourning this fiery embrace of loss, tears and choking disgrace. This was no earth-shaking, tree-falling type of calamity that befell them. It was pure, calculated human disgrace—a hatred unleashed by violent men who simply went on with their lives.

It Doesn't Matter Either

Rachel Bari

A story of betrayal set against the backdrop of the 1984 violence in Delhi, 'It Doesn't Matter Either' pointedly depicts the vulnerability of being a woman, and how religion may not matter when it comes to sexual violence against women. After all, a woman is just a woman.

I

She was eighteen, young and beautiful. With her fair, chubby cherubic face, she was the adored one in the family. Jasleen. The corpse in front of them was not her. She could not be dead. Not like this. Her mother approached the body and slowly removed the white cloth over her face. She shrieked, 'Waheguru' and collapsed on the ground.

Her husband, old and distraught, came and sat at her side. His old eyes could only see the bloodied face of his daughter, if at all it was his daughter. They said it was her. There was nothing to identify. What was left? How would they identify her? Her face was swollen, eyelid closed grotesquely, and there was a deep gash on the side of her cheek where blood had coagulated. Her hair was dishevelled, matted, dirty and the smell of death was overpowering. The body had been on the road with three others. Betrayers and plotters, they were called. They did not utter the name.

'Identify her,' ordered the constable.

'Yes… It is her,' said the old father hesitatingly.

'Haan, haan we know. We just wanted confirmation.' 'Take away the body,' the constable indicated.

'But…where are you taking the body? She needs to be cleaned … gurdwara…cremated properly,' said the distraught mother.

The smirk on the faces of the policemen was open and mocking. 'Cremation ha...haan...we will give you what is left of this body.'

The old man and woman watched the body of their beloved child being dragged away like an animal. As they lifted the body to be put on the cart, the white cloth covering her legs gave away to the wind and lifted. Her pearl-white legs had cuts and bruises up to the knee, which was scraped and looked dislocated. The old woman's motherly instincts and years of fear and protection brought her to her feet and she ran after the cart. The coolie hired to drag the cart stopped, confused. The policeman pulled the woman back. She only said, 'Cover her, cover her...' The policeman guffawed at the old woman.

'She is dead, woman. You can cover her when you cremate her.'

The dust was all that remained on the dirty road, and the old man and woman stood by each other, the empty road in front of them, the dust-laden road.

II

She ran. She didn't know why, but she ran. It was dark. The city she knew looked strange. The turns, the streets were strangers, she turned wherever she could. When she thought that the steps behind her sounded dimmer, she slowed down, waiting to catch her breath. Her body bent down, her dupatta slipped from her head and the dim street light caught her profile. Terrified. She heard shouts. 'This way' and the charge of feet. She straightened and ran. She saw a side street, a dark alley and instinctively ducked into it, only to trip over something and onto a body, which caught her and cupped her mouth to stop the scream. She struggled, and kicked, but the arms around her and the hand over her mouth were strong. She passed out in fear.

Water woke her up. Cold, freezing water. Her body reacted in shock. She spluttered and tried to open her eyes. The light was very bright and she shut them again.

'Open your eyes, girl,' the voice was harsh and she felt a stick prodding her sides.

She started to shiver, and opened her eyes. Her back was aching, so were her arms and legs. Her hair was falling over her eyes and she felt her hand lifting to brush it away. The hair stayed. Confused, she opened her eyes further. She was sitting on the floor, her legs and hands tied. She used her elbows to sit up a little more.

'Who are you?' The gruff voice again.

Her voice croaked, 'Where am I?'

The stick prodded her again. 'We ask questions. You answer, you whore.' She could hear laughter in the background. The light was so bright that she could not see anybody. She bent her head sideways to block off the light and felt the pain on her soles. Her body arched with the pain. When the baton came down the second time, she cried out in horrid pain.

'Don't you dare turn away when I ask you questions!' It hit her again. She did not know that the sound resonating in that dirty, smelly room was her own. She fainted again.

When she regained her senses, she felt pain and something sticky and thick between her thighs. She tried to sit up and felt a sharp searing pain from her knee. She could not support herself on it. She wanted to get up, sit up, but it was as though she had no bones. The room was still dark; she waited for her eyes to get adjusted to it. She heard groans and she called out, 'Is someone there? Who's there?'

All that she could hear was the silence which hung thickly in the air.

III

He stood there, camera in hand. The cold was intense. The cap on his head did nothing to reduce the chill in the air. The shiver which crossed over him was testing.

The bodies lay there: one lying on its side, a wound gaping open on his ribs; the other on his back, a black hole near his heart. The beard was matted, dirty and chopped off in places. The hair was all over his face and there was no sign of the turban. The girl was grotesquely sprawled, her ankle and knee exposed. The knee had shifted as though it was playing hide and seek. The ankle had bruises and the tender veins had erupted in places, an army in camouflage. Her face was turned to one side and the wound was on her stomach. Hers must have been the most painful death, he thought.

His job was to photograph and write. He took out his camera and clicked and with each click emerged a new story. Which would he be able to write? The police leaned on their jeeps and waited.

'Plotters?' he asked.

'Arre, sahib, what do we say? They were running, we caught them. How can you trust anybody nowadays? And turbans, of all things, now! We have orders, you see.'

'Hmmm. And the girl?'

'She is with them; we recovered bits and pieces of paper from their bodies. She had a few tucked…you know where. But we took them…'

'You seemed to have taken everything,' said the man with the camera.

'Ji saab…everything,' said the havaldar.

Back in his cabin he sat motionless, the notebook open. He had to cover the story. It had to go in tonight. The people would know what they themselves did not know. It was a difficult choice. Either he wrote what he pieced together or he did not write. That was not an easy decision to make.

It had been three days since the body of Jasleen had been discovered. For three days, he had striven after the truth. Her body had been discovered, along with two others, in a desolate alley. Her body was near naked. Mud and blood had clung to her, stubbornly refusing to lend any semblance of familiarity to her. She was nobody. He did not know how to begin. The television was still showing pictures of riots in many places. Nobody would report this tomorrow. Nobody would know her. She would be just another plotter, whom the police gunned down, a threat eliminated. He began: 'The year 1984 will go down in history as the worst year in India…'

IV

The evening shift was special today. They were gloating over their prize. And surely they would join the ranks of 'loyal' people. The night, today, was quieter. Fewer sirens and fewer orders with fewer words. They were sitting, sipping their steaming chai from broken porcelain cups.

'Hmmmm…'

'You seem to be satisfied…' said one.

'Yes, for now,' said the other.

'She was easy, isn't it?'

'Yes…how could it not be?' He smirked. 'She broke her knee. Where would she go?'

'Haan…her chunni was useful, wasn't it?'

A cynical smile was the only response.

'Was she with them?'

'Oh no…she was returning from tuition. I see her every day. She lives across my street. When the riots broke out, she came running to me for help. I helped her.' The smile which spread over his face was lecherous. 'She tripped over me in the alley where I was hiding…I helped her.'

He remembered how he had seen surprise and fear in her eyes as he had torn her clothes. He had heard the click of bone breaking as she had tried to knee him when he broke her.

'Was she a Sikh?'

'Who cares? In these times, it does not matter either.'

The Sweets of Mathura

Translated from the original Hindi by the author

Set in a train, this story describes how a mob mistakes a Haryanvi man with the surname Singh as a Sikh. The mob's deafness and blindness to reason and facts is a commentary on the blindness shared by both hatred and justice.

'The next station is Mathura. Get down and buy two kilos of peda. Jyoti loves them. We'd like to give a box to Dharambir's family as well,' said Rajrani to her husband, half-reclining on the berth. Dharambir was a close friend of her husband.

'Let us first see if the train stops there or not. This is not its regular route. And then, it all depends on where the compartment comes to a halt, how long the train stops,' her husband replied.

'No, Mathura is no ordinary station. It's a junction,' Rajrani replied.

'Look at you! Indiraji has been shot and you are worried about buying pedas.'

He was right. All around them a hot discussion was on in the compartment. A similar atmosphere prevailed in other compartments as well. Talking of the attack on Mrs Gandhi, most people were spewing poison against the Sikh community. Calling them 'traitors'. Ever since the news came in the morning that her guards had shot Mrs Gandhi, only such opinions had marked the discussions. Some people were holding Operation Blue Star responsible for this attack. But there were also some others who, taking advantage of the discussions, were cursing the policies of the Congress party. Attacking its policy of supporting the Muslim community allegedly at the expense of Hindus, they were making the discussions anti-Congress.

Rajrani and her husband were returning from the Sunderbans area after having a dip in the Ganga Sagar. Hindus believe a dip in the Ganga Sagar to be very holy. It is at Ganga Sagar that the Ganga river ends its journey that began in Gangotri and meets the sea. Although the place is full of pilgrims and tourists the year round, during the four-month period beginning with the Dussehra festival, lakhs of people from all parts of the country gravitated to this area of natural bounty to enjoy the double blisses of picnic and piety. The temptation of getting a chance to see tigers also brought many animal lovers to the place. There was also a mela on Makar Sankranti, but there being no holidays in January, the rush was greater during the Puja–Diwali holidays in October/November.

On the morning of 31 October, they had got the news about the shooting of Mrs Indira Gandhi, while their train was about to reach Kanpur. It must have been around eleven. Someone, on hearing the news on his transistor-radio, had announced it immediately to everyone. The compartment had fallen completely silent, as if struck with lightening suddenly. Something similar to what Rajrani and her husband had witnessed a few days ago in the Sundarbans...

They had gone to see the tigers and after getting down from the boat they were heading to the jungle. Accompanying them was a thin, lean guide, who was walking a little ahead. In his Bengali-accented English and Hindi, he was telling them that the Royal Bengal Tigers were extremely handsome animals but their numbers were dwindling very fast; falling prey to false propaganda, poachers were killing them and selling their body parts, etc., etc. Suddenly, lightning had struck from the high bushes in front. Before they could discern anything, a tiger had pounced and grabbed the neck of their guide. Poor man, he could not even shriek fully. The tourists were struck dumb. No one said anything out of fear. And then Rajrani had begun to wail, 'Hai Ram! Hai Daiya!' Then the wailing had begun all round. Listening to the noise, the majhis and mallahs—boatmen—had come rushing, carrying sticks—big and small, thin and thick. Some were carrying heavy meat cleavers that they called daos on their shoulders. A similar dao was also in the hands of the guide but, poor him, he hadn't got a chance to use it.

Making a big noise, the boatman had run into the bushes, after the tiger. Scared stiff, scores of tourists had been rooted to the ground. Neither willing to go forward nor wanting to withdraw. After about ten minutes, they had returned—empty-handed, faces fallen.

'Ki korbo! Ehi amaar jindagi—what to do! This is our life, our fate,' one of them had replied in broken Bengali when a tourist asked them about the guide.

Rajrani had continued to sob even after getting down on the other shore.

On hearing the news of Mrs Gandhi's shooting, she had once again let out a big wail. Her husband, too, had rushed to the passenger with the transistor-radio. Other passengers from the neighbouring seats too had crowded around him.

'Now listen to an important announcement. This morning, Prime Minister Indira Gandhi was shot by her security guards at her Safdarjang road residence. At that time, the prime minister was on her way to meet the renowned film maker Peter Utsinov within her residence. She has been taken to the All India India Institute of Medical Sciences, where she is being treated for injuries. End of the announcement.'

With this, began a series of discussions that had been going on unabated since then. They would stop only for a brief while when the music on the radio would be interrupted to broadcast a special bulletin on her condition. Since most of the bulletins were in a similar formal language and there was no new information in them, speculations had started: How many shooters were there? How many bullets had hit her? Where had she been hit? From which weapons had the bullets been fired? Had the shooters been apprehended or had they managed to escape?

On all these questions, people had different views. So much so that it was even being debated whether she was already dead. People had got divided into various groups and were voicing contradictory opinions.

Whenever the train stopped at a station, passengers would ask the people waiting at platforms, and even vendors: 'What news? What have you heard? Is she gone?'

Vendors who came inside the compartments to sell snacks had suddenly changed their manner of hawking: 'Tea, Tea! Coffee! Indira Gandhi shot! Admitted to hospital! Hot tea, coffee!' 'Peanuts! Time pass! Prime minister shot by Sikh security guards! Time pass! Peanuts! Nuts! Nuts!' 'Cutlets! Omelette-slice! Cutlets! Omelette-slice!'

The train appeared to have slowed down ever since the news of shooting had broken. It had also stopped at many small non-scheduled stations, as if the driver was inching forward after seeking directions. The sun had already set by the time the train steamed into Tundla. It stopped there for a long time. No one knew the reason. The railway officials refused to say anything on enquiry. People started speculating again. Someone said that after the shooting of Mrs Gandhi, the entire city of Delhi had been placed under curfew. However, that would have nothing to do with the train stopping at Tundla for such a long time. Someone observed that trains got late generally anyway. Someone else observed that the engine had developed a snag and they were awaiting replacement. As the delay increased, so did the speculations. In between, someone would announce the death of Mrs Gandhi, and someone else would contradict that immediately, observing that if it were so, the radio would be the first to announce it.

Rajrani noted that a woman seated on the opposite seat who had said her name was Dolly—Dolly Sarna—had gone quiet since the news of Indira Gandhi's shooting broke. Although she had been quiet during the entire journey, she had, during sporadic snatches of conversation, revealed that she was returning from her parents' place in Calcutta. Her husband was a major in the Indian army and was posted in Delhi. Ever since the news of the shooting of the prime minister started pouring in, she had covered herself with a bedsheet and had gone to sleep. It was as if she did not want to face people or to look them in the eyes.

It was around six when it was announced that due to an accident on the Aligarh railway route, the train was being diverted and would now go to Delhi via Agra and Mathura. Passengers bound for Ghaziabad, etc. were asked to de-board. The passengers lying on the berths above those of Rajrani and her husband packed up and left, murmuring curses. They had to go to Ghaziabad.

'How would they go now?' Rajrani asked her husband.

'How do I know? Maybe they'll look for a bus or something. What else?'

'Brother, when would this train reach Delhi?' Dolly had asked Rajrani's husband, taking off the bedsheet from her head. From her voice, it was apparent that she was scared.

'Who knows when would it reach? When the route of a train is changed, it becomes like an orphan child,' he had replied.

Dolly had covered her head again and gone back to sleep.

The train had just left Agra station when a hawker standing in the middle of their compartment, while serving snacks to a passenger, said loudly, 'Indira Gandhi shot dead. Riots in Delhi.'

Rajrani's husband lashed out at him immediately: 'What nonsense are you talking! She is still being treated. Don't you dare spread rumours! Get lost!'

'Saab, I heard it in another compartment. Saab, they said that she was dead already. Chana jor garam, chana, chana!' Saying this, he left, picking up his bucket that had boiled Bengal grams, a mix of chopped onions and green dhania leaves and a small box for sprinkling masala.

Another debate ensued in the compartment.

'If she had died, it would have been announced on the radio. The Vividh Bharati music is still on,' someone said.

'Come on, the announcement on radio is made much later…after all arrangements have been made…don't you recall that case…' The person saying this had begun to recount an old instance of the death of a leader but no one was interested in listening to his story. All of them wanted to know what had happened, how was Indira Gandhi's treatment progressing.

Moving up and down, Rajrani's husband had noted that no Sikh family was visible in their compartment. Many of the passengers were, like them, returning after a visit to Ganga Sagar. Also, most people were from either Bengal or Bihar. 'Good,' he thought, 'otherwise there would be a tamasha right here.'

'In India, everyone is sitting on the edge all the time. Everyone is ready to take on another—no matter what the incident, involving whoever,' he thought further.

'Gone! Dead!' announced the man with the transistor-radio who, while holding it close to his left ear, was trying to listen to the news amidst the din of the debate. The manner of his shout was similar to when a wicket fell in a match while listening to the cricket commentary.

'Hai Ram! Hai Daiya! What happens now!' Rajrani wailed aloud as if on the death of a close relation. Then hiding her face in her odhni, she began to sob.

Head still covered with the bedsheet, Dolly had changed sides to face the wall.

The train had still not stopped fully at the Mathura station, when a crowd of people began to run along. They looked different from ordinary passengers. They did not carry bags, attaché cases, boxes etc., in their hands or their heads. Some carried sticks, lathis, ballam etc., and some carried old tyres. In the hands of some were plastic cans, while others were empty-handed.

'Got it! There's one in this compartment! Seat number twenty-seven,' shouted one of them after scrutinizing the list of passengers pasted on the entrance of the compartment.

'Come, let's catch the bastard,' shouted many in unison and forced themselves into the compartment. They came and stood near the seats of Rajrani and her husband. The passengers in the compartment could not comprehend who they were. 'Who's there on twenty-seven?' roared a leader-like fellow. In black trousers and a shiny, checked shirt, he looked quite strange. As if a flute-player member of some local marriage music band.

'Tell me, what is it? I am on twenty-seven,' said Rajrani's husband.

'Catch hold of him! Take him away! Bastard, murderers of the prime minister! Pull him out of the compartment! You kill Mrs Indira Gandhi…sssaaale…sardar!'

'Eh, eh, what are you doing?' Rajrani shouted, standing up from her seat. 'He's my husband. He's no murderer-shurderer.' She moved forward and stood there, holding her husband by the arm. Her husband put her aside and when he tried to free himself from the hold of those people, one of them twisted his arm behind his back and pulled at it. He shrieked in pain. 'Arre, he is my husband. Sube Singh. We are Hindus, from Haryana,' saying this, she held onto her husband's trousers, trying to prevent him from being dragged.

The entire compartment seemed to have been struck with a complete paralysis suddenly. No one had even stirred. As if watching a scene in a play with bated breath.

'See, see! Even the name is "Sube Singh"…a Punjabi Suba Khalistani! Kill him! You mother…sssaaale, a Sikh without a turban! Must also be smoking beedi-sigret etc…Take him away…sssaaale, murderers,' shouted the leader in black trousers and pushed Rajrani back on the seat where the woman was sleeping with her head covered.

'Arre, arre, where are you taking me, we are Hindus…returning after a holy dip in the Ganga Sagar…arre bhai hum Sikh nahi hain— we are not Sikhs. We are Jaats from Haryana,' Sube tried to reason with them.

'We are Congressmen. My father Des Raj Ji Dahia was a freedom fighter. I…we are Hindu…we are already very sad on about Mrs Gandhi's murder. Leave him alone, please…' Rajrani shouted.

'Eh, brother, you heard, they are Congress leaders.' One of the rioters laughed.

'Then take him for garlanding, spray itar on him in welcome,' another said in ridicule.

Pushing him, they pulled him down the compartment. Rajrani followed them, but stopped at the compartment door. Many passengers had also come and stood behind her.

'Arre, arre, where are you taking me? Told you, we are Hindu…I was about to get down and buy some pedas for my daughter. What are you doing…I am not a Sikh,' Sube Singh shouted loudly and began to sob.

'Arre, where is the garland man? Garland him. Also, feed him some pedas,' said the leader-like fellow in black trousers. Then he put his hand in Sube Singh's trouser pocket, took out his purse and put it in the pocket of his own jacket.

'Arre, what are you doing? Where are you taking him? We have to go to Tohana,' Rajrani shouted from behind the passengers crowding the door.

Suddenly, she spotted a railway official in a black coat and shouted, 'Brother, T.T., stop them. They are taking my Sube. Save him!'

The official did not pay any heed to her. He was looking towards the guard's compartment, perhaps waiting for the green signal for the train to move.

From among the rioters, a fellow clad in a lungi put an old scooter tyre on Sube Singh's head, pressed it down hard and fixed it around his neck. Then, he picked up a couple of pedas from those displayed on a vendor's cart standing nearby, pushed them into Sube Singh's mouth and said, 'Now, eat pedas. We have already put Mathura garland around your neck.'

Suddenly, with two pedas thrust down his throat, Sube Singh choked and began to cough: Kho! Kho!

'Take him away to that side. Spray itar on him,' the leader said and pushed him in the direction opposite to the train.

Rajrani was crying, wailing. 'Arre, arre, where are you taking him? The train is about to move. We are not Sikh...Hai Daiya!'

Suddenly, the train jerked and began to move. The group of rioters and Sube Singh moved away from the train. Rajrani tried to jump out, but other passengers stopped her from doing so.

'Behanji, don't worry. Once they discover that you are not Sikhs, they'll let him go. He'll come by the next train. Don't worry,' one of them said.

The train picked up speed. Many passengers standing at the door of the compartment looked back. Suddenly, they saw a circle of fire running—towards the train.

The train was now moving really fast. The circle of fire began to appear smaller and smaller, and soon it disappeared from the vision of the passengers.

Another Kharku

Translated from the original Hindi by the author

This story is about the changing image of the Sikhs after 1984. For a time, it seemed that every Sikh man with a turban was being seen as a terrorist. In this story, a Sikh man buys kerosene oil for cooking and boards a bus to return home. His experience thereafter says it all.

'I say, the kerosene is finished. Get it on your way back in the evening. This Ramesh fellow, the ration shop owner, puts me off every day. "Today, I received no supplies." "Today, you've come late." "Today, the supply truck developed a snag," etc. etc. Everyone says he sells it in the black market,' Satbir said.

'Okay, Ravi's bibi, give me the can. If Parashar Saab, Waheguru bless him, gives me his ration card, I shall get it from the univarshty ration shop.'

'Here it is. The cap got misplaced somewhere. Fix a piece of wood on the top,' said Satbir, handing him the can. Mahender Singh put the empty five-kilo desi ghee oil can in a dirty old bag, hung it from his shoulder, picked up the tiffin carrier in his right hand and moved towards the bus stand. These days, the buses were very difficult to get into. Also, since the beginning of the Gulf War, scarcity of kerosene and cooking gas had increased manifold. There were long queues at petrol pumps for diesel too. They said, the government had no money left in its treasury to buy oil products and was planning to pawn plane-loads of gold. The number of buses plying on public routes had gone down substantially. That's why overcrowding in buses had increased too. Taking advantage of the situation, private bus operators had increased their fares and as usual, the government had ignored this loot. What if in this delicate situation, the private bus operators had decided to go on a strike! That would have brought the entire city of Delhi to a standstill. Now, Mahender Singh had to spend six, sometimes even eight rupees, instead of the earlier four, on the bus fare. Two rupees from Mukherjee Nagar to Sachivalaya and another two rupees from Sachivalaya to the University. And the same on return. And if, by chance, the bus developed a snag en route, then another two gone. No private bus carrier honoured the ticket from another carrier.

'Tell me, sardarji, why are you carrying two items in your hand?' asked Ranbir who was standing there already, as soon as Mahender Singh reached the bus stand. Ranbir was an assistant in the Ministry of Labour and travelled often in the same bus.

'Please don't ask me. For many days, there has been a shortage of kerosene. And this fellow Ramesh, our ration supplier, does not give us our quota. Today, I thought of borrowing my officer's ration card and getting the supply from the univarshty shop.'

'Sardarji, why don't you now get out of this menace of kerosene etc.? Why don't you get a gas connection? Your son is in Dubai, no? Get dollars from him. They say, against that you get the connection immediately,' Ranbir said.

Mahender's only son Ravi, that is, Ravinder Singh Randhawa, had gone to the Middle East for work many years ago now. Right from his childhood, he was fond of going to 'foren'. However, he was very weak in studies. So Mahender Singh had got him admitted to a course in refrigeration repairs in an industrial training institute. After moving from one small job to another for years, he had finally got a chance to go to Iraq. The salary was okay, and being a bachelor, he had a good chance to save. Within three years, he had saved enough for them to convert their kucha house in Garhi into a pucca house. Now, they had permanent arrangement for sewage and power etc. In all this, Ravi had helped substantially, because it was not possible for Mahender Singh to do much. Being a security havaldar in a university, he did not get much—a mere fourteen-fifteen hundred a month. In these days of high cost of living, that was not sufficient even for routine household expenses. However, Ravi being in Dubai—better job and more pay—had helped.

In between, he had also got married.

'But there has been an impact of the war there as well. There is a complete ban on transferring money. For many days, we haven't heard from them either. Waheguru bless us, if all goes well, we shall get the gas too.'

By the time Mahender Singh completed his reply, their bus arrived and they managed to get into it somehow. The buses were extremely overcrowded these days. A boyish-looking conductor would push a two-rupee ticket into your hands as soon as you entered. If you weren't careful, he'd return you torn currency notes while giving change and would look the other way. After that, you alone were responsible for finding space for your two feet, saving your pocket from being picked, saving your stuff from being damaged and reaching the exit gate unhurt before the bus arrived at your destination. The situation had worsened since the time the government had allowed women to board from the front gate. One, women crowded the exit gate to escape manhandling by marauding men and those needing to get down had to do a lot of pushing around. At times, the men had to listen to berating from women—for no fault of theirs. Second, following the example of women, many men too, particularly young college students, had started boarding from the front gate. As a result, those standing in the middle got pressed from both sides. On top of it, the drivers of private buses would press the brakes unnecessarily to give some men an excuse to topple over women.

'Okay, sardarji, see you in the evening. Remember what I said about getting dollars,' Ranbir had said when the bus reached the I.T.O. bus and he had begun to push towards the exit gate although his bus stop was still far off. Today, Mahender Singh had better luck: he got a seat by the time the bus reached Mandi House. Seating himself, he began to ruminate over Ranbir's suggestion.

Blaming the war and mentioning a ban on money transfer were only excuses. The fact was that for the last four-five years, neither had Ravinder sent any money nor had he come home on a visit although

Dubai was just three hours away by air. Of course, once in a while, a letter would arrive, mentioning in a few lines that all was well with them. Rocking on the jerks from the bus, Mahender Singh recalled the events relating to Ravinder's marriage. With great care and fondness, Satbir had managed to find a girl from among her own relations and had fixed his marriage.

Gunwant's father was a private contractor. 'Brother, you've filled our entire house with gifts. For us though, Gunwant was gift enough,' Mahender Singh had told Ravinder's father-in-law.

'But, brother, your son too is one in thousands. And then, he works in "foren",' Gunwant's father had replied. It was customary to praise one another on the auspicious occasion of a marriage. After marriage, Gunwant had stayed with them for four months, although Ravi had gone back after two weeks. He had got leave for only that period.

'Get down, everyone! Empty the bus! This is Sachivalaya,' with the announcement of the conductor, Mahender Singh's reverie got broken and picking up the empty can and the tiffin carrier, he began to walk to the bus stop opposite Gurdwara Rakabganj, the stop for route 680. Since the bus started from there, Mahender Singh had no difficulty in getting a seat. While putting down the bag with the empty can, his attention was drawn to what was written at the back of the seat in front: 'Look under the seat in front of you. Any unattended object can be a bomb. Make a noise immediately and get a reward.' After the 1984 killings, such information was often found written in buses, trains and other public places.

'What can the poor government departments do,' Mahender Singh began to think again. 'There are so many acts of sabotage happening. Only last week, many people had got killed by a bomb blast in a bus plying between Azadpur and Lajpat Nagar. And before that, those bombs planted on two bicycles at the Shahdara bus stand. Dozens had been killed. And a couple of years before that, there had been that incident involving "transistor bombs" throughout the city. In that, many women and children too had been killed. The son of Satbir's aunt was one of them. Always travelling by his own scooter. God knows why he had decided to ride a bus on that fateful day. Perhaps it was destined...'

All such incidents had started happening after Operation Blue Star. Before Mahender Singh's eyes danced the photographs of bloodied corpses that had been published in the newspapers after the shooting of bullets and throwing of grenades by the army inside the premises of the Golden Temple in Amritsar. Besides the kharku (terrorists), thousands of innocent devout persons were also present there at the time of the operation. After this state atrocity, the resentment in the psyche of the Sikh community had increased manifold, which had acted like the pouring of oil on an already lit fire. Foreign forces had taken full advantage of the situation and not only Punjab, but the whole of India, had got embroiled into a phase of killings, the culmination of which was the murder of Mrs Indira Gandhi by her two Sikh bodyguards in 1984. Also arose before Mahender Singh's eyes the scenes of the naked dance of beastliness in Delhi in the wake of Mrs Gandhi's killing. Thousands of innocent Sikhs were massacred, only because the killers of Mrs Gandhi were Sikhs.

'By the same logic, no Hindu should have been left alive after the murder of Gandhiji because he was murdered by a fundamentalist Hindu,' Mahender Singh wondered. 'And this time, the beasts had killed with such cruelty. Husbands, sons and brothers were burnt alive in front of their women. Running households were turned into ashes within minutes. In Palam village, seventeen women in a single household had been widowed in one stroke.'

Ruminating over the beastliness of the 1984 killings, Mahender Singh recalled the Janakpuri house of his son's father-in-law, Sardar Manjit Singh Kohli, where the doors and windows were sealed from outside by the rioters and the place set on fire like the heaps of wood and cow dung cakes are burnt on the occasion of the Holi festival. Scared to death, the neighbours had watched, only uttering 'Hai Rabba! Hai Rabba!' Some neighbours had observed that the rioters had come with household lists from the rations office and were selectively targeting the Sikh households. The entire focus was on finishing off the male members of families and burning to ashes shops and business premises.

Here, in the Garhi area, Mahender Singh himself and the bibi—his son's mother—had been saved by his neighbour, Tiwariji, who had hidden them behind an almirah in a store room without any windows which had been locked from outside. He had misled the crowd of rioters that had collected in front of his house and which included many shanty dwellers from the neighbourhood, by saying that Mahender Singh had fled along with his old wife the previous night.

'Come, let us loot the stuff from the anti-nationals' households!' Hearing this slogan from the leader, Mahender Singh had tried to get up a dozen times, but his wife had put her hand over his mouth, and with a tight hug, had forced him to be seated where he was. The rioters had cleaned out every single thing from his house, not leaving even old, worn-out cycle tyres.

'...If we manage to stay alive, we'll set up the house again!' Sitting in the bus, Mahender Singh recalled his wife Satbir's words repeated many times during the next few weeks. He also recalled how, in those days, Satbir would sleep next to him and, extending her hand repeatedly while asleep, check if indeed he was sleeping close to her.

After those days, for weeks together, the sky over Delhi had been overcast with black soot and the environment filled with a pungent smell of burnt flesh. The whole sight was like what he had once seen in a film called *Tamas* based on the Partition riots. Suddenly, the entire Sikh community had been turned into criminals. Mahender Singh still recalled how in a Peace March taken out on the third day after the murder of Mrs Gandhi, he was the lone Sikh among the marchers and seeing him, a boy playing cricket in a ground near Amar Colony had said aloud, 'Look, a sardar!'

'Kuwait Embassy! Those getting down here, hurry up!' Listening to the conductor's voice, Mahender Singh's attention shifted to the events that had happened in that country a few years earlier. 'Mayhem had descended on Kuwaitis, and later, on Iraqis too. Both countries that offered sustenance through jobs to millions of Indians had themselves become dependent on charity. 'Waheguru be thanked that our Ravi had shifted to Dubai before that happened.' Mahender Singh folded his hands, bent his head down and thanked his God and his lips muttered, 'Nanak tere bhaane sarbat da bhala! (May Nanak look after everyone's well-being).'

In the scare that followed the riots, thousands of households had been uprooted. Selling their businesses which had been running well for scores of years, and well-established households for peanuts, Sikhs from all over the country had gone to Punjab, to live among their own. Similarly, Hindus had fled from Punjab to Delhi, Mumbai, wherever! Within India, an atmosphere prevailed like the one at the time of the formation of Pakistan. Mahender Singh recalled a distant relation of his—Sardar Bami Saheb, who was in the business of selling spectacles and who had closed it to shift to 'Ambarsar'. Young Sikh boys were in bigger trouble. Scared of being either 'recruited' by kharkus or being caught by the police and killed in 'encounters', they were running away to foreign lands, without caring for their older ones. Some used their passports and others, forged documents. Some hid themselves in the boilers of ships and others in the luggage cabins of aircraft.

Mahender Singh thought about the predicament of thousands of Sikhs like himself who could not go anywhere, neither to Punjab nor outside India. Some had no means, while others had no relations—close or distant—living outside Delhi to provide them with shelter. Double quick, they had shifted to those residential areas, bastis and mohallas that had a Sikh majority. Tilak Vihar near Tilak Nagar, Fateh Nagar, Vikas Puri, Mukherjee Park, Jangpura, Bhogal, Gautam Nagar etc.

'We ourselves gave up our pucca house in Garhi and shifted here. Waheguru forbid, if another similar calamity befalls us, we would then be at least among our own people,' Mahender Singh thought. 'In such shifting from here to there, and there to here, the Gurdwara Prabandhak Committees had helped the poor a lot. Had given them money, had appealed to the landlords to rent out their places to Sikhs and had encouraged the mentally besieged Sikh community by observing that this was not the first time in the history of the community that they had been attacked. And this time too they would have 'fateh' (victory)!

In the meantime, Mahender Singh's attention had shifted from the slogans to the phase of bloodletting from which Punjab, Haryana, Delhi and UP had not been able to get out even now—after years.

Hardly a day passed without ten-fifteen innocents being killed. Whether from the bullets of terrorists or of the police, people were being killed. People from the villages were fleeing to the cities and those in the cities to foreign lands. Daily-wage earners were even worse off. Every day an incident or two and the next day a bund or curfew. A strange environment of non-belief and suspicion prevailed. To Sikhs, Hindus had become strangers, and to Hindus every Sikh was a kharku. To terrorists, every Hindu was an agent of the Hind Sarkar (Indian government), and to Hindus every Sikh, a Pakistani mujahideen.

'Waheguru sarbat da bhala', the words wishing that Waheguru would look after the welfare of all, escaped Mahender Singh's lips involuntarily and this time the young man sitting next to him looked at him as if he, Mahender Singh, were insane.

Ten or fifteen days after the massacre, Gunwant and Ravi had come to India from Dubai—for the last rites of Gunwant's parents' family. Guwant's looks were full of so much contempt and hatred, as if Mahender Singh and his wife were responsible for the murder of her parents' family. In front of his wife, Ravi behaved as if he felt guilty about the survival of his own parents. Listening to the tales of terror, his heart had been filled with more horror. Thereafter, they had not dared to come to India. Before leaving, Gunwant had told her mother-in-law in no uncertain terms that they had nothing to do with a country anymore where her old parents and young brothers had been burnt alive in their own locked house and the entire neighbourhood had silently watched like hijras. Of course, Ravi before leaving had observed, 'Patience, Gunwant, patience! Tragedies come and go in human lives.'

'Daughter, time is really powerful. In the course of time, things will be alright,' Mahender Singh had tried to reason with his daughter-in law. But now it appeared to him that he had been trying to convince himself more than both of them.

'University! Those for JNU get down, quickly,' the conductor had hollered and, taking care of the bag with the can and the tiffin carrier, Mahender Singh had got down.

~

'Sahibji, here is your ration card.'

'Thank you very much, Sahibji. I've got the kerosene,' said Mahender Singh while handing over the card to Mr Parashar. What he did not tell Mr Parashar was that the ration shop owner had tried to extract more than the prescribed rate from him by observing that Mr Parashar had a connection for cooking gas and he never drew his quota of kerosene. But Mahender Singh had reminded him that he worked in the Security Department of the university and that the shop had been opened for the convenience of the community. After a little hee-haw, the shop owner had given him the kerosene. However, Mahender Singh had noted that since the 1984 happenings, people's behaviour in the city had become more quarrelsome towards Sikhs. They snapped at them over trivialities. At the same time, the behaviour of Sikhs had become softer; they would keep clear of picking quarrels and would prefer to dispose of contentious issues by apologizing.

'Mahender Singh, you may keep the card with you for now. We do not need it and you may need kerosene now and then. We have a cooking gas connection and we also do not draw any rations.'

'Sahibji, many many thanks to you. Sahibji, I had another request to make. If I could be permitted to leave office a little early, I would arrive home safely with the can of kerosene and well in time. In the evenings, it is terrible on the buses with so much rush.'

After getting the permission, Mahender Singh took off his official uniform, folded it and kept it in the almirah, picked up the can full of kerosene and the tiffin carrier and moved towards the bus stand for route 680. Instead of the stopper of the can, he had inserted a piece of wood wrapped in a piece of plastic. Route 680 buses came from Ambedkar Nagar and were generally packed. Even then, the conductor went on stuffing passengers like onions or potatoes in a sack.

'Okay, route 680 passengers get in. Get in sardarji. You, over there, get in from the front gate,' the conductor was shouting. Although the bus was not packed, Mahender Singh could not manage a seat. He bought the ticket, moved forward and stood in the middle of the bus. Anyway, he had to get down at the terminus. By the time the bus reached Moti Bagh, it became packed very badly. But the conductor went on hollering, inviting more passengers in. And the driver was driving at over seventy. There was so much of noise all around: the shouts of the conductor, quarrels between passengers and on top of it, Haryanvi songs—obscene and out of tune, emanating from the tape recorder next to the driving seat.

By the time the bus came down the Rail Museum flyover, it had picked up more speed. An accident nearly happened while the bus went around the Kuwait Embassy roundabout. While saving a car from a foreign mission, the bus had nearly crashed into the barbed wire fence of the National Rose Garden. With great effort, Mahender Singh saved himself from falling off. The same thing happened at the American Embassy and the Indonesian Embassy roundabouts. People had started murmuring complaints and this angered the driver. When he went around the Teen Murti circle at the same speed, Mahender Singh could not keep his balance and bumped against the person standing next to him. Simultaneously, some kerosene spilled over from the can. At once, the whole bus was filled with the kerosene smell.

'Who is carrying kerosene in the bus?' the driver shouted in his Haryanvi English. Mahender Singh kept quiet.

'Who is carrying oil? Put him down him, immediately,' the driver instructed the conductor and stopped the bus a little short of the South Avenue bus stop.

'Bhai Sahib, I am carrying some for cooking. A little got spilled over due to the jerk in the bus,' Mahender Singh pleaded.

'Oye, Birender, put down this nuisance. You want to set the bus on fire! Son of kharku!' The boyish-looking driver was not impressed with the pleadings of the grey-bearded Mahender Singh.

'Oye sardar, get down quick; can't you hear?' Dressed in dirty torn trousers and a filthy banyaan, the conductor must not have been more than fourteen or fifteen.

'Bhai sahib, I have to go up to daftar. How will I go from here? Rab di saun, I am carrying it for cooking purposes at home.'

Mahender Singh's pleadings had no impact either on the conductor or the driver. Some people began to complain about the 'delay' to the bus. When one of them tried to convince the driver, he lost his temper at him. 'Tainiska mama laagesai? (Are you his uncle?) You get down too. Big supporter of terrorist.'

After this, no passenger dared say anything. Otherwise too, the bus staff and the Delhi police staff both hailing from the same rural areas of Delhi had a big bonhomie between them, which scared people. So, some people started convincing Mahender Singh, 'Baba, aap hi maanjao (Old man, why don't you just agree and get down?)'

Though not wanting to, Mahender Singh had to get down from the bus. There was no alternative to walking till daftar—Central Secretariat. But this whole area was a VIP-zone—MP residences on both sides of the road and the Rashtrapati Bhawan in front! Both Army and Air Headquarters at a little distance. And, halfway, at the Raja Ji roundabout, the residence of the British High Commissioner!

'Anyway, from daftar, I will sit only in that bus in which I can find a seat, so that there is no jhanjhat of the oil spilling over,' Mahender Singh assured himself. Holding the kerosene can in one hand and the tiffin carrier in another, he moved ahead on South Avenue road towards Rashtrapati Bhawan.

~

Today, Ranbir had gotten late leaving his office. 'That's why I don't see Mahender Singh. He must have left by the earlier bus—as usual,' he thought.

~

When he came out of the bath, his wife kept a cup of tea before him and he switched the TV on, to watch the latest news. When the DD news bulletin ended, he'd switch over to the BBC and then to Prannoy Roy's bulletin. Often, there would be arguments with his wife and children since most of the time, this would clash with *Chitrahaar* or some film being telecasted.

'What's so wonderful about the news? Nothing is going to change whether you hear it or not,' his wife would often observe.

'Nor even after you've heard it,' his daughter would never forget to add.

'...an AK-47 and some bullets were recovered from one of them. In another incident, today, the police arrested another terrorist from the VIP area when he was going to set fire to a government office. Some documents and material for starting a fire were recovered from him. The terrorist is alleged to be related to someone in one of the Gulf countries. Next news, from Raman...'

'I say, I forgot to mention something...' said his wife, raising her voice from the kitchen. Ranbir did not at all like this local bulletin by his wife in the middle of the national news. 'Okay, let us listen to your newscast first,' he said, irritated, and switched off the TV. As it was, by now the news telecast was over.

'That neighbour of ours—Satbir—has come twice since the evening, saying that her sardarji has not come home as yet. Generally, he'd be home by seven...she was asking if he had mentioned to you anything about his being late or something...'

Suddenly, Ranbir switched the TV on once again.

'The political crisis in Bihar deepens. Four terrorists arrested in Delhi in different incidents. And violence erupts in Sri Lanka once again. With this ends the newscast. Namaste.'

When Ranbir's wife came into the room from the kitchen, she found that Ranbir's tea lay on the table untouched and he was staring at the Pepsi ad on the TV blankly.

Eyes Don't Lie

Jyoti Verma

The experiences of 1984 impacted Punjab and its youth for another decade, as a generation of religious Sikh boys were perceived as terrorists. The mysteries around the disappearance of several young Sikh boys remain unresolved even today. This story sensitively describes the experiences of one such boy's family.

June 1984

It was a while that we had been on the journey in a bus that day. We were travelling from Delhi to Amritsar. Vir had been restless ever since we left for the bus stop. I had noticed him fidget with his bag several times, shifting the burden from one shoulder to the other. He did it each time a passer-by came close to us. Once or twice, I even felt that his breath was too fast, as if trying to say something, but I decided to let him speak first: 'Do not tell Bibi what I'm about to tell you', he whispered in my ear and pointed to a wad of notes in his bag. I had almost shouted out loud in excitement but managed to compose myself. In a low pitch, I said, 'Where did you get all this money, Vir?' 'I saved. I want to buy a nice transistor for her. I'll find one in Amritsar. So, don't tell her this on the call tonight. Get it?' he answered. 'Only if you buy me my favourite comic', I grabbed the opportunity. He was smiling. 'Promise?' he said, 'Promise.' He looked out of the window, contemplating something. Then after a while, he spoke to me, 'You know you are growing up to be very clever!' We laughed together at that. His face was shining bright enough to turn all the sunflowers towards him. His heavy breathing from before had merely been the effect of the June heat. A jacket of hot air encapsulated our bodies...

'Are you okay, my child?' a voice came, while his laugh still resonated inside me. 'Was I lost again?' I asked myself. I was only coming back to my senses when I saw a stranger kneeling in front of me. 'Why are you sitting in the middle of the street? Are you lost? Let me take you to the police station,' he said. I stared at him blankly. 'Are you hungry?' a middle-aged woman asked me. They both talked and agreed on something. She fed me rice and said a few things, 'You are fine…back home…mother…soon.' Mother…

'Stop fiddling with it. It's an hour now. Here, give it to me!' she chided Vir while fixing his turban for him. She had packed paranthas for our bus journey. 'I am hungry, let's eat please.' Vir replied, 'Not yet.' It was the fourth time I was suggesting eating; he declined the offer consistently. But, the fifth time, he blurted differently, 'You won't listen.' He gave me my share. I giggled when he finished all his paranthas even before I could eat mine first. 'We will reach only at night. You can sleep if you feel like', he said but I didn't want to waste the journey sleeping. I lulled away my time looking out of the window first. Later, a baby and her mother sitting across grabbed my attention. The baby looked at me and babbled. She soon forgot me and slept in her mother's arms only to wake up cooing again.

By the time we arrived, the sun had already set. 'When will we go to Darbar Sahib?' I asked him. 'Tomorrow it's the best day to visit. And we won't be tired then.' I agreed. We headed out for our uncle's place. He was Bapu's friend. We always stayed with him on our trips to Amritsar. 'Noor!' I heard uncle's voice.

My confusion faded away slowly and took along the memories I was lost in…

'Oh, my little girl, you will be fine!' he said embracing me.

'Take me to Bibi', I said. A police officer was surprised to hear my sudden outburst. 'She hasn't spoken a word since she came here. Is her mother in Amritsar?' he asked my uncle. 'No no…' Uncle gave him details of my village and satisfied, he let us go. 'Noor, where is Vir?' I kept looking out of his car's window rendering his question unanswered. 'Beta! You have to tell me. How will I face your mother?' he insisted. 'He went to buy the transistor', I answered. Uncle must have thought something is wrong with me. 'Rest, my child', he said.

But I wasn't wrong.

Memory kept returning to me in bits and pieces. I could still hear the gunshots, echoing endlessly....

'It's going to be okay, Noor', Vir had said. My hands cupped my ears. Each gunshot was as if piercing through my skull, weakening it more each time. A man had said there were tanks too. 'Will I die, Vir?' I asked. I cried inconsolably. 'I wish we had listened to Bapu. We should...we should have never come here', I said crying, still clinging on to him. We all sat in a dark room. Women and children sobbed quietly. The night dragged on. So did the firing. I had slept once when my eyes had started to burn because of the constant crying. Vir held me all that while. And I held on to him. I felt safe with him. As long as he was with me, I was home. The firing had stopped at the break of the dawn. There would be an occasional shot in the sky. These shots didn't pierce through anymore...

December 1984

'Noor?' it was Bibi. I ran to her and held her, tight as ever. She did the same. It had been six months that I had seen her now. Uncle had kept me safe in Amritsar all this time on her request. 'I'm...I'm sorry...we should not have left, even Bapu had said...', I broke down as I said so. She didn't say anything but held me close to her for a while. Uncle had to leave.

'Thank you, Bhraji. You have taken such good care of Noor all these months. I'm indebted to you. I hope I'll be of some help to you someday', she said with folded hands as he left. 'Where is Vir?', she had asked me as I lay in her lap. I had an answer this time. 'He left me at the police station and said that Uncle will find me. He said he will come back soon.' 'But did he say where he was going?' she asked me. 'He said he will go to a safe place', I replied. She nodded as she ran her fingers lovingly through my hair.

I had kept my promise to Vir....

'I think everything is fine now', he said to me. A man had confirmed we could go. 'Look, Noor, I will go out first and if it is safe, I'll come back to take you. We will be home, very soon.' 'Don't go', I said timidly. 'We are safe. We will surprise Bibi with the transistor. She always wanted to listen to the radio while doing her chores. Just imagine how happy she will be. Now don't worry. I'm with you', he reassured. And…he did come back. I rushed over to him. 'There was a curfew but it's lifted now', he told. 'But, why a curfew?' I questioned. 'I'll tell you everything in the bus. Now, we will quickly look for a transistor. I'll explain to Uncle why we had to leave, but only once we get home, safely.' Then he gave me a set of instructions. One of them was to hold his hand as tightly as I could. Another, was to look at our hands only, and nothing else as we exited Darbar Sahib. We went to the only shop we found open. 'I can't sell you anything. Please leave, at once!' the shopkeeper said curtly. 'But here is the money. I have it', Vir insisted. 'Go away!' came the reply. Vir was infuriated. His face didn't shine now. His welled-up, angry eyes had scared me. At a distance, I saw a book vendor closing his shop. I let go of Vir's hand. He had loosened his grip and was busy arguing with the shopkeeper. 'How much is *Chitrakatha* for?' I asked the vendor. 'A rupee', he told. 'Vir! Vir!' I called out. He turned towards me. 'Come back here Noor, now!' he said. 'But, my promise?' I said from where I stood. 'Oh! Is that your brother? I can't sell you anything. Leave now', said the vendor as he put away the book and packed it in one of his bundles. 'But why? What is wrong?' I asked him, but he paid no heed. I turned back to Vir. A man in green aimed his gun toward Vir. Before I could run to him, the piercing sound had come once again. This time it had pierced my heart. I had sat in the middle of the street, numb…

'Where is Bapu?' I asked Bibi as I lay in her lap. It was chillingly cold. These were the December winds that made the weather so. A jacket of frost had enclosed me then. She was quiet first but then soon opened up, 'He has also fled. Just like Vir did.' I looked up to see her face. She was lying. I could tell by her bland expression, she was thinking of something else. Her face was dull and tired. Her eye sockets, black and wrinkled.

'Do you want to sleep, Bebe? Let's go inside. I will cook today.'

'I want to sleep. But…but, how can I? What if they come again? What will I do?' she erupted. That moment, I felt as if my heart was in my mouth. I feared and anticipated the consequence of this revelation.

'It may be months ago but I remembered every horrifying bit of it.'
'Tell me, Bibi, please. Where is Bapu?' I asked nervously.

'It was just past midnight when we heard loud noises. Your father decided to go out when we heard the glass shatter. Someone had hurled a bottle over our wall. As I sat up in bed, I heard him calling my name at the top of his voice', she said while tears poured down her cheeks. I wiped them with my hand. 'Go on Bibi', I said with a trembling voice. 'A mob broke into our house. They dragged him out. I begged them, but no one listened. I heard him cry and plead too. Two policemen stood right there watching it all, as if it were a show. I begged in front of them, on my knees. Nobody paid any attention, Noor. Their eyes didn't flinch once, nor did their hands falter. Their faces were monstrous. They hated us', she said with so much pain in her reddening eyes. 'They burned him alive. I can still recall the ghastly look on his face. His body was snatched from my arms. They didn't even let me mourn him. Heaps of bodies were loaded onto a truck and taken away.'

I cried out loud. I wailed. My face was in her lap as she sobbed too. I could tell only by the droplets that fell on my neck. We stayed that way. For once I wondered if I should tell her too. I knew she wouldn't be able to withstand so much. Who knows if I will?

1991

'Madam!' it was the postman. He delivered only letters since years now. I had been writing these letters to Bibi in the name of Vir. This time I had arranged for something special. 'Bibi! It's okay. Come out. Look what Vir has sent!' I called to her. 'Don't talk so loudly', Bibi whispered as she came out. 'She won't wake up for a long time now', I said, addressing my one-year-old daughter. Bibi opened the parcel patiently. 'A transistor!' she was surprised. 'You have always been such a spendthrift, Noor.'

I was confused when she said so. What did she mean? Did she know? 'You know?' I asked her. My eyes were hazy with tears.

'Thank you, Noor,' she said, with tears pouring down her flushed cheeks, 'After all, I am a mother!' She hugged me. Songs played in our courtyard which had been for years engulfed in mysterious, maddening silences.

WHEN A BIG TREE FALLS

N.S. MADHAVAN

Translated from the Malayalam by
N.P. ASHLEY

N.S. Madhavan had witnessed the 1984 anti-Sikh massacre first-hand in Delhi. He felt that 'the helpless fear and terror would be more inside closed spaces than on streets.' His story 'When a Big Tree Falls' is a story of the interior. He was aware that the Catholic community in Meerut does have a bishop and many Malayali priests and nuns. However, the incident that formed the kernel of this story occurred in Delhi. On one of the curfew nights, after taking curfew passes, he had to drive a Sikh colleague to the airport, to receive her young nephew flying from the U.S. The boy hid himself behind the pillars, within the customs barrier, refusing to come out. Finally, after hours of waiting, when he appeared, his hair was seen to be freshly shorn off. N.S. Madhavan says that he still remembers the look on his face. Thereafter, this story was born. It first appeared in English in 1984: In Memory and Imagination (*Amaryllis*, 2016).

Whenever I check the registers of the monastery, one thing surprises me. Most deaths here happen during the November-December months. In these cold months, the decrepit hearts of the aged inmates of the monastery perhaps stop functioning in the struggle to give them heat.

In this October, there was only one death—Sister Philomena's. When Sister Philomena wasn't seen during breakfast, I asked, 'What happened to Philomenamma?'

Sister Katrina rolled her wheelchair away from the dining table and sat under the pointed arch of the window. The counting of the rosary beads in the hands of Sister Margarita became faster. Sister Martha drank milk drop by drop, keeping her head down. I didn't need to go and see Sister Philomena in the long hall with beds on both sides. I called up Father Thomas of the bishop's house and asked him to come down immediately.

I clearly remember 1984, October 31. That morning, I went to the Meerut railway station. A nun was arriving from Orissa to become an inmate in the monastery. By the time we reached, the train had already arrived. Seeing me, two people, a young nun and an aged nun with tiny wrinkles spread all over her face, stepped forward.

'Sister, are you a Malayali?' the aged nun asked me almost immediately.

'Yes.'

'Where in Kerala?'

'Varappuzha. Near Ernakulam. Where are you from, Mother?'

'I am from the north. Thiruvambady. My father had migrated from the south of Kerala to the north.'

The young nun was from Orissa. She had to go back the next day itself. Sister Angelica—that was the name of the old nun. The young nun told me that Sister Angelica was diabetic and hence she shouldn't be given anything sweet. 'I was in Orissa throughout my life,' said Sister Angelica. 'Cuttack, Rourkela, Kalahandi and last, Bhubaneswar. I was teaching Mathematics and Science. And finally, I arrive here in Meerut. Doesn't everything end here?' she said on our way to the monastery, turning back at the cemetery dense with crosses.

This monastery for aged nuns was founded by the bishop who passed away last year. Earlier, nuns used to spend their old age in the place they had been working and living. A complaint kept surfacing in the bishop's meetings that they weren't given adequate care.

When I returned from Germany after my higher studies in nursing, the then bishop of Meerut sent for me. 'You are a child of the Church.' The Bishop, who was from Changanassery, knew of my growing up in the orphanage, of God's calling at a young age, and of the church sending me to Germany for higher studies.

'I thought of this monastery keeping you in mind. A haven for our aged nuns who can no longer do God's work. You should run it.'

I didn't sleep through that night. Since childhood, my mediator on such occasions was Gabriel, the angel of angels. I prayed for a long time. At last, I heard the flapping of wings behind me. The messenger of God had come. 'Oh, the one close to God, Jesus built the Holy Church on the rock of Peter. Can the monastery sustain on me, this fragile white pebble?'

'Sister Agatha,' my own mind whispered in the voice of Gabriel. 'This is the Almighty giving you an opportunity to be the salt of the earth.'

Oh salt, that has lost its sourness, I cried with my face pressed on the bed.

From the first group of inmates in the monastery, only Sister Karuna is alive now. Sister Karuna, a native of Spain, used to run a training centre for destitute girls in Bihar. She came to the monastery with a grand piano.

By the time I allotted the bed and arranged other things for Sister Angelica, it was eleven. It was then that Father Thomas called from the bishop's house, 'Did you hear? Apparently, Indira Gandhi has been shot.'

'Oh God!' I was petrified.

'Everybody says she is dead. But the radio is still reporting that she is only injured.'

'Jesus Christ,' Sister Angelica said when she got to know the news. 'She was in Orissa the day we were starting from there.'

While feeding her light-green soup with a spoon, I told Sister Davis. 'Indira Gandhi has been shot.'

The mind of Sister Davis had flown away like a bird a couple of years ago. She said nothing other than opening her mouth for the next sip.

Sister Karuna went and sat near her piano when she heard the news. Its open lid gave her asylum like a tree. She sat flipping through the song books, without playing the piano. At two, Father Thomas called again, 'Radio Australia has announced that Indira

Gandhi is dead. Some newspapers in Delhi have also brought out one-page editions.'

'AIR?'

'They are still saying she is injured.'

'TV?'

'They too.'

When I got out of the phone-room, I saw Sister Katrina reading the prayer book while sitting in the wheelchair. I told her in Malayalam, 'Did you hear? Father Thomas called up and said Indira Gandhi has been shot dead.'

Sister Katrina had almost stopped talking after the death of Philomenamma. They both had come to the monastery from Delhi together. She lifted her face, trying to ask something, but was defeated by the struggle to form words. She pushed the wheelchair into the inner room. I noted in my mind that it was time to oil its wheels.

When I reached the office room, I saw Sister Margarita hovering near the open almirah stealthily.

'Sister,' I said in an admonishing tone. 'What are you doing?'

'Nothing.'

'Lie. Aren't you looking for the medicines so that you can throw them away?'

It was the gardener who found out that Sister Margarita was throwing away the blood pressure tablets she was supposed to have thrice a day. Seeing red and blue tablets trapped in chrysanthemum plants and petals of dahlia flowers, he was amazed. When he picked them up and showed them to me, I immediately understood these were Sister Margarita's tablets. From that day onwards, I made sure that she had her medicines in my presence.

Suddenly, Sister Martha came into the office room. Noting how agile she was, I often wondered whether she reached Meerut a little too early.

'Is the news true?'

'Mmm.'

'How sad! Indira Gandhi had once come to address a meeting in Indore at the ground of the school I used to teach in. She threw the garlands and bouquets she got to the children. She apparently did that all the time. Adivasi boys, on their bare feet, ran around deftly catching them. Indira got excited. She started extracting flowers from bouquets and tossed them. But the smart children didn't allow a single one to fall on the ground.'

At nightfall, the news that Indira Gandhi had been killed came on TV for the first time.

That night very few inmates came to the dining room for dinner. The ninety-six-year-old Sister Mary, who usually had her meals sitting in bed, came leaning on a walking stick to the dining hall, 'I want to sit with everybody else. It has been a long time,' she smiled.

Sister Davis, who had grown senile, sat staring into the TV set without muttering to herself. Sister Katrina rolled her wheelchair away from the TV.

Sister Martha was crying, 'I can't forget the volleyball with the bouquets.'

Nuns lay down to sleep in the red glow of room heaters. I switched off the light in my room on the first floor after saying my prayers. I was shivering under the woollen blanket. This shiver was not due to the November cold; it was my share in the fever that had caught the nation.

After some time I heard somebody knocking on the door. When I opened the door, Sister Sicily who accompanied Sister Angelica was standing outside.

'Sister Agatha,' she said. 'I feel scared.'

I looked into the foggy night behind her. It lay like the sea created at the beginning of the world. It was silent. God had not put a voice in its throat.

'Sister, you can sleep in my room.'

The next morning, Father Thomas phoned from the bishop's house, 'Trouble has started. Sikhs are getting massacred in groups. Lock up the doors properly. The sister from Orissa shouldn't go back now.'

The Gothic doors and windows were all shut. Sister Sicily, Sister Angelica and Sister Katrina sat around a room heater warming their hands. Sister Mary was lying down hugging a hot water bag. All of them were looking at the hospital room off and on, as they could hear Sister Wilfred wheezing. When the sound increased, I got up and went to give her oxygen from the cylinder.

Gunshots sounded outside. When I looked out at the city from my room on the first floor, I could see frozen trees of smoke. By evening, the trees of smoke became a great forest.

The watchman, a Gurkha, sat inside, after having locked up the iron gates. He kept giving news about what was happening outside.

All the shops of the sardars in Clock Tower had been destroyed. The taxis of sardars were being set on fire by the rioters. The dead bodies of sardars could be seen on the way to Sadar Bazaar.

Gunshots could be heard throughout the night. Like sky glow brooding over faraway cities, the red luminescence of fire could be seen on the horizon.

The next day, 2 November, the sound of gunshots only increased. The inmates spent the day in the hall. Even the face of Sister Davis, who had lost her mind, had fear spread all over it.

The next day, we saw the last journey of Indira Gandhi on television. Young Sister Sicily kept describing the scenes to ninety-six-year-old Sister Mary who couldn't see very well.

'The crowd is quite small,' Sister Angelica said. 'People might not have come out fearing attacks. Nehru's funeral procession was something to see. I was in Delhi then.'

Sister Sicily continued her narration based on the TV visuals. Other than Sister Mary, Sister Martha and Sister Margarita sat around her to hear the commentary.

Now, through Delhi's Vijay Chowk, Indira Gandhi's funeral procession was moving. The visual was the same in two dimensions on the TV. Sister Sicily translated the TV images into words. I couldn't take the same tragedy enacted in three platforms. My entrails started stretching heavily. I bent over the washbasin and vomited. Thus, for the first time in life, history touched me physically.

On 4 November, curfew was declared. The inmates stayed in their beds the whole day. Sister Sicily and I took food to their beds.

At night, Sister Katrina pushed her wheelchair up to me and said, 'I want to go out to the verandah.'

'No sister, you shouldn't.'

'Aren't the lights off? I want to go out. I am feeling suffocated.'

'Okay, I will also come with you then.'

Even as they heard the hinges of doors squeaking, the inmates didn't raise their heads to look. The wind through the open doors pierced cold holes in the room's brooding heat.

'Let me walk around a bit,' Sister Katrina said. She moved the wheelchair to the other side of the verandah and back. I stood pressing my face into the darkness.

I got a shock when I heard Sister Katrina's sudden cry from the other side of the verandah. 'Oh Lord, murderers!' The wheelchair came rushing at me sounding like the wheels of a train.

Sister Katrina was gasping, 'Murderers in the darkness...'

I ran to the kitchen. Sister Karuna swiftly came out and locked the door after pushing Sister Katrina's wheelchair inside.

I selected the sharpest of the knives and hid it under my clothes.

The sisters were silent. Inside the hospital room, Sister Wilfred was struggling to reduce the sound of wheezing by pulling back her muscles. Then we heard somebody banging on the door. Sister Karuna and Sister Martha stood touching me. The banging got louder.

'Open, please open,' a woman was heard saying in Hindi. A child's cry followed.

We could hear motorcycles roaring up and halting outside the monastery. Their headlights ran around the walls like the searchlights of a circus.

'Open, they have come to get me,' the woman was wailing. When I opened the door, we could see a woman clad in a salwar-kameez with her head covered by a shawl and a Sikh boy who had his hair tied up with a white handkerchief.

'They killed my husband. They killed my elder son Bablu. They are saying they will kill me. And this boy too,' she said, teetering on the ridges of madness.

When those motorcycle riders started pounding on the gate of the monastery, Sister Karuna ushered the woman and the child inside and locked the door. Until the gang of motorcycle riders left the place, saying something to the Gurkha, nobody spoke a word.

'Who are you?' Sister Martha broke the silence in Hindi. 'My name is Amarjeet. They killed many people in our colony. As a protest against the army's entry into the Harmandir Sahib, the Sikhs of our colony didn't celebrate Diwali this year. That was why they were so terribly angry with us.'

'Didn't the policemen come for your help?'

'The police station is right in front of our colony. The people in the colony had gone to meet the station in-charge. He said he couldn't do anything as there weren't enough police personnel. He also hated us.'

'Then?' Sister Martha continued.

'We left our homes and moved to the gurdwaras.'

Nihang Sikhs who wore blue clothes and blue turbans with quoits of steel kept vigil outside gurdwaras. The singers sang the praises of the Guru, accompanied by harmoniums hung from their shoulders. Kirpans, the daggers worn by the Sikhs, were hanging from everybody's waist. Some had guns too.

Adi Granth, the Sikh holy book, sat on a stool covered with a red silk cloth. The Granthis respectfully waved the yak-hair fans over it. Devotees dropped coins in front of it. At a corner of the gurdwara, the devotees were heaping up wheat flour for the langar, the common kitchen.

Only one Akali from Gurdaspur gave a speech: Khalsa Panth, the community of initiated Sikhs, needs blood today. The blood of the Gurus' own Sikhs. Oh Sikhs, oh, you who had been baptized by the Amrit, to be immortal even while dying for the Guru, what the Guru needs is sacrifice, sacrifice. In the blood of the listeners, the genes that carried the clan's memories swam around. All of them called out loud: Sat Sri Akal!

'When policemen started their rounds, some of us returned home. Others stayed back in the camp of the gurdwara.'

The attack took place at night. They picked up Amarjeet's husband and killed him. Then the elder son. A man clutched on to Amarjeet's hand. When she savaged his flesh with her teeth, he had to let her go.

'I ran dragging my boy,' she said. 'I remember the face of the man who grasped my hand. Ramji. My husband has an iron store at the junction. Ramji has been trying to snatch it somehow for a while now. If both of us are finished off, he can have the shop.' They spent an entire day in the gurdwara. But Ramji and his friends were circling around the gurdwara on bikes and jeeps. Policemen must have been bought off by them. Once it got dark, Amarjeet and her son ran out stealthily from the gurdwara. At night, stepping through the gaps in the wall of the monastery, they entered the compound.

Sister Sicily brought a cup full of milk and gave it to the boy. He drank it in one go.

'What is his name?' Sister Angelica asked.

'Joginder Singh. We call him Juggy at home.'

'Do you want more milk?' Sister Katrina asked him.

Juggy nodded yes, unabashedly. Sister Martha got a glassful of milk, bread and a couple of boiled eggs from the kitchen.

'We have no hope here. We have to leave this place,' Amarjeet said. 'We have to go to Delhi. I have relatives in the camp in Fatehpur gurdwara. Can we stay here till we manage to escape to Delhi?'

Oh Jesus, you give us opportunities to be compassionate. I took Amarjeet's hand and led her to the now-vacant bed of Sister Philomena, who died in October.

'You can sleep here,' I said. Then I prepared a bed on the floor for Juggy. After eating a long loaf of bread alone, he slipped into a sleep in which he was unlikely to see any dream. The sisters also went to bed after saying their prayers.

Next morning, 5 November, the sisters got up earlier than usual. I thought they were waiting for Juggy to wake up.

Juggy's attention first went to Sister Karuna who looked different from the other nuns. Her light blue eyes amazed him. Sister Karuna walked to the piano holding his hands. He stood looking at the black and white keys. Sister Karuna pressed on one key. 'Do,' she said.

Hesitantly, Juggy also pressed the same key, 'Do.' The inmates of the monastery heard the voice of Juggy for the first time.

'Re, Mi, Fa,' Sister Karuna said rhythmically pressing the keys.

Sister Angelica went to Juggy smiling. She pressed on the hair tied with a white handkerchief. Then she looked at me and said, 'Doesn't this look like a spider's egg?'

Juggy's face went red. He forcibly removed Sister Angelica's hand. He was so agitated that he even pushed her away from him. From that moment, Juggy's hair became off-limits for us. We understood that the historical sense of a clan lay braided in that.

Sister Margarita asked for her medicines that day. Sister Katrina hovered around Amarjeet and Juggy in her wheelchair. Sister Karuna got busy baking a cake for Juggy.

I contacted the bishop's house to take permission for allowing Amarjeet and Juggy to stay at the monastery. Father Thomas said he would consult the bishop and call me back. Even before I started thinking whether the bishop would agree or not, the phone started ringing.

'The bishops order is to go ahead on the path shown by God,' Father Thomas said.

As it was curfew time, the doors and windows of the monastery were kept open without fear. After years, the ninety-six-year-old Sister Mary got out into the garden. One end of her walking stick was held by Juggy. Through Sister Mary's cataract, sunlight lay bleary like the Milky Way.

'What is the name of this flower?' Juggy asked.

'What does it look like?'

'Like the moon. Round and big.'

'Colour?'

'Yellow.'

'Does it have many petals?' Sister Mary asked.

'Petals? Yes, much more than lotuses have. Small, not-so-broad petals.'

'Then the name of this flower is dahlia.'

Sister Mary and Juggy moved to the next flower. Sisters looked at them curiously from the verandahs. While they were climbing back into the monastery, Sister Mary said, looking at everybody, gasping and with a smile, 'Juggy has become Adam, by christening all objects, moving and unmoving today.'

The next day there was a relaxation in the curfew. Trains started running. We sent Sister Sicily, who had to go back to Orissa, Amarjeet and Juggy to the railway station with the Gurkha. When they were at the steps, Sister Wilfred came out of the hospital room. 'Juggy, Juggy,' she called out loud, and placed an engraved locket of the Virgin Mary in Juggy's hand. He took it, waved at everyone one last time and ran to join his mother.

Just as life was getting back to normal in the monastery, a military vehicle came and stopped outside the compound. From it, the Gurkha, Amarjeet, Sister Sicily and Juggy climbed out. Juggy stood motionless with his eyes closed. Sister Sicily made him walk holding his hands. As soon as they entered the monastery, he disappeared somewhere.

'What happened?' I asked. The Gurkha narrated the story.

'We had walked only some distance. A jeep came and stopped near us. A person jumped out of the jeep to grab Memsahib. By then Juggy had started crying "Ma, Ma, those people, those people." The mother and son started to run.'

'They had been lying in wait for us for hours,' Amarjeet said sobbing.

'They sped up the jeep to chase them and run them over.' Though the Gurkha was shivering with fear, the ability of his contracted eyes, joined eyebrows and sharp jaws to express emotion was limited.

'Luckily they were saved because an army vehicle arrived right then,' said the Gurkha.

'Don't worry,' Sister Karuna said. Sister Martha found Juggy sitting quietly under the stairs in the darkness.

'You can live here for as many days as you want. Nothing will happen to you,' I said.

The words of this sinner, uttered without the consent of the Almighty, had already gone astray. I got a call: 'CIA agents, if you don't leave the sardarni and child for us, we will bomb your monastery out of existence.' Before I could say 'hello, hello?' with my parched throat, he had hung up.

Though the police force was deployed to give protection, stones were pelted at the rear of the monastery. One of the stones hit the stained glass painting of Jesus with a sheep. It broke the heart of the shepherd.

The next day, on 7 November, Father Thomas called early in the morning from the bishop's house. 'They have demolished the statue of Our Lady of the Lourdes outside St. Mary's School. They are calling up frequently asking for custody of the sardarni and the child.'

'Will the unrest turn against *us*?' I asked.

Father Thomas didn't say anything.

'What should I do?'

'Bishop said God will continue to show you the way ahead.'

I went and knelt down in the prayer room. *Angel Gabriel, give me a message. Don't you have any message for me from God?* Other than shadows moving ahead through the frontiers of the mind like a train of refugees, nothing else came to mind.

My mind was empty. I started weeping. After some time, I felt an ethereal peace. By then, Amarjeet and the other inmates reached the prayer room.

I asked the driver of the ambulance, George, to bring a coffin.

The road that God showed to this sinner was this. I said looking at the inmates: 'Amarjeet will wear the habit of a nun. Juggy will lie in the coffin inside the ambulance. Some of us will stand around praying. We will get into the eastern gate of the cemetery in a way people can see and drive out of the western gate. Then we will reach the church near the railway station. It won't be difficult to get to the railway station from there.'

Sister Sicily went out of the room and brought Juggy there. Sister Angelica held his hands tightly. Sister Martha sat down on the floor and pressed down his legs. Even then Juggy was trying to free himself ferociously like an animal. Sister Mary created a trap for his knee with the crooked side of the walking stick. Sister Margarita closed his eyes with her hand. When he started crying out loud, Sister Karuna covered his mouth with her hand.

Amarjeet removed the white handkerchief from Juggy's hair. I untied his hair that was tied to the crown of his head. It stretched down to his shoulders. I sprinkled water to make it damp and then with a big pair of scissors, started cutting his hair. As strands of hair fell on to the floor of the monastery, he became more and more naked.

'Waheguru wahe,' Amarjeet whimpered.

Juggy's helplessness grew. He stopped crying. Sister Karuna withdrew her hand from his mouth.

'Jo bole so nihaal,' Amarjeet said to lead Juggy.

'Sat Sri Akal,' Juggy said mechanically. By that time his hair had become very short.

I noticed the skin-colour change on his face only after the haircut. The part that came under the head cover, as it hadn't seen sunlight for years, had a different colour and shape. That would definitely give him away. Mixing charcoal in mustard oil, I made a paste and smeared it on his face to make the colour look identical across his face.

The ambulance had reached by then. In the coffin inside the ambulance, Juggy lay down. The coffin was closed in such a way that air could get in. Amarjeet, in the garb of a nun, Sister Sicily who was going back to Orissa, Sister Angelica, Sister Karuna, Sister Martha and I sat around the coffin to cover it and started saying our prayers.

Initially the journey was calm. After some time, motorcycles came racing towards us. They rode the bikes parallel to George and asked him to stop. George started driving faster. We had the motorcycles roaring behind us, changing gears quickly. Sister Karuna placed her long hand on George's shoulder and asked him to stop.

She opened the back door of the ambulance and stood at the step. Her veil, caught in the wind, flew like hair left open. Her blue irises, with dark pupils contracted to pinpoints, confused the motorcyclists. Holding up the hand with the thurible, Sister Karuna asked in Hindi, 'Satans, won't you spare even the dead?'

Sister Angelica and I increased the speed of the Malayalam prayer song we were singing. After hesitating for a minute, the motorcyclists went away. We went through the cemetery and got out of the other gate. The journey up to the church near the railway station was event-free. When the ambulance stopped, Amarjeet and I opened the lid of the coffin.

'Get up, Juggy,' Amarjeet said. Just like a butterfly coming out of its pupa, he got up. He ran his hands through his hair with the sorrow of broken clan continuity. The knowledge that the hair I cut off had sprouted in his mother's womb started suffocating me.

Amarjeet, Sister Sicily and Juggy got into the women's compartment of the train. He stood pressing against the window panes of the train. Without him realizing it, his hands went to his head.

The next day the riots practically ended. There was no curfew during the day. Sister Mary didn't get up from her bed. Sister Katrina moved her wheelchair as far as possible from everybody else. Sister Margarita refused to take her medicines. Sister Angelica tried talking of old matters. Sister Davis lay murmuring. Sister Karuna sat in front of the piano doing nothing. Sister Martha prayed throughout the day. Sister Wilfred returned to the hospital room.

As for me, I went to the prayer room and locked myself in, with the experience of the deaths foretold in November hanging heavily in the air like static electricity.

Dear Friend! The World is an Enemy

Satya Vyas

Translated from the Hindi by
ISHMEET KAUR CHAUDHRY

This excerpt from Satya Vyas' novel, Chaurasi *(Hind Yugm, 2018) is perhaps the first fictional account set in Bokaro, Bihar, during the anti-Sikh violence. Many people are not aware that the violence had spread outside Delhi and across India. Bokaro and Kanpur were particularly badly hit. This important novel highlights the composite culture of Bokaro before the riots, followed by the actual violence against Sikhs. In this excerpt, Rishi is in love with Manoo, the daughter of his Sikh landlord, and to save her and her family, he finds himself participating in mob violence against other Sikhs.*

There is a haunting silence of its own kind during the night of a riot. Different from all other silences. Totally different. It doesn't scare you off, just makes you listen to the silence before death. How abnormal amongst everything normal! I wonder why the crickets are the first to listen to this silence. This silence breaks when the rebels shout and the crickets are silenced. When such a noise was heard from the crossroads, Rishi had just reached there. He saw that a group of about ten people were burning a jeep. The First man recognized him.

'Why party! Are you in a great hurry? Are you interested in the woman or in their belongings?* Arre…! We all were just coming

---

* The author puns on the word 'cheez', literally meaning 'thing'; in its singular form it refers to the girl in the house, while 'things' in plural refer to the belongings. Violence involved simultaneously killing, looting and assaulting women.

to start the ceremony.' The First laughed shamelessly and spoke in a vulgar way while placing his hand on Rishi's shoulder; Rishi was helpless and pretended to be ignorant despite the fact that he understood what First was implying.

'I have come to inform you about that only, brother. I feel that they are suspicious and are leaving. The house-owner has asked me to call for a taxi. I have come running for that,' said Rishi breathlessly.

'Haven't they already left! They will not leave till you return with a taxi…and all the better if they have left; we will comfortably rob their entire house,' the Second man interfered in their conversation. Rishi was horrified at hearing them speak like this; but he also relaxed at the same time as he realized that the first aim of this group was looting and robbery.

'But the police?' Rishi expressed his fear.

'Police! See there in the khaki pants. Everyone is pouring water on the jeep. You don't worry about the system. Tell me would you like to take the rod or rampuri?' The First asked while showing him a small knife.

Rishi had been quite involved in fights, brawls and disruptions, but he had done them all boldly, relying on his own strength. He had never felt a need for weapons, nor had he ever thought about them. He had always understood the difference between beating and killing. But right now, he was concerned for Manoo, and he couldn't risk the danger of being suspected. So, he said, checking himself, 'Whatever I can get.'

'Okay, do one thing, you keep this rod. As it is, the ammunition is less,' the First said, while handing over a rod to Rishi. They had not yet finished talking when a mob shouting, 'Kill him, kill him! Catch him, catch him!' joined this group. Everyone headed together for the main lane. The crazy mob had just reached Chhabra Sahib's house, while yelling slogans like 'Blood in revenge for blood and Four will die for one; one by one, the Sardars will die', when they saw Mad Gurnam in the light of the lamp-post.

Mad Gurnam did not belong to this lane. Wandering, he had reached here by mistake. He was not even a sardar. Seeing his unkempt long hair, someone had made a bun on his head. Mad

Gurnam had liked the bun and the lane so much, that he never left it after that. By being teased, and teasing the children here, this gumnam (anonymous, 'lost name') had become Gurnam.

Most of the people in the mob ran towards Mad Gurnam. 'He is the one, he is the one, he was eating sweets in the morning.' Shouting, the crazy people surrounded him. Mad Gurnam could not understand that though he was insane, why were the others behaving insanely! And what could this insane man have understood about why other insane men had surrounded him? In any case, the mob did not spend much time on him. With one stroke of the iron rod, Gurnam shivered and fell down. The same rod was inserted in his chest and turned around. When the rod got stuck between his ribs and bones, it was driven in like a screw. Gurnam did shout in pain, but his shrieks were suppressed under the noise of the wild crowd. When the hot blood splashed on the road, Gurnam fell cold. The mobsters had had their revenge: 'Blood for Blood'.

When the rest of the mob ran towards Chhabra Sahib's house, Rishi also followed them. One could enter the house only after opening the iron outer gate, which was locked. The crazy mob was too impatient to have inquired about the keys from Rishi himself. The First shouted, reaching the gate, 'Break it! Break it! Saala, they have locked it! They have locked it from inside! They are still upstairs, saale!' The mob was getting excited. 'Move away bhencho! Insert the rod. Like this, yes, turn it, turn it! Good job!'

The lock at the outer gate had been broken.

'Bring them down from upstairs! Bring the saale down! Kill these sardars! The nation-betrayers!'

'No, no! Let us kill them upstairs itself! We'll kill four-for-one today!' Shouting, when the mob surged forward, Rishi was the first one to enter. He carefully stood protectively in front of his door while making way for the others to move upstairs. When about ten or more people had gone upstairs, he, too, followed them and started pushing at the door with others.

'Break the door! Break it! Break it! Break the door!' The noise got louder. 'Move away bhencho! It will not open by pushing. Insert the rod in the centre and move it diagonally. Yes, just like that! They are inside! They are inside! They have kept something against the door from inside. Mader—!' said the Second, pushing at the the door.

'Hit him hard with the rod! He tries to be a leader!' The Third was heard saying.

'Break it! Break it! It is broken! It is broken!' The door, which had resisted for some time due to the sofa supporting it from the inside, finally broke open. The mob rushed inside.

'Where are they? Where are they?'

'Arre, arre look for them in the bathroom!'

'In that room! In that room.'

That room! That room was not an empty room. Guru Granth Sahib had been installed in that room. A room with an eternal peace-giving ambience, even in this situation of the angry mob. The mob saw the room but couldn't dare to enter inside. They turned aside and got busy robbing the house.

'They were cooking, saale!'

'What is it? Just see!'

'Potatoes!'

'Arrre, re, re! This door in the back is open. They have run away, seems they ran away from here. Yes, must have run just now. The cupboard is open.'

'The girl is also with them. Mustn't have been able to run far off yet,' Rishi said this intentionally; but no sooner did he say that than the mobsters divided themselves into two groups. Those who were in a hurry to steal things and run away began running with whatever little they had found. The remaining were thirsty for blood. Taking them along, Rishi ran out with them.

With the rod in his hand, Rishi was the first one to go out, so that he could show his eagerness to find them. Taking everyone along, he moved away from the street, shouting the slogans.

~

When Rishi left, he knew that he had to drive these people away from his street. So far that they may not be able to return before morning.

But he had forgotten that this night was not an ordinary night. It was catastrophic in nature. The route he had taken was not an ordinary route. It was a mirage, and he could never have guessed where it would finally take him. He was not even aware that now he was a mere pawn. The control of the night was in the hands of those who were with him and what it was that they controlled: some houses that had been marked; chaos; the thirst for blood; rumours, such rumours that may excite people to the core of their nerves:

- 'Sweets were distributed after the assassination of Indira Gandhi.'
- 'They said, "Take some sweets, Nani has died."'
- 'The gurdwaras were decorated with lights that night.'
- 'Yesterday, all Sardars wore saffron turbans in celebration.'
- 'The Prime Minister's assassin said that only he is Khalis, pure.'
- 'In their Khalistan, everyone else but the Sikhs will be marked and killed.'
- 'Trained by Pakistan, truckloads of terrorists have entered every district of the country. These people are supporting them.'
- 'Just see their boldness! If the leader of the country is not secure, we will have to protect ourselves. It is Indiraji today; tomorrow our mothers will be picked off. Day after, our sisters.'
- 'Fourteen girls were found in the Dashmesh truck owned by a sardar in Dhanbad.'
- 'Moreover, things might change altogether, upside-down!'
- 'Their weapons are about to reach, the train has already started from Punjab. They are being assisted by Pakistan.'

It did not take long for the mob searching for Chhabra Sahib and his family to find another job. Rishi and his companions listened carefully to the noise coming from a distance. The sudden noise attracted Rishi and his friends' attention. Five to seven boys were chasing a thin boy into Sector Two. The boy, who was running, did not appear to be a sardar. He was running fast, so fast that the boys chasing him could not maintain the pace and had stopped, exhausted.

On seeing that the chasing mob had halted, not only did the boy slow down, but he also fell, coughing. In his bad luck, Rishi's team was standing there. No sooner did the Second lift him, holding his collar, than Rishi was stunned seeing something. There was some hair stuck with sweat on the neck of the boy. The boy was a Sikh and it seemed that he had got his hair cut, just a few hours back to remain safe. Some of the cut hair remained stuck on his neck with the sweat.

'He is running having stolen things. He is not a Sikh,' Rishi said, putting his hand in the boy's pocket, before the Second man could begin his inquiry.

'Then let him go. Take the money and hurry. It is about to be eleven and we have not spotted even one person,' said the First. Rishi turned the boy's pockets out and took all the money and pushed him towards the other side. The boy was saved again, a second time. He was convinced that now his life would be saved. But that was his mistake. The direction in which Rishi had pushed him, there was a deadening silence in that street. Rishi wanted the boy to run away, moving through that haunted street; but perhaps the boy's house was towards the other side, or perhaps, death was awaiting him towards the other side. He got up and, dusting himself, started moving towards the other side. As soon as he reached the lamp-post, the turban's marks on his forehead became visible to the First. He shouted: 'Aye, hold him! Hold him! Squeeze him! Squeeze! This saala! From his neck! Yes! This way! Just see! Saallaa…is a sardar!' Hearing this, the boy tried running again, but he had already exhausted all his strength. The Second caught him right in the middle of the road. Another group of mobsters approached from the front on their cycles and proceeded ahead, making a loud noise, 'See, the mark of the turban, see.' The First caught the boy by his hair and pressed his nose. The boy thrashed, and in this attempt, he was released from the clutches of the Second.

He ran again. But this time, he was stoned from behind; a stone hit him in the centre of his head and disturbed his balance. He fell on the road again. The First lifted him again, holding him by his hair.

'Please let me go. What have I done?' The boy could just speak this with his dry throat.

'You didn't do it, did your community do it, maderchod? And if you get a chance, you will also do it. Aye boy! Bring a rope fast,' First told Rishi.

Rishi thought that they would tie him, beat him and leave him. With this misconception, he began searching for a rope around him. He felt that the sooner he would be able to find the rope, the better it would be. He remembered that in the last street a banner advertising 'Saree Kendra' was loosely hanging. He began running in that direction. But in his haste, he forgot to see that the Second was also looking for something across the road.

'You people have become so arrogant? Yah. Betrayers! Saalon! You people will enter our houses tomorrow?' said the First, clutching the boy's face.

He was still expressing his hatred while the Second brought the tyre of a motorcycle kept outside a garage in the corner. Even before the First could understand, the Second twisted the arm of the boy to his back, such that the boy's mouth opened in pain. This was what the Second wanted. He clogged the boy's mouth with a piece of cloth and closed his mouth. Before the boy could settle, the Second asked the First, 'Do you want to watch bhangra?'

Since the First could not understand the question, he didn't reply.

Without waiting for the First's reply, the Second put the tyre on the boy's chest in such a way that it tied both his hands. Then, the Second quickly took out a bottle hidden in his waist and bathed the tyre with it. That was kerosene oil. Seeing this, the heart of the First also filled with pity. Before he could say anything, the Second had already lit the oil-smeared tyre with a matchstick. The boy, surrounded by the flames, fell to the ground. He tried rolling to put out the fire but none of his efforts could bear fruit.

Rishi was late in reaching there. Seeing the boy from a distance, he ran towards him. But before he reached him, the boy had already lost his life. The fire had turned the boy's body into coal. Now there was no meaning in standing there.

As the mob proceeded, the First asked the Second, 'Do you have liquor? Doing all this is not possible without liquor.'

'I have it, sure,' said the Second, taking out another bottle from his waist.

'Saale, hope this is not kerosene?' asked First, laughing, and took the bottle.

'No,' the Second gave a one-word reply.

'Achha, tell me one thing, where did you get the oil from, particularly at this hour?' asked the First, and drank from the bottle.

'Everyone stands by you in trouble.' This was the Second's answer. Rishi had only questions.

SECTION III
PLAYS

THE OLD MAN SPEAKS

GURSHARAN SINGH

Translated from the Punjabi by
TEJINDER KAUR

This play was written in 1984, the year when Punjab crisis was at its peak. It is significant as it is one of the few voices that emerged, not after, but very much during the crisis. Gursharan Singh was very popular amongst rural people in Punjab as he performed street plays in villages; truckloads of people came to see him perform. 'The Old Man Speaks' was a revolutionary street play, which critiqued the situation in Punjab. Its audience could immediately relate to its experiences. A Hindi translation of the play is also available on the Gursharan Singh Trust's website.

The play is dedicated to those who consider it their duty to continue to fight against political corruption on the one side and religious fanaticism on the other.

Characters:

Baba (an old man)
Congress Member
Jathedar (Sikh leader)
Newspaper Seller (a young boy)
Other folks

The play is set in India immediately following the assassination of Prime Minister Indira Gandhi.

The Newspaper Seller enters the stage.

NEWSPAPER SELLER: Today's breaking news…which will not be making headlines tomorrow; will turn stale day after and will be forgotten on the fourth day…has been assassinated/killed.

(Three to four people buy the newspaper. Baba enters. He is holding some things in his hand and a bag is hanging from his shoulder. He seems to have come from a long journey. His shoes are laden with dust.)

BABA: Has been assassinated?

OTHERS: Yes, has been assassinated.

NEWSPAPER SELLER: Spend some money, buy a newspaper. A very big/well-known personality has been assassinated.

BABA: A very well-known personality?

NEWSPAPER SELLER: Yes, spend some money, buy a newspaper. A very well-known personality has been killed. The country was known by its name.

BABA: The country was known by its name.

NEWSPAPER SELLER: (*Aside*) Baba is very cheap. He doesn't want to spend any money but likes to know all the news. (*To Baba*) Baba, a renowned personality has been killed, the country was known by its name, was killed in its own house.

BABA: Was killed in its own house, that is very bad.

NEWSPAPER SELLER: What is bad about it?

BABA: Was killed in its own house.

NEWSPAPER SELLER: Who was killed?

BABA: Whose name was known in the country.

NEWSPAPER SELLER: Whose name was known in the country?

BABA: The one who was a well-known personality.

NEWSPAPER SELLER: Who was a well-known personality?

BABA: The one who was killed.

NEWSPAPER SELLER: Who was killed?

BABA: This is what I am asking, who has been killed?

(Others laugh)

NEWSPAPER SELLER: (*Aside*) Baba is a real rascal. He wants to know the news for free, but he is not getting anything from me. (*To Baba*) Baba, government flags have been lowered.

BABA: Let them do whatever they want, how does it matter to us?

NEWSPAPER SELLER: Mournful music is playing on the radio.

BABA: Has some big man from the radio gone to heaven?

NEWSPAPER SELLER: It is not a he, but a she that has gone to heaven. Television cameras are focused on her dead body.

BABA: As if television cameras ever focus on living people.

NEWSPAPER SELLER: The workers are on strike in the market.

BABA: I don't need to buy anything in a hurry.

NEWSPAPER SELLER: Distinguished dignitaries are coming from all over the world.

BABA: Why, is it their mother that has gone to heaven?

NEWSPAPER SELLER: No, not their mother, the country has lost its mother.

BABA: What happens when a mother dies?

NEWSPAPER SELLER: The country becomes an orphan.

BABA: The country is already an orphan.

NEWSPAPER SELLER: What do you mean?

BABA: This country has been an orphan for centuries. Is there anyone to take care of her? That is why the hungry and homeless die in hundreds of thousands. Those who are not hungry just read the newspapers and fight among themselves (*Newspaper readers frown at Baba and leave the stage*). There is only one news here. It was the same news yesterday, the same news today and it will be the same news tomorrow. Now don't say, Baba is a miser, that he does not spend money. Here take the money and put the newspaper in this bag.

NEWSPAPER SELLER: (*While putting the newspaper in the bag*) Baba, there are many newspapers in this bag already.

BABA: Not just newspapers, these are the essences of life, my boy. Now tell me what is your news? They say a murder has taken place. Murder of a well-known person. A person by whose name the country was known. She was killed in her own home. The flags have been lowered. The radio is playing continuous mournful music. Television cameras are focused on her dead body. The workers are on strike in the market. Distinguished dignitaries are arriving from around the globe.

NEWSPAPER SELLER: (*Loudly*) Baba, the Prime Minister has been killed.

BABA: (*Without showing any surprise*) So then. Now her son has become the Prime Minister.

NEWSPAPER SELLER: He has asked the people to remain calm.

BABA: And the people are setting fires.

NEWSPAPER SELLER: Baba you know all the news already…

BABA: Because I know how to read between the lines.

NEWSPAPER SELLER: How?

BABA: Okay, you read your news and I will tell you mine.

NEWSPAPER SELLER: (*Reading the newspaper*) The Prime Minister has asked the people to remain peaceful in the country.

BABA: It means that riots are taking place on a large scale in the country.

NEWSPAPER SELLER: The government intends to start a campaign against poverty.

BABA: It means that millions of people are dying due to poverty. (*With emphasis*) Listen to me, if the Prime Minister says that unemployment will be eradicated, then it means that the number of unemployed on the streets has increased. If the Prime Minister says that corruption will not be tolerated in the government, then understand that corruption has peaked. If the Prime Minister says that the country's unity will be protected, then the country is ready to split into pieces. (*Walking away*) Now that is enough for today.

NEWSPAPER SELLER: No, Baba. You have to tell me, what is there in this bag?

BABA: Your mother's head. (*Changes his tone*) There is the history of 1947, 1964 and of 1984.

NEWSPAPER SELLER: Forty-seven, sixty-four, eighty-four? Tell me what is their relationship?

BABA: There were riots in 1947. Houses were burned, innocents were killed, and children were orphaned, married women were widowed. There were riots in 1984. Houses were burned, innocents were killed, and children were orphaned. Married women were widowed. Those who ruled in 1947 were white skinned. Those who are ruling in 1984 wear the home-spun white cloth. The wheel of time has come full circle. People are crushed, the rulers keep ruling.

NEWSPAPER SELLER: Baba, what is the relationship between 1964 and 1984?

BABA: In 1964, the father died and the daughter was enthroned. In 1984, the mother has died; the son is enthroned. A billion people ruled by one clan. All others are useless.

NEWSPAPER SELLER: Baba is very clever. He says one thing but means something else.

BABA: Son! I have suffered over and over again. In 1947, I lost my father. In 1984, I lost my son-in-law. My mother became a widow in 1947 and my daughter became a widow in 1984. In 1947 a son was orphaned, today a grandson has been orphaned. What a coincidence—then, a grandfather was ruling, today a grandson is ruling. Now don't say Baba makes up stories. Baba only narrates what he suffered.

(CHOOK, CHOOK. *The sound of a train is heard. All characters line up as a train.* CHOOK, CHOOK. *Suddenly the train stops.*

Three passengers are pulled out and doused with petrol. Baba wants to extinguish the fire but he is pulled and thrown away. When all this is being enacted the news keeps pouring in from behind.)

1st News: Today's breaking news. Three passengers belonging to a particular religion, travelling by Rajdhani Express, were dragged out, sprayed with petrol and burnt at Tughlaqabad station, outside Delhi.

2nd News: The railway minister claimed that there was no problem in railway operations. Everything was functioning normally as it should.

3rd News: The railway minister has assured that all rail passengers will be given full protection by the police and the army.

BABA: (*Picking up ashes from the burnt corpses*) Will be protected or turned to ash. (*A satirical laugh*) It will be turned to ash. No, already turned to ash. Yes, the law of the land, the conscience of the country and the constitution of the country, everything turned to ash. In this country, everyone has the right to live honourably. All turned to ash. (*Changes his tone*) Sprinkle this ash over the Himalayas and immerse it in the Ganga. Take this ash to the deep sea of Kanyakumari. (*Changes his tone again*) From Kashmir to Kanyakumari, we all belong to one country. (*Rubbing it*) But we have become foreigners in our own country.

(While Baba is speaking, the dead characters go off the stage walking like zombies. They repeat, we have become foreigners in our own country.)

(A Congressman enters the stage from the other end, followed by a lumpen bully who is copying his gestures.)

CONGRESS MEMBER: So Harichand, what is the progress?

HARICHAND: The progress is remarkable, sir. Dragged three turbaned Sikhs off the train and sent them to hell. Burnt four taxis and turned them to ashes. Torched eight houses and taught the Sikhs an unforgettable lesson.

CONGRESS MEMBER: Well done. Now I can tell the Prime Minister that when a tree falls tremors are felt all around. Now, what should we give you as a reward.

HARICHAND: Sir, there is no need for any reward today. I have done well already. A lot of looted stuff has come my way.

CONGRESS MEMBER: What did you get? I would like to know that.

HARICHAND: Silk saris, transistors, VCRs, steel utensils, gold ornaments and ten thousand rupees in cash.

CONGRESS MEMBER: The policemen didn't stop you, did they?

HARICHAND: Not really. Superficially, they told us to go away. But softly they told us to burn them all. We provided the fuel and they lit it up. Even though the army was all around, still we had great fun.

CONGRESS MEMBER: In other words, the army and police have done their duty as they were supposed to.

HARICHAND: Yes sir, done their duty and also lent a helping hand in looting.

CONGRESS MEMBER: That was the expectation from them.

HARICHAND: Sir. What are the orders now?

CONGRESS MEMBER: Wait for the signal. The next programme will probably be to hold a peace march.

HARICHAND: Peace march?

CONGRESS MEMBER: Yes, a peace procession.

HARICHAND: How many people will be needed?

CONGRESS MEMBER: You are responsible for getting around one hundred. But they should all be innocent-looking.

HARICHAND: Sir, we are always waiting for a signal from you. It will be the same people. Yesterday they took part in looting. Next, they will participate in a peace march. Yesterday they were gangsters; today they will be gentlemen.

CONGRESS MEMBER: How is that?

HARICHAND: Like this! (*He takes off the scarf from his neck, buttons up his shirt up to the neck, combs his hair. Takes out a cap from his pocket and wears it. Shouts the slogan)* 'Whoever incites a fight between Hindus and Sikhs will be called an enemy of the country. Hindu and Sikh are brethren.' Sir, you will lead the march and we will follow you.

CONGRESS MEMBER: Very good. Okay now you leave.

(Harichand prepares to leave but comes back.)

HARICHAND: Sir?

CONGRESS MEMBER: What now?

HARICHAND: Sir, people of our constituency have come.

CONGRESS MEMBER: What people?

HARICHAND: Those whose homes were looted yesterday.

CONGRESS MEMBER: Okay you leave from this side. Our next programme begins.

HARICHAND: Yes, sir. *(He leaves)*

(The Congressman acts as if making a phone call. Baba and two men stand in the door.)

CONGRESS MEMBER: *(On the telephone)* What are you saying? The mob has torched the shops of the Sikhs? Where was the police? Inform the SSP to send more forces. Suspend the SHO. Sikhs are the pride of India. They have contributed immensely towards the Independence struggle. What did you say, the mob is enraged that two Sikhs have assassinated our mother, Indira Gandhi? But they were only two, the entire community can't be blamed for this? Yes, yes, take full action. Peace should prevail at any cost. Depute the forces. Enough is enough. Yes. Yes…enough is enough. What happened so far is enough. Nothing more should take place. A few hooligans tarnish the image of India and we just sit and watch and do nothing. It is impossible. We will protect the people of our constituency at any cost. Even if we have to sacrifice our lives.

(He puts the telephone down and addresses the people who have been waiting while he was talking on the phone. He speaks in a clever way to outsmart everything they say.)

CONGRESS MEMBER: Come in. I am extremely sorry that some social misfits have caused immense harm to people of your religion. Such wicked elements take advantage of every opportunity.

FIRST MAN: But the police…

CONGRESS MEMBER: I know that the police did not do anything. These people do not recognize their duty. They only know to live by cheating and deceiving. 'You bastards, homes of innocent people are being burnt in front of you. And you are just watching the fun.' There has to be a limit to this wickedness.

SECOND MAN: But even the people at the police station…

CONGRESS MEMBER: Even the people at the police station did not do anything. Yes, I have come to know that they took the phone off the hook at the police station. I called there many times. There was no reply or the line was busy. When I walked down to the police station myself; the SHO told me the phone is out of order but I could see that the phone was taken off the hook. Then I really took him to task. I am sure he will remember it for the rest of his life. Crooks, they play tricks with us, as if we are idiots. We ourselves do such acts (*Stumbling*). I mean…let's see what we can do. Bloody young rogues think they can take us for a ride (*Shifting*). Well, tell me, what did you lose?

FIRST MAN: The loss…

CONGRESS MEMBER: I know that enormous loss has occurred. They did not leave even a single thing behind. They took silk saris, transistors, VCRs, steel utensils, gold jewellery and cash worth thousands. First, they looted the houses, then torched them. But we will not sit still, these criminals will be forced to return each and everything. What do they think? Each one of them will be sent to jail. There is still a government in control in this country. Isn't it? I am meeting with the Prime Minister immediately today. I will demand that everything, to the last paisa, should be returned.

SECOND MAN: But we are absolutely homeless now.

CONGRESS MEMBER: I know that you have become homeless. Your houses are no more. Winter is approaching. Where will you go? The government is setting up camps for you. After all the government also has a responsibility. The PM is giving five lakhs from his fund.

SECOND MAN: Five lakhs? This amount is...

CONGRESS MEMBER: I know that five lakhs is not much. But this is the first instalment. More funds will flow from World Red Cross, you will also get blankets. Tell me if there is any other issue.

FIRST MAN: Issue, you did not...

CONGRESS MEMBER: I did not leave any issue untouched, I know, this is what you want to say. Now, if I do not understand your problems, who will? You people have elected me. I know that during the last election people of your religion were completely united and voted for me. You didn't vote for Bhartiya Janata Party. We all know that that is a sectarian party which guards only the interests of the Hindus. Their slogan is Hindi... Hindu... Hindustan... But our party believes in secularism. Mahatma Gandhi taught us— *Ishwar, Allah tero naam, sab ko sanmati de bhagwan.*

BABA: (*He has reached a point where he can't control himself now*) What else did Mahatma Gandhi teach you?

CONGRESS MEMBER: (*Shaken*) What do you mean?

BABA: He taught you to tell lies in front of people; fool them with your dramatic acts. We have not come to beg alms from you, because we know that all that has happened, has happened because of your schemes and conspiracies. We have come to tell you that the PM has been assassinated. We are not happy about it. Some mean-spirited people distributed sweets, which is not a good thing. The same way, some stupid people distributed sweets during the action on Darbar Sahib, when thousands of innocents were killed. Deception and stupidity has become supreme in our country. On one side, people are killed, and on the other side, sweets are distributed. Those who distribute sweets have not lost their sons. Their daughters have not lost husbands. Their kids have not been orphaned. (*Getting excited*) We condemn those who distribute sweets when others die. We despise the government, which is riddled with lies, killings and deceit. (*Baba turns while saying this. The Congressman gets very enraged. Baba turns again*) Damn you. (*Loudly. He exits from one side.*)

CONGRESS MEMBER: (*The Congressman leaves angrily from the other side*) They have killed our beloved mother and they are also damning us.

(*Jathedar, Baba and two other Sikhs appear.*)

JATHEDAR: The Sikh Community is in a crisis. The religious order is in danger.

BABA: What did you say Jathedar ji?

JATHEDAR: There is danger to the religious order.

BABA: (*Sarcastically*) The religious order has always been in danger.

JATHEDAR: What do you mean?

BABA: Jathedarji, it has been thirty-seven years since the country became independent. On the one hand, the government always kept saying that the country faces danger and you, on the other hand, kept saying that the religious order is in danger.

FIRST SIKH: It is not the faith that is in danger now; it is we the people that are facing danger now. We have no good reason to stay in India.

SECOND SIKH: What sort of life is this. We are especially targeted and killed, our properties burnt. What have we not done for this country?

BABA: What did you do? No one did anything for the country, everyone looked after their own interests.

FIRST SIKH: Babaji, you always take the opposite view. If we did not contribute anything then who did?

BABA: When did I say someone else did? No one did anything. Everyone looked after their own interests.

SECOND SIKH: What we need to think about is what should be done now.

BABA: Ask the Jathedar. But, what will he say? His politics in the whole of twentieth century has always revolved around religion.

JATHEDAR: Politics and religion can never be a separate thing for the Sikhs. Our Gurus have said so and this is our history.

FIRST SIKH: Jathedarji is saying the right thing.

BABA: What is right? You and your Jathedar have become expert historians without reading or knowing a thing about history and are trying to fool people. Do you know why and when the Gurus gave this advice?

JATHEDAR: When?

BABA: At the time when Sikhs were selfless and fearless warriors. They were fighting against Mughal rulers' oppression and atrocities. Aurangzeb said that only Muslims will live in Hindustan. That time the fight was between religions and that is why the response was from a religious perspective.

JATHEDAR: So, should we go against the teachings of our Gurus now?

BABA: The Gurus mandated us to stand firm against the oppression and fight for your just rights. We need to follow that order. But tell me what rights your wealthy Sikhs are going to fight for? They are the ones who rob others of their rights. What do they have common with ordinary Sikhs or other ordinary folks?

JATHEDAR: (*Irritated*) People like Baba are always willing to divide our religious community, the Panth.

BABA: Yes, if someone suggests a sensible thing, it creates division in the Panth. As if the Panth is a group of fools. You should know that the government under which the Sikhs suffered a holocaust is headed by a Sikh. The city in which all this happened has a Sikh as its mayor. Now go ahead and say that they are out of the Panth.

JATHEDAR: Yes, they are traitors to the Panth.

BABA: Yet you are the one voted for these traitors. Why? Because they are Sikhs. You garlanded them. Invited them to your gurdwaras and honoured them. Didn't you do that?

FIRST: What is it that you really want to say?

BABA: I want to say that the time has come to stop this song of the Panth being a separate entity. Be part of the mainstream of the country and use the new political sense of the twentieth century. Understand that the politics and the divisions are not based on religion but rather on classes. The wealthy classes of your Panth have been on friendly terms with the Congress Party leaders and on the other hand have been funding Sant Bhinderanwale in Amritsar. Someone gave you a slogan that such a country should be created where Sikhs were in power. Those Sikh feudal lords rob the poor agricultural tenants. Those Sikh factory owners live on the labour of poor workers. The capitalist Sikhs want to advance their own agenda by using you so that they can also grab a piece away from Birlas and Tatas of this land. They want to see a place where they are the Birlas and Tatas. There is nothing more to it than that.

JATHEDAR: But how can we live in this country now? Where we have been treated like this and so much loss has been suffered by us.

BABA: We should think about this. We need to think about it. We should have thought about it when the innocents were being killed in Punjab.

FIRST: What should we do now?

BABA: What should we do? Search within for answers. Change your thought process. Figure out who is your friend and who is your foe in this country?

SECOND: Who is our friend? No one.

BABA: Well, if you keep thinking this way, then really no one will be your friend in this country. If you look to foreign countries for kindness, they will sympathize with you superficially but will laugh at you from within. What did America, Canada, England do when the Golden Temple was attacked and destroyed in an army action? No one did anything and it wasn't their responsibility anyway.

JATHEDAR: But we do not have a friend even in this country.

BABA: Why not? This is a country of seventy crore people and many people support you. When you were being attacked in Delhi or other parts of the country, who were the people who were raising their voice in protest? They were printing and distributing leaflets all around. Open Maharashtra's newspapers and see how editorials after editorials were being written. They were saying that one Nathu Ram Godse killed Mahatma Gandhi, that did not mean there was no place for all Marathis in India. Who were those people who have risked their lives in Calcutta to save the Sikhs? Yes, there are many enemies here, but at the same time people who have faith in humanity and democratic values are not few either. Recognize them. But you will be able to recognize them only when you change your own vision and have a more sensible approach to politics. This is the twentieth century, not the fifteenth or sixteenth. (*Taking out a newspaper from his bag*) Read this news. People's Union of Civil Liberties, People's Union for Democratic Rights have called for a massive rally. For whom? For you. Why? Because they understand the character of the rulers. They know that the army boots who suppressed the Nagas and Mizos in the Northeast yesterday are creating havoc in Punjab today. The only difference is that there the majority of army men were Sikhs and here they are non-Sikhs. They know that the forces that do not let the Assam issue be solved will not allow the Punjab issue to be resolved either. They know that this country is ruled by plunderers who will never want the people united. These rulers will initiate riots and communal fights. But we should recognize the power of the people. They are emerging and are in the process of awakening others. Match your steps with them. Add your voices and words with theirs. Do not ask for a piece of land where Sikhs can rule, rather ask for the whole nation, where the worker is recognized. The question is will you do so?

JATHEDAR: Leave it. Forget it. What useless talk Baba has started.

FIRST SIKH: But Baba speaks the truth.

JATHEDAR: What truth? It's a sin to stand here even for a minute. (*Angrily*) *Wahe Guruji ka Khalsa, Wahe Guruji ki Fateh*. Goodbye.

BABA: (*Speaks after them*) *Wahe Guruji ki Fateh*. Go to the Singh Sahibs and have Baba chastized for religious misconduct.

(*The Newspaper Seller enters the stage. Pause a little. The same scene is repeated as in the first Act.*)

NEWSPAPER SELLER: Today's breaking news is…which will not be making headlines tomorrow…will turn stale day after and will be forgotten on the fourth day. (*Three people take the newspaper and start reading. The newspaper seller repeats 'today's breaking news'.*)

BABA: Stop this nonsense. What breaking news? There is no breaking news in this country. All news is stale. Hindu-Muslim quarrels. News of hatred among Hindus and Sikhs. Lok Sabha elections. Same old news, same old abuse. The games rich play involve millions. The poor are used only as a tool. News of torching Dalit colonies. News of jobless youths committing suicides. News of sky-rocketing prices. News of the leaders switching political parties. All stale news.

OTHERS: (*Lifting their faces from the newspapers*) Yes, all stale news.

BABA: O dear newspaper seller, get some fresh news, at least sometimes. Tell us of a new sunrise on this land.

OTHERS: New sun?

BABA: Yes. When the hard-working people of this land will not be oppressed. Hindus will be there, Sikhs will be there, Muslims will be there and they will also be there who do not wish to side with any religion. The news of that sun is awaited by millions of Indians.

(*Baba says these last words slowly. Then he looks to one side, as if seeing a sun in his imagination. Everyone looks to that side and becomes still.*)

Seekh Kabab*

A TRAGICOMEDY

Kuljeet Singh

Translated from the Hindi by
ISHMEET KAUR CHAUDHRY

A tragic comedy that delves into issues related to the transformation of Sikh identity and their experiences after 1984, 'Seekh Kabab' centres around the character of a retired soldier of the Indian Army who comes to inquire about his missing son at t he police station, and what he experiences there. The play has a Brechtian setting and experiments with light and music. The grim times after 1984 have been dealt with sensitively, as the play mocks at the frailties of life and human desire, as well as fear.

Stage set-up

The play is set at the Police Station, Sadar, New Delhi in November, 1984.

The stage is divided into two spaces: the main space represents the room of the officers with table, chairs, files, almirah and other stage props, while the other space is the waiting area with a few chairs kept in a vertical line. The actors may change this arrangement according to their convenience and stage design.

The play moves from one scene into the other without any black out. For the sake of reading, it has been divided into scenes.

---

* The title is derived from Uma Chakravarti's book *The Delhi Riots: Three Days in the Life of a Nation* in which she writes, 'A popular joke reverberated through elite schools in Delhi: "What is a seekh kabab?" The answer was: "A burnt Sikh!"' (pp. 166-7)

Characters (in order of appearance)

Tiger	A man in white kurta and pyjama
Stand-up Comedian	
Musicians*	Six to eight musicians (harmonium, percussion & vocals)
Kaushik	Senior police officer, around forty years old, intelligent, balanced, righteous
Mehr	Junior police officer, around thirty-five, impulsive, aggressive and gross
Ravi	A teaboy
Sunder	Junior police officer, around thirty–thirty-five, works in the field to resolve cases
Pritam Singh	Retired subedar of the Indian Army, in his fifties
Barber	
Bridegroom	
Sex-worker	
Man with a shaving kit	
Boy with tyre	
Elderly woman	
Other characters (as per convenience)	

As the audience stands outside the performance space in the open foyer, they come across a few unrelated activities happening:

>An artist painting
>A boy collecting hair
>A woman searching for her family
>A bridegroom getting ready
>A man standing, shaving his body
>A boy playing with tyres
>A boy trying to tie a turban
>A boy (Ravi) making tea

---

* The number of musicians may vary as per requirement and availability.

These acts may be played as per requirements and interpretation.

Audience enters/Preset

(Tiger is reading the voter list and addressing his imagined supporters in a spot. A flashlight falls on him like somebody clicked his photo. He gets alert. Asks who's there in the same direction, abuses and runs out.)

Opening Spotlight

A well dressed and well educated stand-up comedian addresses the audience with a six- to seven-minute long piece focusing on sardar jokes [mainly Santa-Banta jokes]* to let everyone have a great laugh. The initial jokes should be really funny and should arouse laughter in the audience.

His address ends with the question:

What would you call a burning Sikh?

Pause

He asks the audience.

No reply.

Asks again.

No response.

Fade Out.

Scene 1

Police station inside room—Slow light fades in on Mahatma Gandhi's photo—Police officer smoking a cigarette.

Another police officer enters.

MEHR: Jai Hind, janab! You came early?

KAUSHIK: Yes, for the match today…kids don't let me watch it at home.

MEHR: Janab…? What…scared of children…?

---

* Santa-Banta Jokes are popular jokes poking fun at the sardar community.

KAUSHIK: Yaar…children are all powerful…anyway, has the match started…?

MEHR: …is about to start, Janab.

KUSHIK: What's the team?

MEHR: The same old one…

(Ravi, the tea-vendor, enters)

MEHR: Keep the tea here, Chhotu…give one to Sundar outside too.

(Ravi exits)

KAUSHIK: Oye…who is this boy?

MEHR: Janab, he is our Chhotu…. Joginder Singh's son…

(Points to the boy, a Sikh who has got a haircut recently.)

KAUSHIK: Is that so?…seeing him for the first time

MEHR: He is the same boy who delivers tea everyday.

KAUSHIK: He is looking different…. *(stares at the door)*

MEHR: Janab…you are aware of the entire situation…what happened Janab…?

KAUSHIK: Nothing…see if the match has started.

(Tiger enters)

TIGER: Come…I'll show you the match.

KAUSHIK *(completely flabbergasted)*: Please … please Come sit, Sir.

MEHR: Sundar please order a hot cup of tea for Sir.

TIGER: Are you sitting here to watch the match? Despite the large number of policemen here, how come someone managed to click my photograph with the mob? Tell me how come?

KAUSHIK: Which photo?

TIGER: When that sardar manages to publish that photo in the newspaper…you'll come to know.

MEHR: Sahib where did this happen? When did this happen?

Tiger: Bhenchod…are you a policeman or am I? Get the information.

Kaushik: I think there is a misunderstanding, Sir…

Tiger: The news is confirmed and by evening the matter should be dissolved.

Kaushik: Sir, relax, I'll submit the entire report, by evening to you, by hand….

Tiger: Every thing should be clear by evening…

Song:
>   Tiger Tiger Tiger x3,
>   Tiger Tiger Tiger Tiger x3,
>   Tiger Tiger—Tiger burning bride x3,
>   Tiger the magic box;
>   Our Tiger,
>   Tiger landed on a plane,
>   Long list; many a name;
>   Not enough oil nor matches;
>   So many shops, offices, cars, houses and thatches
>   How will they manage this! A chance…
>   This is their chance, the right chance
>   It comes once
>   not again and again.

Mehr: Shut up! Oye…

The song goes on:

>   Snatch, steel and run…
>   Don't see the price
>   Tiger, Tiger, Tiger x3
>   We don't fear anyone
>   We control the system, government and everyone
>   Sajjan and Bhagat are with us
>   They saw the world turn to ash x2
>   Tiger, Tiger, burning bride x2
>   Tiger Tiger
>   The city has become a jungle where the tiger has his might.

(*While the song goes on, light from the inner room of the police station starts moving on to the waiting area outside. The entire stage is lit and the stage clearly shows a distinction between the main room and the waiting area. We see a lot of people there awaiting their turn, including the barber, bridegroom, sex-worker and man with a shaving kit.*

Kaushik and Mehr are sitting in the office. Sunder returns with three cups of tea. He enters the room. Kaushik and Mehr look up.)

SUNDER: Sir, we have lost the toss, we'll have to do the fielding…

MEHR: This is the problem of our team…nothing can come of it… why, Sir?

KAUSHIK: Where is Omveer? Inquire about Himmat too…

MEHR: Yes, Sir…

(*Kaushik stares at him.*)

KAUSHIK: Ask Sunder what's the score? (*Goes out*)

(*All actors look at the man who is shaving. Mehr enters.*)

MEHR: Hey Sunder…what's up…today??

SUNDER: Sahib, Omveer has completed the Nabi Kareem's job and Himmat is coming.

MEHR: And…there was a complaint of theft in the market…?

SUNDER: Sahib, Omkar has been sent there and those who have their complaint have been called here.

MEHR (*Looks at the man*): O ho! He has come again! Ask him to sit.

(*The man, Pritam, is continuously shaving his body. Mehr goes to Pritam, comes back and tells Sunder something.*)

SUNDER: Sahib, this sardarji has been sitting since a long time. He isn't telling anything; says he has retired as a subedar from the army. Wants to meet sahib, says he has some urgent work.

MEHR (*to Pritam*): Haanji Sardarji…what happened?

PRITAM (*with a photo in his hand*): I am Subedar Pritam Singh, this is my son's photo, I need to meet your sahib.

(The phone rings. Mehr invites Pritam Singh inside.

Scene 1 and Scene 2 are in continuation. Only the space outside is unlit when the action takes place in the main room.)

Scene 2

KAUSHIK (*on the phone*): Ji Sir…hmmm…ji…I am working on it Sir… I've understood that… Don't worry, it'll be done…

MEHR: Janab

(Kaushik, gestures to him to stop talking)

KAUSHIK: Give me sometime Sir…but Sir… But I am trying Sir… Ji… Fine Sir…fine…fine. Jai Hind Sir.

MEHR: Janab, this is Pritam Singh 1799, Wazir Singh Gali, Chuna Mandi, Paharganj.

(Pause. Kaushik looks at Pritam.)

KAUSHIK: Sit…

(Pritam Singh sits.)

KAUSHIK: Tell me, what happened?

PRITAM (*enthusiastically*): My name is Pritam Singh, Sikh Regiment, 19 Sikh Battalion…have served this country for twenty years, look at my photo of the 1965 war, *(shows the photograph)* I was twenty-five years old then, this is my CO, Solanki Sahib, he used to praise me in front of the entire battalion, I had a valour, would swallow any kind of pain considering it to be a sugar-coated medicine. Solanki Sahib always remained very happy with me, he never overlooked my proposal, he knew if Pritam Singh said something, he must have thoughtfully proposed so.

MEHR: So, where all were you posted Sardarji…towards Rajasthan? or…did you go towards Kashmir too…?

PRITAM: Yes…yes…I have stayed in Rajasthan, at Jaisalmer…also in Jhansi and… Assam as well…

KAUSHIK: When did you retire?

PRITAM: Three years ago…in 1981…the regiment was in Kapurthala, all Jawans attended, they gave me this big memento (*gestures with his hand*), army canteen gifted three suitcases, Solanki Sahib gave me the address of his house…said…Pritam do come to my house.

KAUSHIK: Did you go then…?

PRITAM: Where?

KAUSHIK: To his house?

PRITAM: I didn't have any work to visit him for…

KAUSHIK: How come in Delhi…?

PRITAM: My son completed school about three years ago… What better place for academics than Delhi…? Had saved some money in the APF…so bought a house with it…

KAUSHIK: Oh! You used the entire saving. So, what is your means of earning now?

PRITAM: I work in a school… I receive some money from there and some from my pension… As it is, we are just three people at home…my wife is very religious…she goes to the gurdwara every morning…doesn't miss at all…the day she is not able to go, she remains disturbed the whole day.

MEHR: That's right…it is our tradition, we also alight the lamp every day. I do it in the morning and my wife in the evening….

KAUSHIK: Okay…who is the third one?

PRITAM: My son, Kartar Singh. I have come to you for him, he is studying right now, very stubborn, does what he decides…then he doesn't listen to anyone… Last year he came and said, I don't feel like studying… I am not interested…get me a camera. I had some money, I bought a camera with it. I thought he is my only son and he had never demanded anything ever, I could do at least this much for him… The camera was a bit expensive but I didn't hesitate, just wanted Kartar to stay happy… I bought it from my friend, Jagbir's uncle's shop in Chandni Chowk, since he knew us, he gave us some discount, had we bought it from somewhere else, it would have cost us much more, don't know how much.

(Kaushik and Mehr look at each other as Pritam Singh continues talking.)

(In the waiting area.)

SUNDER: What do you do?

BARBER: Sir, I am a businessman

SUNDER: What business?

BARBER: ...business, I am a barber

SUNDER: What?

BARBER: Am I not a businessman?

SUNDER: Speak up!

BARBER: Sahib, do you know why have I been called?

SUNDER: There is a complaint by the colony members that you have blocked the drains of the colony, and you make a lot of noise at night in your shop, what is happening?

BARBER: Sahib, all of them are jealous of me.

SUNDER: Why man, are you in a powerful position, that they are jealous of you?

BARBER: Sir, God is graceful, I am prospering every day.

SUNDER: How much do you charge?

BARBER: Sahib, Rs 30.

SUNDER: Sala, what kind of service do you render, hain?

BARBER: Sahib, my shop is different than others, God is merciful, I tell you, your job is useless, you may also start a similar business as mine.

SUNDER: Sala...how much do you manage to earn in a month?

BARBER: Monthly? Your salary of a month is my daily earning.

SUNDER: Sala…what is it that you do? Do you sell drugs?

BARBER: Sahib, it is that, they come at night to get their hair cut. You won't believe that I used to charge Rs 2, now I take Rs 30 from them, and why shouldn't I charge them this, I have to erase the mark on their forehead. Just that God remains graceful, I have admitted my son in a public school, one day he'll get educated and become an officer.

SUNDER: …and…why is this drain jammed?

BARBER: Sahib, where could I have disposed the hair? Threw it in the drain! Tell me what should I give you, these days… God is graceful, whatever you tell me, we'll send to your place for your wife and children.

Scene 3

KAUSHIK: Don't worry Pritam Ji … since when is your son missing?

PRITAM: He left home on 2nd, hasn't returned since then.

KAUSHIK: Didn't you inquire in the neighbourhood?

PRITAM: I inquired…but no one knew anything… Initially I was worried but he called up on 6th…he said everything was fine and he'll return in a couple of days…. I thought everything was fine…and then Gursharan also stopped me.

KAUSHIK: He didn't tell you where he was?

PRITAM: He didn't tell me this and I was also in a hurry…forgot to ask him.

KAUSHIK: Your son has been missing from so many days and you are coming now to inquire… What kind of a father are you?… Anyways, Mehr write down… What name did you say?

PRITAM: Kartar

KAUSHIK: Kartar Singh…?

PRITAM: Kartar Singh Khalsa…

KAUSHIK: Khalsa? But aren't you Pritam Singh…?

PRITAM: Ji, Kartar has been baptized. He has consumed Amritpan.

MEHR: You retain a knife in that…no?

PRITAM: It is called a kirpan.

KAUSHIK: You didn't consume Amrit…?

PRITAM: Since I was in the army, it was difficult to follow the discipline.

KAUSHIK: What is Kartar's age?

PRITAM: Twenty years

MEHR: Is Kartar married?

PRITAM: Oh no! He doesn't listen to us. We are tired of telling him. You know children do what they want to. He says, it's not time for marriage yet.

KAUSHIK: Where do your relatives stay? He might have gone there…

PRITAM: Some people are here in Delhi…others in Punjab, maybe he has gone there but whenever he goes there, he informs us.

MEHR: Did you check with his friends? Is he alcoholic?

PRITAM: He doesn't have friends in Delhi. All his friends are in Gurdaspur. He doesn't take alcohol like other boys.

KAUSHIK: And you? You were in Army na…?

PRITAM: Ji …we drank sometimes.

KAUSHIK: How come sometimes…? As it is you people eat a lot of chicken-vicken.

PRITAM: Let chicken-vicken be aside…when I was posted in Punjab in Amritsar, we all roasted mutton together.

KAUSHIK: Butchered it yourself…? Weren't you scared…?

PRITAM: What scare ji…? When we butchered so many enemies… these were just goats and accompanied with alcohol that was sanctioned…it was fun.

(The tea vendor enters.)

KAUSHIK: Will you have tea?

PRITAM: No.

KAUSHIK: You don't take tea...then what do you drink Sardarji...? *(laughs)* Did Kartar have an enemy?

PRITAM: What Sir...?

MEHR: He means to ask if Kartar had an argument with someone?

PRITAM: No Kaushik Sahib, Kartar is a very calm person. He used to get angry in his childhood. Once a child made fun of his turban. Kartar hit him in his head. He would have been rusticated but I scolded him and asked him to apologize. Since then, he became very calm. *(Sundar shouts and Mehr exits)* Don't know what happened, no argument with anyone...no fight... I tried asking him many a times but he would stare thoughtfully. I once pulled him and sat with him, asked him, 'Oye what do you keep thinking? Why don't you speak out your thoughts?' Sir, that day, he shouted angrily, 'Daddy don't worry, now time will come, all of them will get an answer.' Then he'd start writing something in his dairy quietly and then he wouldn't be seen.... Sometimes, he said, 'Daddy don't worry the big day is about to come.'

MEHR: What is Kartar's education?...

PRITAM: After completing two years at Khalsa College, Kartar had lost interest. Said he enjoyed photography.

MEHR: So, what does Kartar do now?

PRITAM: Now...he does photography only...

KAUSHIK: Of what kind...?

PRITAM: Every kind, he loves taking pictures of cars, leaves home early morning. He has taken a lot of photographs of Delhi... you can visit entire Delhi through his photographs... Shishganj Sahib, Bangla Sahib, India Gate, Teen Murti, Gyarah-Murti, Rashtrapati Bhawan. One evening he took us to India Gate to eat ice-cream, he clicked my photograph with his mother, we have framed that photo and have hanged it on our wall, but his mother's favourite photo is of Harmandir Sahib...

KAUSHIK: Amritsar...you went to Amritsar...

PRITAM: We didn't... Kartar did.

KAUSHIK: When did he go?

PRITAM: He keeps visiting the place.

KAUSHIK: When did he visit last?

PRITAM: I don't remember, Sir.

KAUSHIK: Don't remember...? Hmmm

(Sunder enters abruptly.)

SUNDER: Sir, three wickets down...

KAUSHIK: Who took them?

SUNDER: Two by Kapil and one by Shashtri.

(Kaushik gets up. Kaushik orders Sunder.)

KAUSHIK: Get water for sardarji...

(Kaushik moves out to ask the score and tells Sunder to bring the diary and photo from Pritam's house. Sunder leaves.)

BRIDEGROOM: I always thought about my marriage, when will I get married? When will that day come in my life, when I'll get married? I had turned thirty-five and wasn't getting married, friends had a lot of fun at my cost. One of my massis brought an offer...the girl's name was...she was a little dark but I liked her. I was happy in my hearts of heart that I am about to get married. Cards were printed, sweets were distributed, the relatives had come. My mother was very happy, her daughter-in-law would look after her once she came home. One night, friends asked me, 'Oye Sattu have you kept a condom?' I asked them what it was? They asked me if I wouldn't sleep with my bride on the first night? Ohhji, I really enjoyed listening to them. I brought a condom...ji, and put in the pocket of my sherwani. On the day of my marriage, I was about to ride the horse, the band was beating and friends were dancing. I rode the horse and my father circled a Rs 20 note around my head. I was holding the kirpan and wearing a sehra. Wahji, I really enjoyed it. I saw that around ten to twelve people were coming, they killed Daarji, more so, they even carried my bride with them. I am still waiting for Kaalo with this condom.

Scene 4

MEHR: Sardarji what do think…where must have the boy gone to…?

PRITAM: Had I known this, why would I have come to you?

MEHR: That is fine…but think again carefully…maybe something is left out… Think carefully.*

PRITAM: I have told all that I knew, you tell me what more should I say…

MEHR: Okay, tell me what was he wearing that day…?

PRITAM: Yes! Kartar was wearing a check shirt, black pant and a royal blue turban…he was wearing sports shoes…

MEHR: Sardarji, what do you think…why did he leave home on 2nd November itself…?

(Phone rings and Kaushik enters the waiting area. Mehr picks up and talks.)

SEX-WORKER: Sahib, I am from 55 number kotha. Your people have forcefully picked me up and brought here. They say that they found a turban and a knife of a sardar from my room. Sahib, he was my customer.

He came to my house on the night of 31st October. Sala, he always came prepared, would play with three-three fairies, but that night he was not prepared. He was in a state of a shock, completely jacked-out, he was asking me to hide him. He was hiding in my chest like an infant. He was considering me to be his mother, as if I will offer him milk and caress him in my lap. He always considered himself a brave and chivalrous Singh (*bangs*)…and now he was no-one, minuscule…meek and very

---

* The sentence used in the original translation literally means 'pressurize your mind'.

scared...there was no erection...it kept hanging. Some people came to inquire about him outside, I thought of handing him over to them, but then...what to do, he was my regular customer. Sala...was saved. Sahib, he forgot his kirpan and turban, what is my fault in it? (*Speaking to herself*) It would have better, had I not opened the door...

(Sunder enters and hands over the photographs. Mehr keeps the receiver of the phone and goes in the waiting area and whispers something to Kaushik. Kaushik enters the main room with photos.)

KAUSHIK: Okay sardarji, did you have water...when did your boy leave home...?

PRITAM: Around 1st or 2nd.

KAUSHIK: On 1st or on 2nd?

PRITAM: Either on 1st or 2nd, one of the two days.

KAUSHIK: Or was it 31st...try to remember clearly, Sardarji...it must be 31st...there was a lot of disturbance on the 1st and 2nd....

PRITAM: Ya...must be so, Sir...

KAUSHIK: Okay...so your son often visited Harminder Sahib? *(asks while showing the photograph of the demolished Akal Takht)* So...he was there on the same day...? Why?... What do you say?

PRITAM: Sir, this photograph was taken by Kartar... I told you that our relatives stay there...he visited them often...that is why he took this photograph.

KAUSHIK: *(Shows the photograph)* So all of you were there at this time...?

PRITAM: Yes...we may have been there...

KAUSHIK: So sardarji, your son Kartar Singh Khalsa is a photographer? And he often visits his people at Amritsar...he also writes a diary that he keeps secret from you...he wears a kirpan too, he is Amritdhari, doesn't have any addiction means he is a devout Sikh...and you told that he is also stubborn...is determined about what he wishes to do..., am I right, sardarji?

PRITAM: Ji, you are right.

KAUSHIK: Okay, Mehr get his signatures...

(Pritam Singh hesitates.)

MEHR: This is the paperwork required for us to proceed, once we register the complaint, we'll be able to locate your son...come on sign the register...

(Pritam Singh signs the papers...hesitatingly, with scepticism.)

MEHR *(change of tone; from normal to stern)*: Now you tell us, where did you send your son?

PRITAM: Send my son...where? I am searching for him myself and have come to register a complaint...?

MEHR *(aggressive)*: Gyani. Kartar had phoned you... No...? Where did he call up from...?

PRITAM: I told you, Sir...that we received a phone call on 6th...

KAUSHIK: We have understood what you told us... Now tell us what you haven't told us...

PRITAM: Meaning...?

MEHR: You'll understand the meaning immediately...once I give you one under your ear...

PRITAM *(reacts sharply)*: I am a subedar...talk to me politely...

MEHR: Politely...? Okay we'll talk politely, absolutely polite...sardarji, care for a glass of water? *(Pritam doesn't reply)* No, no, here drink it *(Throws a glass of water on his face)*.

PRITAM: What are you doing? Why such misbehaviour!

MEHR: Speak the truth now? I am an extremely polite person.

PRITAM: Are you threatening me?

KAUSHIK: No, it is not so...we are only asking you...where is your son?

PRITAM: Had I known this, I wouldn't have come to you?

MEHR: Enough of subedarji and all that business...stop fucking...tell us straight away...

PRITAM: You may quit such blabbering... I'll look for my son myself...

MEHR: Where are you going, Gyaniji, the procedure has just begun...?

(Pulls Pritam and makes him sit him on the chair. Pritam tries getting up again, he pushes him to settle on the chair.)

MEHR: Sunder, close the door. Hey, look Gyani, Sir is speaking, listen to him...

KAUSHIK: Subedar Pritam Singhji, your son Kartar Singh Khalsa, who is Amritdhari, wears a kirpan, doesn't have any addiction means he is a Pakka Sikh, you told us that he often visits his friends at Amritsar. In the second week of June, when this event *(shows the photo of Akal Takht)* took place, he was there with his fundamentalist friends, your son was waiting for his big day and that day was 31st October, Pritamji he left home around 9 a.m. with his diary and camera because...he had to elope with his friends around 9:45 a.m., a camera so that people mistake him for a reporter, and there is no problem. But when his friends were caught here in Delhi, he ran away to Amritsar and Subedar Sahib you didn't receive any phone call or so...all this was happening right under your nose and you didn't get any news...? Do you think that policemen are foolish...? You came here so that no one suspects you...now tell us where is your son...terrorist son...Kartar Singh Khalsa??

(Fade out.)

A few people from Singh Band start playing instruments and singing as chorus:

Ooooooooooo
Stop it...stop it...stop it right away
We were playing the instruments in the baraat
these buggers picked us up from there and
have imprisoned us here
Is this the way?
What anarchy? I am shocked at what has happened to us

We haven't committed any crime,
moreover they have beaten us so much…
beaten us so much, beaten us so much, beaten us so much that
his bump has been turned red…he hasn't been eating nor drinking
he is sitting silently…quiet…very quiet…
(*To the fellow musician*) Everything will be fine…
'Don't worry' I asked the police, 'Why have you arrested us?
If we have made a mistake tell us, why have you brought us here
and locked us up?'
He said, you are from the Singh Band!!
(*To self*) 'Of the Singh Band?'
'So what, if we belong to the Singh Band?'
'No, No' He said, 'Your Singh is that Singh…'
'That Singh?'
'Arre bhai which Singh?'
He said, 'Your Singh is that Singh…'
I asked him again 'Bhai which Singh?'
Let us also know 'Which Singh?'
'Which Singh is he?'
'This Singh is which Singh?'
'This Singh is which Singh?'
'This Singh…that Singh…?'
'This Singh…that Singh…?'
'This Singh…that Singh…?'
'This Singh…that Singh…?'

Goes on

(*frustrated and angry*) Stop it…don't you understand?
ONE OF THE MUSICIANS: The brothers explained them
that our employee's names are Rakesh Singh and Ashok Singh…
not, Manjeet Singh, Hardeep Singh.
But they were not ready to listen to anything…
They said that 'Your Singh is Manjit Singh…'

> I said, 'My Singh is Rakesh Singh'
> They said that 'He is that Singh...'
> I said that 'He is this Singh...'
> 'This that; this that; this that; this that; this that; this that'
>
> *Repetition. Reaches a state of confusion.*
>
> Stop it...
> They brought us and locked us up.
> Our payment is due and we didn't get the food as well.
> When sahib comes, we'll tell him clearly to get us our payment.
> Let them keep playing Singh Singh.
>
> *Cross Fade*

Scene 5

Mehr searching Pritam Singh

MEHR: Get up sardarji.

(*Mehr pulls out everything from his pocket.*)

MEHR: What is this?

(*Pritam Singh is silent.*)

MEHR: See Gyani, I am a temperamental person. Your boy is at fault and you have hidden him...maadarchod...tell the whereabouts of the boy...tell his address.

KAUSHIK (enters): Mehr (*with a cigarette in his hand, loud*).

KAUSHIK (*realizing Pritam Singh's discomfort, throws the cigarette*): See your son is spoilt...let us know the address, otherwise you'll be in trouble...the entire family will have to come to the police station...

MEHR: Look, Sir has been sitting here since morning and you are beating around the bush with new stories...look, Gyani, tell us the truth otherwise we'll turn you into a pigeon.*

---

* The original text has a rhyme that couldn't be retained in the translated text.

KAUSHIK (*firmly*): Sardarji, understand, that your son has taken a photograph which is not in favour of the government…we want that photograph…get us that photograph from your son, I promise, nothing will happen to your son.

PRITAM: Sir, I am searching for him myself.

KAUSHIK: There is a lot of pressure on us, understand.

PRITAM: Kartar can't do any such thing, he is a Sikh, Guru's Sikh…

KAUSHIK: That's it subedar sahib, your son has been misled, those doing such misdeeds are not a few but many in number, we are in such a situation that your son's belief in religion has qualified him to use the gun…in the name of Guru, many innocent people have been de-boarded from the buses and killed…and such a massacre has been called freedom of the sect, Kartar is also a victim of this strategy… You have sacrificed for your country, I am sure you will help us.

PRITAM: Sahib, had I known anything I would have told you truthfully… I have shared all that I knew.

KAUSHIK: So, you feel Kartar is innocent…?

PRITAM: Ji if he had done something wrong, he should definitely be punished…

KAUSHIK: He has helped the terrorists in assassinating the Prime Minister,… he should be punished…

PRITAM: If he has done so, then he should definitely be punished.

KAUSHIK: Do you feel that he hasn't done anything of this kind…?

PRITAM: Sir, do you have any evidence?

MEHR (*comes with a photo*): So, was he fucking his mother with this photograph?

PRITAM: Look, you are forcibly tainting him as a terrorist. He is absolutely innocent.

(*Mehr slaps Pritam. Pritam falls down.*)

A child playing with a tyre enters:

CHILD: My papaji had a tyre shop
   One could get all kinds of tyres there
   Think, flat, thick, big ones, you could even get scooter's tyres there
   My papaji was very fat, his shop was at Rani Jhansi road,
   Have you seen the crossroad there?
   Satguru Tyres
   I play a lot of games with my friend Guddu, racing and all
   One day, Guddu's father, Ajay uncle said, 'Children don't play with the tyres, it's not good to play with them'
   I asked, 'Why Uncle?' Uncle didn't reply.
   After that Guddu never came to play with me. I don't know why!!
   One day I saw that Guddu's father Ajay Uncle and my papaji were playing together...
   with a tyre. I was surprised that Ajay Uncle was playing with a tyre...
   He had told me not to play with a tyre and now he was playing with a tyre himself
   that too, he was playing strangely...with a new tyre
   a game with a new tyre!
   A game in which they hang a tyre in your neck...
   That day I realized that a tyre can be used for many things...
   (*looks out*) yes Bunty... I am coming...wait, wait for me... I am coming...coming

   (*He runs out.*)

(*As the narrative ends Mehr slaps Pritam again. Scuffle between the two. Mehr and Kaushik hold him tight on the table.*)

KAUSHIK: Look Pritam Singh, don't you take undue advantage of my innocence, speak the truth otherwise I have a lot of ways to get the truth out of your gut, let us know, where did you hide that photograph?

   (*Pritam remains silent.*)

KAUSHIK: We have already told you that there is an immense pressure on us, tell us where your son is (*shouts*) Speak out… you bhenchod!

(*Phone rings.*)

KAUSHIK: Ji, ji Sir … we have caught a man… Okay, he has been identified…? What is his name? Okay, Roshan Singh…? Kk… (*Puts the phone down*) Mehr listen to me … what is his son's name?

MEHR: Kartar Singh Khalsa…

KAUSHIK (*on phone*): Yes Sir, okay sir. Jai Hind Sir.

(*Long pause.*)

KAUSHIK: Leave him, let him go…he is not that boy…they have identified that boy, he has been found…

KAUSHIK: Subedar Sahib, you can go, now.

(*Mehr leaves him, Kaushik collects all photos and hands them to Pritam. Pritam looks at them…collects his stuff which is thrown all over.*)

PRITAM (*about to leave, as an afterthought*): Sir, is Kartar a terrorist?

(*Mehr and Kaushik look at each other and are speechless.*

Pritam in a very tight spot.)

PRITAM: Guru Gobind Singh…now…speak…

(*Lights Fade out.*)

Seekh Kebab Song

Good bye blue skies (x4)
Now we don't need you…why do you stand still…silent
Now we don't need you…why do you stand still…silent
Speak out—speak out—or just say goodbye—goodbye
Goodbye-goodbye-goodbye-goodbye-goodbye
If noise is not the answer then just that Seekh Kebab is

If noise is not the answer then just that Seekh Kebab is
You are a participant of this evening, of all the happenings
Of all the happenings
Thunder or storm—or just say goodbye
Blue skies goodbye, goodbye-goodbye-goodbye-goodbye
Hardeep, Ashmit, Jaspreet, Kuljeet
Hardeep, Ashmit, Jaspreet, Kuljeet
No one bothers for you ... no one cares
You are a messenger of peace—namesake ... just namesake.
Goodbye blue sky ... goodbye-goodbye-goodbye-goodbye-goodbye
The big tree will fall again ... the earth will shake again
the earth will shake again
The head will be slain again ... the dreams will burn again
The Seekh-kebab will be cooked again

(*While the song continues we see lights fade in at the waiting area.*

Pritam Singh waiting with other characters.)

MEHR: Sundar, what is today's score?

You'll watch, just watch and would just keep watching...still–
You'll watch, just watch and would just keep watching...still–
Goodbye blue sky...goodbye—
Goodbye blue sky...goodbye—

(*Mehr enters again. Asks the same question. Another victim is being called in. Song continues.*

Lights fade out in order of this sequence: Waiting area, then main room, then Mahatma Gandhi photo frame.

The same stand-up comedian comes here. Laughs. Laughs. Goes on laughing.

Fade Out.)

One Day from Chaurasi

Harvinder Paul Singh

Translated from the Hindi by
ISHMEET KAUR CHAUDHRY

A musical play singing the 'song of injustice', 'One Day from Chaurasi' was written in 2012 and first performed at Jantar Mantar, Delhi on 31 October 2012 in the presence of Nirpreet Kaur, an activist struggling for justice for her father against a local politician who had burnt him in front of her own eyes. The play received an extremely emotional reaction from the audience, who raised slogans against the system. It brings out how the killings of 1984 have set up another history of impunity and how justice has been delayed and thus denied.

Scene 1

(All artists are sitting in a circle. They are sitting in a frozen position. One of the older artists addresses the audience as a narrator.)

NARRATOR: Friends, thirty-one years ago, on this day, the Sikhs were massacred in Delhi. They were picked, identified and killed—burnt alive. Still, thirty-one years after the event, the tears of that pain well into our eyes. *(All actors circle the narrator and start singing in a chorus)*

CHORUS: The eyes rain tears, we die every moment
The eyes rain tears, we die every moment
My son doesn't return—tormented with memories of daughter;
The thought scares me, the thought scares me
With the burning tyre in their neck, never be they born again—

With the burning tyre in their neck, never be they born again—
Let's pray together—lets pray together—let's pray together[*]

(All sit down.)

NARRATOR: But even after thirty-one years we haven't got justice, what we have received is a date after date.

LEADER: O, sardarji, forget the past—what is there in it. (*in a lighter mood, sings*) *Chodo kal ki baatein; kal ki baat purani.*

NARRATOR: Then why don't you forget the old tales too—you have been burning Ravan for centuries—why do you burn him every year? Forget the past—release the Sikhs from the closed prisons—those who are still in jail despite completing their sentence.

LEADER: No, they are dangerous, they'll disturb the nation's peace.

NARRATOR: You mean to say, that those perpetrators who killed Sikhs in 1984 and are roaming around scot-free, they don't threaten the peace of this nation?

ONE PERSON: O Uncle! Why are you shouting thus?

NARRATOR: Yes, yes, we will shout and keep shouting asking for justice. We will keep shouting: 'We want justice!' 'We want justice!'

ALL: Yes, we want justice

ONE BOY: Uncle, we were born after 1984—let us know what happened in 1984.

ALL BOYS: Yes, let us know what happened in 1984—what happened in 1984.

NARRATOR: Okay I'll tell you, listen, listen to a story from 1984, a tale of 1984.

Scene 2

All artists move in a circle and sing

ALL: Listen everyone, listen! Let me tell you a tale—
Listen, listen and pass it on

---

[*] These lines are from Babu Maan's popular song.

A story that can melt hearts—
A story that brings tears to eyes—
Let me tell you a tale—
Listen, listen and pass it on—
A story that can melt hearts—
A story that brings tears to eyes—
Come, I'll tell you a tale—Come, I'll tell you a tale
A tale from Chaurasi! A tale of Chaurasi!
A tale from Chaurasi! A tale of Chaurasi!

(All sit together; one young boy stands up; one lady, Baljeet Kaur, finds a corner and sits there.)

YOUNG BOY: This is a story of this old lady Baljeet Kaur who, for the last thirty-one years, comes and sits on this bench outside this court. Come, let's ask her why does she come here.

SECOND BOY: Amma! What are you doing here?

BALJEET KAUR: I am WAITING.

ALL: Waiting? For whom?

BALJEET KAUR: Hunn!... (*with a smirk on the face*) what can you get from the court?

ALL: Justice.

BALJEET KAUR: That's it! I wait for Justice here.

THIRD BOY: Is it that, you haven't still got justice, even after so many years?

BALJEET KAUR: No, my sons, no. Justice hasn't been done to me. Something inside me pricks me...troubles me and haunts me... (*sobs*) and I get up and walk out...come here, and sit outside the court. Someday I may find Justice!

FOURTH BOY: Amma, do you come alone...isn't there anyone to accompany you?

BALJEET KAUR: No son, none of my family members are alive, so who will come with me?

FOURTH BOY: At least bring someone along.

BALJEET KAUR: No one comes along, son, no one—130 crore people of this country are dead—all have died.

FIRST BOY: Amma! It seems you are put of your mind. All these people are alive—living and walking around—they are alive, they are not dead.

BALJEET KAUR (*shouts*): No, their conscience is dead. The entire country came to life for justice to one Damini; but why did they remain silent to give justice to thousand Daminis in 1984? That is why I say—all of them are dead.

ALL (*in a chorus*): This is a land of the dead—All have died—This is a land of the dead.

FIRST BOY: Amma! Don't give us riddles to solve, tell us clearly what happened with you.

BALJEET KAUR: I'll tell you! I'll let you know. Thirty-one years ago, I also had a family, my husband Inder Singh, my sons, Monu and Sonu. (*Takes a round happily*) We all lived happily in Delhi.

Scene 3 (Flashback)

INDER SINGH: (*Enters the stage happily with his son Sonu*) Baljeet, Baljeet, our Sonu stood first in school.

BALJEET: (*Kisses Sonu*) Wow! That's a great accomplishment by my son.

INDER SINGH: (*Caresses his moustache and says proudly*) After all, he is Inder Singh Fauji's son.

BALJEET: No, he is my son!

INDER SINGH: (*Pulls the child towards himself*) No, my son.

BALJEET: No, he is my son!

INDER SINGH: No, he is my son! (*Both repeating the lines pull the child towards themselves*)

INDER SINGH: Okay. Let's ask Sonu, he will tell us whose son he is? Beta whose son, are you?

SONU: Of both. (*Both of them start laughing loudly*)

(Sonu and Inder Singh leave the stage, Baljeet Kaur looks serious and thoughtful again.)

Scene 4

BALJEET KAUR: It was then that, all of a sudden, on 31 October 1984 Indira Gandhi was assassinated. This was the only sin committed by us. Some veteran politician said, 'When a big tree falls, the earth shakes', the next day a local politician came in our street and said…

(She is thoughtful…and the scene shifts.)

Scene 5

LOCAL POLITICIAN: *(Addressing the crowd)* Indiraji has been killed by these Sikhs. These Sikhs have killed our mother, these blood stains should fall on their houses too. *(Raises slogan)* Kill the sardars!

CROWD *(Replies)*: The anti-national Sikhs!

LOCAL POLITICIAN: Kill these sardars!

CROWD: The anti-national Sikhs!

LOCAL POLITICIAN: Kill these sardars!

CROWD: The anti-national Sikhs!

FIRST MAN: There runs a sardar. *(A Sikh man wearing a turban crosses the mob running in front of them.)*

SECOND MAN: See, I have caught this sardar.

THIRD MAN: Lo! Have killed the sardar.

FOURTH MAN: Have burnt the sardar

FIRST MAN: Arre! See…his stomach has been ripped apart.

SECOND MAN: And…they have put a burning tyre around that sardar's neck and have burnt him alive.

ALL *(Together)*: Ha, ha, ha *(laughing)* see how this is sardar struggling… ha, ha, ha *(they continue laughing).*

FIRST MAN: Everywhere, wherever you can see...bodies of Sikhs are lying...as if animals sleeping everywhere.

SECOND MAN: All sardars have been killed.

THIRD MAN: All sardars have been killed.

LOCAL POLITICIAN: Wait, I have a voter's list—and list of ration cards of this area—(*Sees the list*)—Inder Singh Fauji is still alive...let's go to Inder Singh Fauji's house.

ALL: Let us all go to Inder Singh's house

ALL: Go to Inder Singh's house

Scene 6

(*The mob reaches Inder Singh's house.*)

FIRST MAN (*Knocks at the door*): Inder Singh open the door.

SECOND MAN: Inder Singh open the door.

LOCAL POLITICIAN: This door will not open, break it open. (*Breaks the door and pullout Inder Singh. He struggles to free himself but to no avail, he is helpless*)

INDER SINGH: What is my fault? What have I done? Why are you killing me?

LOCAL POLITICIAN: We'll tell you your fault...we'll tell you... You Sikh have killed Indiraji.

INDER SINGH: No, I haven't killed her...let me go...leave me...

LOCAL POLITICIAN: Take him to the crossroads and burn him alive there.

(*The mob enacts tying Inder Singh's hands and putting a tyre around his neck and burning it. Inder Singh struggles, shouts, shivers helplessly.*)

Mehar Chand removes his shirt and tries to put out the fire.

FIRST MAN: O Mehar Chand...what are you doing? Why are you trying to save this sardar?

SECOND MAN: You are not a sardar!

MEHAR CHAND: But…am I not a human being?

THIRD MAN: You are a man of our party.

MEHAR CHAND: No, I belong to the party of humanity.

LOCAL POLITICIAN: Throw him in the burning fire…he is favouring a sardar.

(*Mob picks up Mehar Chand and throws him on Inder Singh.*)

(*Inder Singh's son Monu runs after his father.*)

MONU: (*Weeping*) Daddyji daddyji.

LOCAL POLITICIAN: Ae…you also follow your daddy…daddy ji's son.

(*Politician indicates with his hand, the mob picks him up and throws him in the burning fire. Inder Singh, Mehar Chand and Monu struggle and shout for some time and then return to silence.*)

MOB: (*Laughs*) Ha hahaha… (*leaves the stage*)

Scene 7

BALJEET KAUR (*Yelling*): Sardarji, Sardarji,

(*Weeps and then takes control of herself*)

Oh, ho! I should at least save Sonu…Sonu…Sonu…where are you?

(*Sonu appears*)

Sonu these mobsters are killing the Sikhs, they will not leave you alive son, remove your patka, I'll cut your hair and you escape from the back door, run away, my son, run away.

SONU: No, I will not cut my hair, you were the one who taught me that my hair is my identity, a proof that I am a Sikh.

BALJEET KAUR: Yes, dear son, hair is our identity, identity for the Sikh (*hugs him and begins crying*) but what should I do son, you father is burning, your elder brother has also been killed. These beasts will not leave you, get your hair cut. If you are saved go to the gurdwara and ask forgiveness. Keep your hair again.

Sonu: No mother, I will not cut my hair.

Baljeet Kaur: (*Hugs him and cries*) Okay do one thing...remove your patka. I will plait your hair like girls do, wear this skirt and run away.

(*She removes his patka and hurriedly plaits his hair and makes him wear a skirt.*)

Go son, run away...run away...run away...come on...be quick...Sonu.

(*Sonu runs away.*)

Scene 8

Local Politician: (*Addressing the crowd*) Sonu, Sonu...according to the ration card... Inder Singh has another son, named Sonu... look for him...find him.

Mob: Catch hold of Sonu...find him and bring him here...

(*Sonu is running but finally the mob manages to get hold him.*)

First Man: Hey doll, where are you running?

Sonu: Just like that... I was going to my aunt's house.

Second Man: (*Holding Sonu's hand*) Everyone watch...see he is wearing a kara.

Third Man: And see, watch this...his forehead has a mark of the patka.

Forth Man: He is a sardar's child—he was trying to escape in girl's clothes.

Local Politician: He is Inder Singh's younger son, Sonu.

Mob: Kill him, he is a sardar's child.

(*The mob kills Sonu mercilessly.*)

All sardars have been killed...all sardars have been killed.

Local Politician: There were 340 Sikhs in this area, all have been killed. Come let's move ahead.

Scene 9

(The mob is progressing while raising the slogans, two young boys speak to each other.)

FIRST BOY: Sardar's sardarni is very pretty.

SECOND BOY: Really, come let's see that.

FIRST BOY: Wow! Sardarniji Wow! What pretty eyes, lovely and big.

SECOND BOY: Her cheeks are like apples from Kashmir.

BALJEET KAUR: You dogs...you have killed my entire family—you have robbed my house—now I have nothing left for you.

FIRST BOY: A lot is still left with you.

SECOND BOY: Your body...

FIRST BOY: Your youthfulness...

(The mob surrounds Baljeet Kaur, move in a circle around her. Baljeet Kaur begins shouting for help.)

BALJEET KAUR: No...no...no...

(The mob snatches her dupatta and throws it away... Baljeet shouts... inserts her head in her knees and weeps...then she gets up.)

BALJEET KAUR: Haaye what is this...what has happened to us?... Sardarji you fought at the border to protect the people of this country and these very people have done this to us... (*sobs and then controls herself*) I will go to the police station... I will call the police and will fight for justice... Everyone says that this is a democratic country...the judiciary is autonomous and supreme...tell me isn't judiciary supreme in this country.

ALL: (*chorus*) Yes...yes...judiciary is supreme in a democracy.

FIRST BOY: Whether rich or poor; high or low.

SECOND BOY: Whether a politician or a lay man.

THIRD BOY: Whether Hindu or Sikh.

FOURTH BOY: Whether Muslim or Christian...all are equal for the judiciary.

First Boy: The defaulter is punished.

Second Boy: Yes, the murderer is hanged too.

All: Yes...yes...the murderer is hanged too.

Baljeet Kaur: If so...then I am going to the police station to file a complaint.

Scene 10

(Police Station)

Baljeet Kaur *(crying)*: Inspector Sahib...the mob has killed my husband and both my sons...they also raped me...please file a complaint... Inspector Sahib, please file a complaint... I know each one of them, I recognize each one of them... Inspector Sahib please file my complaint...please write it down....

(Inspector does not pay any attention to her.)

Baljeet Kaur: Inspector Sahib file the complaint...take my report.

Inspector *(In a Harayanvi accent)*: What are you watching? Out, out you go from here...whatever will happen to others, will be done to you too...get lost from here...they walk in laundering...file a complaint...file a complaint...

(Baljeet Kaur returns hopelessly...takes circles on the stage...)

All *(singing in chorus)*: We are all dead!... Here everyone has died... they are skeletons...no feeling...no emotions...no conscience... all are dead...

Baljeet Kaur: I'll go to the court now.

Scene 11

(Baljeet Kaur reaches the court and pleads to the judge.)

Baljeet Kaur: Judge Sahib... Injustice has been done to me...the mob killed my children and my husband...they raped me.... Judge Sahib I need justice.

JUDGE: Mishra Commission is sitting on the cases, once we receive their report, the procedures will start.

(Baljeet Kaur takes two circles of the court. In the background, all sing in a chorus.)

ALL: We are all dead!... Here everyone has died...they are skeletons... no feeling...no emotions...no conscience...all are dead...

(Baljeet Kaur returns to the court.)

BALJEET KAUR: Judge Sahib has the report been received.

JUDGE: Yes, the report has been received but another committee, Kapoor-Mittal Committee, has been set. We need to wait for that report now.

(Baljeet Kaur takes two circles of the court. In the background, all sing in a chorus.)

ALL: We are all dead!... Here everyone has died...they are skeletons... no feeling...no emotions...no conscience...all are dead...

(Baljeet Kaur returns to the court again.)

BALJEET KAUR *(To herself)*: This time justice will be done.

BALJEET KAUR: Judge Sahib has the report been received?

JUDGE: Yes, the report has been received but another committee, Nanavati Commission, has been set. We need to wait for that report only then will the procedure begin. This is a legal institution...understand...

ALL IN A CHORUS: Yes, yes this is a legal institution....

FIRST MAN: Rich or poor.

SECOND MAN: Politician or actor.

THIRD MAN: Hindu or Sikh.

FOURTH MAN: Muslim or Christian...all are equal in front of the court.

FIRST MAN: The criminal is punished.

SECOND MAN: The murderer is hanged to death.

ALL: Yes, yes, the murderer is hanged to death.

Scene 12

(Baljeet Kaur returns to the bench where the play began.)

BALJEET KAUR: I have to go to the court today, I have a hearing today… maybe I will get justice today…

ALL: Amma, this time you will get justice. *Amma abb to achhe dinovali sarkar bhee aa gayee—iss baar to ensaaf mil hee jayega* (Amma, now the government has changed, they promise better days, now justice will be done to us!)…okay we need to go now…okay Amma. (*They leave.*)

(Baljeet Kaur gets up and goes to the court.)

Scene 13

(Court is in action, two bodyguards dressed in red clothes are flanking the judge.)

JUDGE: Start the procedure.

A VOICE: Baljeet Kaur and Netaji present yourself to the court.

(The local politician and Baljeet Kaur reach the court. C. Singh, Baljeet Kaur's advocate is standing next to her.)

LOCAL POLITICIAN: Your Honour, I'd like to defend my case on my own.

JUDGE: Permission granted. (*Points towards the second advocate*) Proceed Mr Singh.

MR SINGH: Your Honour…the day after the assassination of Indiraji in 1984 this politician came to their street with a big crowd… and he raised slogans like 'Kill these sardars…kill these sardars'… Your honour…and in no time they killed her young children and her husband by hanging a burning tyre around his neck…

Your Honour...hanging such a brute not just once but thousand times is not sufficient.

LOCAL POLITICIAN: That's a lie, Your Honour... I wasn't there that day.

JUDGE: So where were you that day?

LOCAL POLITICIAN: Your Honour, that day I was with the Prime Minister's dead body at Teen Murti Bhawan from 7 a.m. to 3p.m...this recording of Doordarshan is a proof of my presence there.

MR SINGH: Your Honour...there is no proof of time on this tape and anyone can reach Teen Murti Bhawan from the crime spot in five minutes. Therefore, it is wrong to say that this politician was not there on the crime scene... This politician was present on the crime scene and was very much a participant in the mass-killings... Your Honour.

LOCAL POLITICIAN: Your Honour...that day there was a curfew in entire Delhi...how could I reach there with a curfew on...you know it very well that not even a dog can come out in a curfew.

MR SINGH: Definitely not a dog can come out in a curfew but politicians like you can come out to instigate people...to kill others.

JUDGE: Mind your language, Mr Singh.

MR SINGH: Sorry, Your Honour... Your Honour, this politician was spotted on the crime scene by witness Surinder Singh and Gurcharan Singh as well.

LOCAL POLITICIAN: Your Honour, Surinder Singh and Gurcharan Singh have died.

MR SINGH: Your Honour, it is a matter of investigation as to why the prime witnesses of this case are dying one by one.... Your Honour, this politician was present on the crime scene and a participant in mass-killings.

LOCAL POLITICIAN: Your Honour...this is a lie...none of the inquiry reports bear my name and the CBI has also given me a clean chit—see here. (*Keeps the paper in front of the Judge.*) Your Honour, that day, I was distributing blankets, it was the month of November and it was a bit cold…if she did not get one, I can give her one now. (*Moves ahead to offer a blanket.*) I have been saving the Sikhs and have been rendering the relief aid to them.

BALJEET KAUR (*Throws the blanket on his face*): I don't need your charity, I need justice.

MR SINGH: Your Honour … he is lying … he hasn't been distributing relief items but death… I have a question: if this politician was saving life of the Sikhs then how come 5,000 people died in Delhi?

LOCAL POLITICIAN: Your Honour…when a big tree falls the earth begins to shake.

MR SINGH: Yes, Your Honour…this is not a law of a civilized society but the law of the jungle…when a big tree falls…the birds lose their nests, they get destroyed and they get crushed under the weight of the tree…the birds in this country are the Sikhs.

JUDGE: Order… Order… Mr Singh, the Court gives its judgement based on witness and proofs and not on emotions, and according to the police investigation the Court has decided that since there is no evidence against the local politician that can prove him a criminal, he is acquitted respectfully of all charges from this case.

BALJEET KAUR: (*In a loud voice*) Judge Sahib…he is a murderer—he should be hanged till death.

JUDGE: Silence.

BALJEET KAUR: (*With a sad face*) Thirty-one years have passed… Judge Sahib, when will I get justice… First, Mishra committee, then Kapoor-Mittal committee, then Jain committee and then Nanavati committee…till now eleven commissions have looked into this…ten different governments have completed their tenure. (*cries*) I want justice Judge Sahib, I want justice.

JUDGE: Guards draw her away from this room…she is disrespecting the court… (*Guards hold Baljeet Kaur by her arms and push her.*)

BALJEET KAUR: (*Shouts*) Judge Sahib…remember…when law cannot provide justice then people attain justice for themselves.

NARRATOR: (*Begins singing the song, which everyone sings moving in a circle.*)

Song:
The heart irks when Chaurasi hits
Injustice for the Sikh—its memory burns them still

The arid eyes have dried rivers
Little life, endless tales of injustice
Those who have butchered sons of mothers
Burning tyres on the necks
have become spectacular for the office bearers

The heart irks when Chaurasi hits
Injustice for the Sikhs, its memory burns them still

Burns them still, burns them still…
Burns them still…

SECTION IV
POEMS

Ajmer Rode

Trilokpuri 1984

A COLLECTION OF THREE POEMS

THE POND IN MY SOUL

When will you clean up
the Trilokpuri pond
with the dead and half-dead,
sunk suspended
rising slowly to float.
The breath of dying water
travels across oceans
reaches my soul
fills it with Trilokpuri pond.

The pond
and people of ordinary doings
belonged to each other.
The thirsty stopped here
to drink a mouthful or two and carry on.
Children splashed each other
with water and laughter, and sang.
Shamans summoned small gods
to help them do rituals, charms, cures.
It was a pond of small men and small gods.

1 november 1984.
Rain god Indira descended to see
who turned his rainwater red and sore—
drowned in shame.
Lord Shiva swooped down
to see who on earth had engaged
in Rudra Tandava deadlier than his—
holy Ganga drifted off his head,
suffocated in the pond.

When will you clean up my soul
of the Trilokpuri pond
with its dead,
sunk suspended afloat.

BONES IN HER HANDS

White bones of her son
glowed in dark silence
as she entered the place
once her home.

Ghost words escaped her lips
as she sat sifting the ashes
collecting the pieces. Precious.

With the bones in her hands
she's been wandering in search
of a clean river where she could
dip the bones, let go, free her hands.

Reaches Yamuna
flowing through Delhi—
the water is polluted more
than ever before.

Drowns
with the bones in her hands.

THE SIXTH FINGER

No, it's not mine,
this sixth finger on my right hand.
It's my dead husband's

Someone cut it off his hand
removed the gold ring
and hurled the finger
onto my folded hands.
The finger rooted itself
between my index and the right thumb.
While thousand others still fluttered
in the pools of blood
in this galli. Silent as the dead.

No matter where I ran to
what direction I travelled in
the sixth finger,
like a compass pointing to the North Pole,
always pointed
to this galli of Trilokpuri.

Still does
after more than three decades.

Bishnu Mohapatra

October–November 1984

Translated from the Odiya by
GANESHWAR MISHRA and JATINDRA KUMAR NAYAK

A pitch-dark night.
The tame owl's
Dance of death
Makes the earth shudder
Fear piles up
On the roads of the city
Death's long shadow captures
Its lanes and by-lanes
On the still waters of the Yamuna
Float corpses of heart-rending shrieks.

Who knows
How this night will end
The sun's grey face
Will emerge from the forest of dense smoke,
Around a curtain of nightmares
Nervous eyes will peep,
Bearing no traces of life or tenderness
Their wings flapping loudly,
Countless flocks of vultures
Walk through the heart of the city.

The city is full of memories
This road that runs from my village to yours,
From the king's palace
To where his subjects live,
Layers and layers of skin.

Old memories—
The sepoy's harsh voice,
The sound of horse hooves
Shattering the stillness
Of quiet village paths.
Who comes?
Whoever the sepoy takes away

Never returns.
Whoever he ties to his horse and drags away
Turns into a tale
That takes on a life of its own.

Any animal that gets caught is sacrificed
To be served at the grand feast.
The city has set the forest on fire today.
Everyone excitedly waits for the grand feast.
They know not what happens
When the jungle gets burned to ash.
Who knows what terrible calamity
Waits to strike this place?

How can I have the heart to tell you,
The one you are waiting for
Will never come back,
How can I tell you
Waves of hatred
Have washed your father away?
On a stone at the end of the street
Dreams lie shattered.
Smiles shatter into splinters,
And feelings of helplessness
Force their way into every heart,
Like a cruel winter night.

What can one write of today,
What can the idiom of files capture?
Eyes swollen from crying,
A widow's grief staring out of the eyes of a woman
Whose husband is still alive,
The oppressed hearts of orphans, defeated time—
All this slips through the net of empty words.
All that remains includes
One's hushed voice,
And a few government and non-government reports.

Do not let history be written
In the language of files.
May everyone's tears and grief
Course through the veins,
Till the hand
Turns stone-hard
And smashes
History's countless ribcages.

Pashupati Jha

A Riot Victim

Shouting the name of God,
they raided my house
in the dead of night—
the time fit for thieves and sinners.
They smashed the doors open,
and, despite my pleas and cries,
hacked my hapless parents
before my stunned eyes.

And then, again in the name of God,
they did something much more terrible;
unmindful of my welling tears
they mutilated in minutes all the gifts
I had preserved for years.
Since then, however I try, I fail
to utter the name of God, how sad;
they leer at me, and call me mad.

A Godless Country

Suddenly my town is all aflame,
pundits and mullah are at their old game
of grabbing for themselves worldly fame.
People are rushing to mass prayers
in mosques, gurdwaras and mutts;
to gore another's god in the guts
with knives, swords and rifle-butts.
This is how to ensure their way
through such bitter and blatant lies
to the golden gate of paradise,

and be assured there of eternal stay.
There is something serious amiss
ignorance is now no more a bliss,
like serpent, it is bound to hiss
and drown all the wounded cries;
who says, there are human ties!

Idea-Obsessed

When an idea
does not remain an ideal
but becomes an obsession
winning a thousand impulsive minds,
militancy of myriad hues
spreads its roots
in the soft tissues of the heart,
hurtling ahead with mad rush
hurting insanely all around
in a grand illusion of gallantry.

But bravery
needs something quite different--
a calm mind and cool courage
to rise above the intoxication,
above the scarlet perversion
and to descend down
to something very mundane--
to the level of the lowly earth
of solid action.

Not the spilling of sporadic blood
but the constant sweating
for the cause of one and all.
A difficult task indeed,
as arranging everything afresh
after a smashing storm.

Harnidh Kaur

Eighty-four

'The air smelled like fear,'
says my mother, her face
suddenly younger, as young
as the face that peered out
of the dried-up water tank
in the middle of the night,
money tucked into the folds
of cloth that covered her in
layers and layers, more than
she could count—the Delhi
winters have always been
unkind, and the onset of that
year's cold was marked by
more than just a chill that went
to the bones—scorched plastic
has a heady smell, mixed with
kerosene and blood, it smells
quite like death, and death it
saw, yards of wound cloth,
crimson red, stained darker with
fresh hues of anger, pain, and
loss, found itself thrown on the
ground, and off the heads of
those it adorned, but what was
most telling was the pin drop
silence of those who could help
for studied ignorance of anguish
is abetment unto itself, and

the silence that followed, was
the worst of all, because those
who survived, hoarse and scared,
had no voice to call their own.

Fleeing

She sat across the table, and
clutched at the ceramic in her
hand, spotted with age and grips,
the mug too large, and too at odds
with the narrow, bent fingers that
wrapped around it, just as she
was at odds with the world she inhabited.

Her hair was slicked back with the
smell of coconut, and it snaked down
her back, a narrow tale of the faith
that she fostered, and its signs were
there to see for those who noticed,
a flash of silver on her wrist, and the
little prayer book she clutched to her chest.

The colours she wore, hues of the plains
made her stand out, stark, against the
city of pastels she was living in, and her
skin, the colour of a wheat harvest, stood out
against the pale pinks and creams,
underlining, highlighting, demarcating
her tangible otherness, and vulnerability.

We spoke for a little while, and her voice
sounded hesitant, wrapping itself into
the language we shared in slow, careful
movements—her words flowed in a cacophony
of accents that chafed at each other's very
existence—one she was born into, and one
she learned in order to survive her transitions.

'Why did you leave?' I asked, overriding my
own feelings of intrusion, flinching at my
own demand to unravel bandages she had
struggled to cover herself in, and she smiled,
resignation shading her eyes like the shade
of rainless clouds over dusty land, one that
she had left, afraid and circumspect.

'This isn't your home.' I said, surprised at
my own boldness (I don't often try to
shock someone into revealing their most
hidden depths), and she sighed, softly,
and her face reminded me of lullabies
hummed to me through the evening fogs,
layers of wool, and winter smells.

'Will you have some more tea?' she asked,
as though my questions were irrelevant,
and in that moment, I knew they were,
because the home I spoke of, and the land
I lived on, had cut into her heart, cut deep
enough to cut themselves out of what she
had left, of her identity, of herself.

The Portrait of a Man

My father's silhouette is incomplete
without the shadow of his turban,
one I've seen him tie every day, often
twice, with careful, measured grace
filtering through his movements.

He ties one end of six metres to a
solid anchor as he wraps the cloth
into folds, upon folds, upon folds,
each careful tuck and tug tying him
closer to the identity he holds.

One corner of each of them is faded
by the smallest shade, holding teeth
marks from where he clenched at
the cloth, draping it around his neck,
across his forehead, and down again.

He does this slowly, calmly, standing
still, brow furrowed in concentration
till each fold mirrors the next, and he
pins them down, crisp overlappings
underlining a history he chooses to tell.

My earliest memories are of him as a
magician, tying impossibly long stretches
of colourful cloth into intricate knots,
looming over me as I saw him condensing
practice, faith, and culture into his impression.

But sometimes when I see him perform
his artful meditation, honed to precision with
years of repetition, all I can think of is the
people who sobbed as they held scissors
to the most prominent expression of themselves.

I think of how they must've felt, as the throngs
fuelled by anger and bloodlust pressed against
the gates of their homes, voting lists in hand,
chasing down men who had, till then, carried
their turbans so proudly on their own heads.

I imagine the turmoil they faced, with the
choices they presented to themselves,
caught between faith and massacre,
the helplessness in the face of reckless,
unwarranted, unjustified executions.

I wonder if they look at their reflections
and see the faintest silhouettes of what
they were forced to give up, and give in,
and I imagine that the history that it signifies
isn't a wound that heals, or forgives.

Bargains

The dawn of tenth November,
nineteen eighty-four, saw a dawn
of grey and pink hues, the skies painted
a faded reflection of the colours
that had been splattered on the roads
almost all week, before, and the
city bustled like it did, as always.

As mornings go, it was an ordinary one,
wisps of fog trailing around ankles
as they collapsed under the rays of weak
winter sun, cut across in giant swaths
by the shuffling of early risers setting up
the day's stock—they sat on their haunches,
beedis in hand, waiting for their sales to launch.

The rates of the day were usually decided
by a common agreement of sorts,
a flexible number that was attached
to various goods, as they were dispatched,
and the prices were bemoaned, paisas haggled
over, and free condiments demanded,
all little traditions followed as commanded.

And on the tenth of November,
nineteen eighty-four, another price of sorts
was defined; Fifty rupees (less than a
dollar today, if you'd believe the rates) was
handed over to terrified, attacked mothers
and their children in Sultanpuri,* and
they were told, 'You're free, and safe to go.'

---

* Them v Us, quoted in *The Assassination & After* (1985), Arun Shourie, p. 85.

Muscle Memory

'Your body remembers, even when you hide,'
says my mind, as I walk through the narrow
lanes of Trilokpuri, dusty red and scattered
grey, chipped bricks casting meandering
shadows over rapidly fading paths in the
weak winter sunlight.

'Your fingers know, though you don't,'
affirms my body, as I feel cold wrought
iron, after warmed stone, after pliable mud
after scraggly, overturned, roots, brushing
against my hands, leaving smears of faded
remembrances against them.

'Your hands tremble, and you know why,'
whisper my fingers, as the stories I've
heard, and the numbers I've read, weave
in and out of half-heard radio reports
and state-sanctioned commission outlines
gather, like witnesses.

But they remain silent, party to my own
avoidance, as the loss is snatched away
under acquisition acts, broken down into
statistics, and filed away into comfortable,
byte-sized pieces, a broken inheritance of
crippling loss and pain.

Jagjit Brar

When the Sky Darkened in Shame

Upon orders of the Tree Carnivore
    boundless bullets rained
    on the holiest of the Holy.
And countless canons thundered.
All that was sacred was plundered.
Five centuries of history were turned into ashes.
The sacrosanct Sarowar was filled with blood
    virtually all of the faithful worshipers.
Yet the 'others' stood on the side and cheered.

It took only two blazing, tall, courageous 'bullets'
    the Tree was felled.
The 'others' living high on its branches
    or under its canopy
    were fuming, seething, livid, angry.
They let loose packs of their pet coyotes
    to go on the killing binge
    in revenge.

Coyotes didn't have to journey far
    the blameless lived next door.
Yet they came riding chariots of hate, spitting fire
    and singed innocent raw flesh
    that smelt selective death
    of a child, a grandpa, an expectant mother
    or any other
    of the two bullets' faith.
The screams of the victims' fell on ears deaf
    even though they resonated high across the sky
    that darkened in shame.

Centuries of amicable living
    to the blinded meant nothing.
So much more even a butcher is forgiving.

With vicious, wanton carnage
    of many a thousand souls.
They filled the streets with blood
    that coursed to the Parliament,
    from there to India Gate, to Qutub Minar
    and in Chandni Chowk it stopped
    to pay homage to a Holy Man's sacrificial essence,
    offered willingly centuries before
    in protection of the very 'eighty-four'
    savage killers.
Verily, O yes.

Where is hiding justice?
It has turned over the business to its antonym
    who will sit on it silently for endless decades more.
Surely one day
    the army of my words will drag
    justice out of its safe haven 'cause
    the grisly era of my history it cannot ignore
    not anymore.

Gurcharan Rampuri

Dwarf Heads

Translated from the Punjabi by
AMRITJIT SINGH and JUDY RAY

Dwarf Heads are at the top
But their intentions are down under
They store their wealth abroad
And even lose their sleep

They don't know
Who is going to use this money

They lose their pride and repute
Their greedy eyes ever remain low
They have evil intentions, heartless actions

The stone-hearted monsters
Depart from the palace every night
They hold daggers in hand, darkness in head
Gunpowder in their bags
They burn towns and villages at will
Innocent people are set afire

Royal statements are useless words
Nobody believes them
Wherever the royal prince goes
People spit on his back

How can one expect justice
From such a royal court
Where the judges are on sale

False are committees, courts, and councils
The kings and queens are deceitful
Only the Dwarf Heads are at the top!

Duryodhan Still Rules Hastinapur

Translated from the Punjabi by
AMRITJIT SINGH and JUDY RAY

The prince told a lie:
When a huge tree falls
The earth shakes at the impact
And he let loose fierce wolves at innocent people
While he hid himself safely in the palace.

Pyres of live men and women were set afire
Lovers like Ranjha were consumed by flames
Burnt were houses and bazaars
There was a hue and cry in the city

When gunpowder was showered like rain
On my fragrant garden all over
The tops of cyprus trees were shorn with tridents
And roots were cut to pieces with swords
Thousands died in the holocaust
The earth shakes not anyway
With the weight of a huge tree falling
The prince is telling a lie indeed

Hastinapur is actually being ruled
By Duryodhan, the evil prince of Mahabharata
He dons the gown of Kautalya, the wise minister
Which he has captured by stealth

When I asked the frightened priest
How distant was the dawn of justice
He advised me in hushed tone:
Be quiet, keep thinking, continue dreaming

It is midnight yet

When the earth actually shakes
A thousand huge trees would fall

Hardly can I sleep now
There is loud crying inside and outside
The prince is telling a lie indeed
He is committing a heinous crime.

Parvinder Mehta

Shadows

They come every year
asking me the same questions:
'How did it happen?
How did you deal?
Can we have a picture?
A sad face will look real!'
I have become a stone
to their pelting queries.
Hard grief penetrates
again and again. A broken
sculpture re-sculpted
to fit their mould. An image,
of burning now blurred beyond
memory, hammered by grief,
chiselled with loss haunts me,
yet they ask me again to describe
my feelings and anger.

Between the image and the words
the horror and the emotions
there is a bulwark of reality
asking me other questions.
How will I get my children their
next meal? Will my son's miseries
end his life sooner? What is the future
of my daughter's traumatic past?
They never ask these questions.
Stuck in that forced, desiccated past
plastered upon me, they try to peel off
dry layers in hopes of finding something
new. The dead stone keeps growing
nourished with this barrage of queries,
a dead cocoon and a dead gaze
only shows a barren ground
trampled upon by curious explorers
hoping to discover ignored histories
and painful memories.

They fruitlessly ask me about them—
the killers that ageing justice can't see
anymore. These naïve reporters know not
their predecessors who also
asked, wrote yet failed like them.
Those dusty police files, pages torn
lest hideous secrets be revealed,
are submerged in cobwebs of apathy
and hollow compassion.
Justice knows not me
nor my plight. She simply left me,
a mere shadow of a dark past,
a mystery that will never see the light.

SMUDGES OF HISTORY

A dark smudge on that glassy façade
bothers the eye of cautionary present.
To clean all smears and splotches,
they collaborate, codify, hide narratives.
Yet traces of hushed memories,
whisper repressed stories and
invisible apparitions peck from
a slanted gaze. Watering the stubborn
smudge with excess lies, they try
to erase it, yet minuscule bacteria
of protest grows and spreads like spilt
milk. Meandering its way, seeking
possibilities and audience,
it finally looms in a revolution
demanding thought, penitence and
belated acknowledgements.
The smudge remains, an apparition
of imagination, untraced yet not vanished
in hoary existence. Haunting with an
absent presence, erased etchings,
ignored knowledge, it continues to
portend the foggy future built
on blotches of omissions.

Aphasia

furies unleashed
    taboos emboldened
        mobs frenzied
            agendas disguised
                no rhyme or reason
                    neighbours in treason
                      fanatic rivalries
                          dragging victims
                              ripping hairs
                                  tearing clothes
                              snatching dupattas
                          shameful groping
                      lustful attacking
                  disgusting honour
              stabbing foetuses
            unbirthing life
          strangling shock
        killing chores
      clipping beards
        garlanding tyres
          splashing kerosene
            smoking cigarettes
              forcing cigarettes
                afraid lips
                    horrified eyes
                      evil smiles
                          deadly ambers
                              fiery dragons
                        rising fire
                      exhibiting deaths

                              moving on
                           teaching lessons
                         looting riches
                       dancing mayhem
                  another victim
              check-marked list
killing more
       uncovering hide-outs
             revealing informants
                   discriminating demons
                      cleaning crews
                          resuming normalcy
                              shovelling bodies
                                 dying half-deaths
                                    eternal oblivion
                                        no-name victims
                                     unnamed predators
                                  no memorials
                              buried secrets
                          reluctant forgetting
                      ghosted spectacle
                  erased memories
               etched nightmares
           punctuated emotions…
failed hope
       failed justice
              failed ideals
                     … failed words
                        failed…
                             fai…
                                …

Manroop S. Dhingra

A Moment

A moment changed my life!
A happy-go-lucky girl once, only joyous tears to shed.

Now,
Only darkness prevails,
Silence conquers all,
Every being—a lonely planet.

I sit and ponder,
A moment changed everything,
How, a living city turned into a morbid town.

A moment brings devastation, my grandmother told me.
I witnessed the same, which I'd heard once.

Who would save us from this devastation?
A Saviour shall arise.
A Saviour again in this age of vice?
We need to make us Saviours,
To thrive in this burning jungle!

If Everyman awakens,
A Brave New World shall rise!!

Mother

Wild fire in front, open swords following,
There's no place to go O' mother, your daughter shall ruin today!

What's with the city? I see enemies all around,
My brothers till yesterday, snatching my dupatta away.
There's no place to go O' mother, your daughter shall ruin today!

I have knocked all doors, there's no way,
I need a Krishna now, there's no help,
There's no place to go O' mother, your daughter shall ruin today!

My soul's aching to leave this body,
My each pore is burning to get a glimpse of you,
I have lost all hope and I am losing my breath too,
There's no place to go O' mother, your daughter shall ruin today!

Gautam Vegda

Cinders

A couple of half-burnt cadavers,
howling and horror-struck in
razed down houses,
crippled with leaving gruesome streaks behind,
the streaks blending blood and melted flesh.
Fire embraces one, the other embraces fire.
The corpses are skinless
like entire mutton hung in butcher's shot.
Now they don't pelt stones,
they slash with swords,

set fire on tyres…bodies stuck in it.
Maybe cadavers are Dastar-less,
hairless, nameless and lifeless now.
The fire evaporates them like
a moth burning in the kerosene lamp.
The earthen pot is still clung to one's neck.
The other's hand didn't release the Kara.
Khaki watches python swallow the hunt slowly.
Wails and shrieks wade to quiver the chair but fail.
The houses are silent like deserted ant colonies.
Blaze of Varnashrama scorches bodies but the earthen pot
that promises unjust and hips of burnt corpses.
The pot is stuck deep in melted throat.
Obdurate to budge as if the mule.
Spittle is boiled over the pot,
it appears as corrosive as nitric acid.
Beware, vicious hands, behave.
Are you ever scorched?
The spittle will be spilt one day over you too.
Kirpaans ablaze along with carcass,
Tyres are extinguished but man's body's cinder.
Blood dried up but not tears.
Spatters on the walls tattooed our hearts.

Inside the Borders

He was vigil at the barbed border
where bleak wind brings bullets or snowfall.
Dastaar stands tall with warm breaths,
clonking of the cannons would mean death.
It's fire, everywhere, on your houses.

What were you protecting from?
Your sons are slain and houses are stained.
All have united to revenge their mother's death,
the heaps of many mothers' corpses lie loaded in trucks,
of fathers and sons; tarnished bodies of daughters loath
the gory drainage full of their dissatisfied aversion.
Don't return home, barbed wires shelter you.
You are not a soldier here in your city, your dastaar and kara will
    write your death.
Can't you see the fumes everywhere?
The fume of hatred and atrocity spurting out of their lungs.
You protect the nation but you are not part of the nation.
Your people are projected betrayers.
You shed your blood on the border, unaware that
they cause bloodletting of your blood in your house.
You are not a soldier when you walk on the street
just like that Dalit soldier walking down the road to his home.
Gamblers at the pasture intoxicated and engrossed mark him
    Chamar.
For them, a Chamar is back, filthy and lower.
Caste, for them, is greater than nation,
emptied guns vomit the ungrateful smoke,
porous body falls lifeless and reward-less,
roads are polluted, wish he could have the bush hung at his back,
stains would have been vanished with a drift.
Your turban irks in their eyes,
your service is rewarded with slashes, thumping and choking.
Oh Country! Pages of your history are smeared with everlasting
    tears and blood of the innocent.
Who will rub it off?
A mother's life cost thousands of mothers' honour and…life.
Would these corpses demand the same?

Ishmeet Kaur Chaudhry

Rest in Peace

When someone dies they say
'Rest in peace'
But if the brutal hands of politics
Burn your men and children
Rape your women
Rip naked your daughters
Kill you with burning tyres and arson powder
Humiliate you
Mock at your identity
Make fun of your hair
Handcuff you with your kara
Tie the string of your kachairah to your neck
and hang you till death on the tree
burn your kanga with your burning body
stab you with your own kirpan
blame you for the crime you haven't committed
followed by decades
and decades
and decades
and more years of injustice
how do you rest in peace?
Alive or dead?

A Chapter of Indian History

We are the living dead
Skeletons of our past
Our bodies remind each one of you
That we are a chapter of Indian History.

Born in this country
we owned it, protected it,
were proud of it
 loved it, and even nurtured it

Our field yielded gold
we were the soldiers and
the farmers:
the proud Indians

Till on a fateful day
history wrote an ugly chapter;
and reasoned it 'well'(?)
A mother was killed

Instead they kill her own children
maybe we were the foster children
but innocent
we did not kill our mother.

They called us militants
terrorists and anti-national
They called us many names
and we became a stock of jokes for them.

Then years passed
we lost our children to drugs,
depression and fatigue
a struggle for survival.

They did charity on us
We needed involvement.
They took mercy on us
We needed empowerment.

They said they will be brothers to us
We said we needed justice.
They said they will help us forget the dark chapter
We said we needed an apology.

The fatal history
is adding on to the dark chapters
and prolonged years of injustice
and indifference.

Notes on the Contributors

Rachel Bari is a Professor of English and Chairperson, Department of English at Kuvempu University, Karnataka. Her doctoral thesis on Eugene O'Neill has been published as *Paradoxical Women: Irigaray, Femininity and Eugene O'Neill* (2012). Her articles have been published in *Discoursing Minority: In text and Co-text* (2014) and *Growing Up as a Woman Writer* (2007). She has edited four books and written a monograph on South Asian writing.

Dhiren Bhagat (1957–1988) was an Indian journalist, poet and short-story writer. He was known for his provocative and distinctly unconventional conservatism. He contributed regularly to the *Spectator* (London), the *Sunday Observer*, *Indian Post* and the *Illustrated Weekly of India*. Though he was born in Tokyo, he acquired his education from Mayo College, Ajmer, before graduating from Merton College, Oxford in 1981. Bhagat was writing a book on the Punjab at the time of his death in a car accident in November 1988.

Jagjit Brar was born in 1941 in Bawalnagar, now in Pakistan. His much talked-about novel, *Dhup Darya di Dosti* has been translated into several Indian languages. His poems and short stories have been published in translation in Hindi and English. Jagjit immigrated to America in 1968 and received a Ph.D. in Economics from Oregon State University. He taught at a state university in Louisiana, where he received the President's Award for Excellence in Research. In 1980, the Punjab Department of Languages honoured him with the Outstanding International Writer Award. He retired from Louisiana University as Director of Business and Economics Research Centre, and now lives in San Diego, California.

Uma Chakravarti is an Indian historian and feminist who taught at Miranda House, University of Delhi. She has also been an activist associated with the women's movement and the movement for democratic rights, participating in several fact-finding committees including the 'International Tribunal on Justice for Gujarat'. A leading scholar of feminist history-writing in India, she has been called the 'founding mother' of the Indian women's movement.

Ishmeet Kaur Chaudhry teaches at the Centre for English Studies at the Central University of Gujarat, Gandhinagar. Her translations include the works of Bushra Ezaj and Veena Verma, as well as Jeanine Leane's book *Dark Secrets: After Dreaming (AD) 1887–1961* (2010) into Punjabi. She is the editor of *Patrick White: Critical Issues* (2014), co-editor, *Violence, Subversion and Recovery: Women Writers from the Sub-continent and Around* (2019, with Rachel Bari) and author of *Texting the Scripture: Sri Guru Granth Sahib and the Visionary Poetics of Patrick White* (2016). Chaudhry was an IUC Associate at IIAS, Shimla in 2016.

Manroop S. Dhingra has been teaching English language and literature for the last twenty years in both Punjab and Gujarat. She had been associated with J.G. Group of Colleges, Ahmedabad. She has presented papers at national and international conferences. She is a poet and writes in Hindi, Punjabi and English. Her poetry has been published in reputed journals both in translation and the original.

Nandita Haksar has worked as a human rights lawyer, campaigner and writer for more than three decades. Her work has especially focused on various aspects of nationalism and the rights of minorities. Haksar's publications include *Nagaland File: A Question of Human Right* (1984, with Luingam Luithui); *Delhi Riots: Three Days in the Life of a Nation* (1987, with Uma Chakravarti); *Framing Geelani, Hanging Afzal: Patriotism in the Time of Terror* (2007); *Rogue Agent: How India's Military Intelligence Betrayed the Burmese Resistance* (2009); *The Judgement That Never Came: Army Rule in North East India* (2011, with Sebastian Hongray); *ABC of Naga Culture and Civilization* (2011); *Across the Chicken Neck: Travels in North East India* (2013); *The Many Faces of Kashmiri Nationalism: From the Cold War to the Present Day* (2015); *Framed as a Terrorist* (2016, with Mohammad Aamir Khan); *The Exodus is Not Over: Migrations From the Ruptured Homelands of Northeast India* (2016); *Flavours of Nationalism: Recipes for Love, Hate and Friendship* (2018) and *Kuknalim, Naga Armed Resistance: Testimonies of Leaders, Pastors, Healers and Soldiers* (2019). She was awarded an LL.D. (Honoris Causa) from NALSAR in 2015 in recognition of her work in the field of human rights.

Pashupati Jha is a senior Professor of English and former Head of the Humanities Department, IIT Roorkee. He was the Chairman of the Indian Association for English Studies (Now AESI) from 2006 to 2011. Besides numerous academic publications which include a book on Sylvia Plath, the co-edited anthology, *Reflections on English Studies* (2002), and over sixty research papers and book chapters, he has also published three widely read and reviewed poetry collections, *Cross and Creation* (2003); *Mother and Other Poems* (2005) and *All in One* (2011). *Awaiting Eden Again* is his fourth poetry collection. He holds a Ph.D. from IIT Delhi.

Harnidh Kaur is a policy analyst and poet. She spends her time between Mumbai and Delhi, and understands new cities through the poetry they elicit. She can be contacted at kharnidh@gmail.com.

Tejinder Kaur is a freelance copywriter. She has been teaching English for the last fifteen years and speaks several Indian languages. She has a master's and M.Phil. in English from Panjab University, Chandigarh.

N.S. Madhavan is one of the foremost writers in Malayalam, with five short-story collections, a novel, a book of plays and a volume of articles to his credit. Some of his most noted stories are tales narrativizing events of communalism, such as the 1984 riots, the demolition of Babri Masjid and majoritarianism in Mumbai. He is the winner of the Crossword Award and numerous State Akademi awards. Sashikumar's 2004 Hindi feature film, *Kaya Taran* was based on his story 'When a Big Tree Falls'. His Malayalam titles include *Choolaimedile Savangal, Higuita, Thiruthu* and *Puram Akapuram*. The English translation of his acclaimed novel was published as *Litanies of Dutch Battery* (Penguin, 2010). Madhavan retired from the Indian Administrative Service and lives in Cochin.

Harsh Mander is a writer, human rights and peace worker, writer, columnist, researcher and teacher, who works with survivors of mass violence, hunger, homeless persons and street children. His books include *Unheard Voices: Stories of Forgotten Lives* (2001); *Untouchability in Rural India* (2006, co-authored); *Fear and Forgiveness: The Aftermath of Massacre* (2009); *Ash in the Belly: India's Unfinished Battle Against Hunger* (2012);); *A Fractured Freedom: Chronicles of India's Margins* (2012); *Looking Away: Inequality, Prejudice and Indifference in New India* (2015); *Fatal Accidents of Birth: Stories of Suffering, Oppression and Resistance* (2016) and *Partitions of the Heart: Unmaking the Idea of India* (2019). He edits the annual *India Exclusion Report*. His real-life stories have been adapted for films, such as Shyam Benegal's *Samar*, and for Mallika Sarabhai's dance drama *Unsuni*. He regularly writes columns for the *Indian Express*, Scroll and thewire.in He recently organized a journey of solidarity for families affected by hate violence across India called Karwan-e-Mohabbat (a Caravan of Love).

Parvinder Mehta is a Sikh-American writer and educator living in Michigan, USA. She earned her Ph.D. in English from Wayne State University, focusing on immigrant identities in selected works of contemporary Asian-American writers and filmmakers. She teaches Liberal Arts and English courses at the undergraduate level. Her publications include academic articles in *Journal of South Asian Diaspora*, *Journal of South Asian Popular Culture*, *South Asian Review* and *Sikh Formations* as well as book chapters in edited anthologies. Some of her poems have been published in *Muse India*, Sikhchic.com and other literary venues. She is currently finishing her book manuscript, tentatively titled, *Mimic Women: Cultural Camouflage, Affect and Global Modernity*.

Bishnu Mohapatra is a social theorist and poet, an educator and a commentator on society, politics and culture. Bishnu taught politics for more than twenty-five years at the University of Delhi, Jawaharlal Nehru University and Azim Premji University. He has held visiting appointments at Maison des Sciences de l'Homme, Paris, National University of Singapore, University of Kyoto, Japan, and National Institute of Advanced Studies, Bangalore. From 2002 to 2010, he headed the governance portfolio of the Ford Foundation's South Asia office in Delhi. Mohapatra has authored four books of poetry and translated two volumes of Pablo Neruda's poetry into Odiya. A volume of his poetry in English translation, *A Fragile World*, was published in 2005. He has a Master's in Political Science from University of Delhi, an M. Phil in Politics from Jawaharlal Nehru University and a D. Phil. in Politics from the University of Oxford. He is currently a professor at Krea University.

Harish Narang is a writer, translator and a scholar of Literature and Culture Studies. A former Professor and Chair at the Centre of English Studies, Jawaharlal Nehru University, New Delhi, he is currently a Visiting Professor at Ambedkar University of Delhi. He has two published collections of stories in Hindi, *Pakistani Bachcha* and *Sunte thhe Sahar Hogi*, and is preparing his first collection of stories in English. Narang translates both from English into Hindi and vice-versa. He has translated renowned writers like Chinua Achebe, M.G. Vassanji, Saadat Hasan Manto and Marta Tikkanen. His well-known translations include *Manto My Love*, *Qatil ka Geet*, *Janata ka Aadmi* and *Is Sadi ki Prem Kahani*. He is married and lives in Gurgaon, Haryana.

Gurcharan Rampuri (1929–2018) was a Canadian poet of Punjabi descent who wrote in Punjabi. He lived in British Columbia. In May 2011, Weavers Press in San Francisco published *The Circle of Illusion*, a collection of Rampuri's poems translated into English by Amritjit Singh and Judy Ray.

Ajmer Rode has published poetry, drama, prose and translation in Punjabi and English. His book *Leela* (1999, co-authored with Navtej Bharati), is considered a landmark of twentieth-century Punjabi poetry. His English poem 'Stroll in a Particle' is among eight international poems inscribed on a public wall outside the Bill and Melinda Gates Foundation in Seattle, and his poem 'Kalli' is included in *100 Great Indian Poems* (Bloomsbury, 2017). Rode is one of the founders of Canadian-Punjabi drama. His latest play 'Tainted Hands' premiered to a full house at Surrey Arts Centre in March 2018. He was invited by the Sahitya Akademi of India to read at the Commonwealth Writers' meet at New Delhi (2010) and by the Words Without Borders at the 2018 Brooklyn Book Festival, NY. Rode is the recipient of many awards and honours, including the Punjab government's Best Overseas author award (1994) and the Lifetime Achievement Award by the University of British Columbia in 2013.

Daman Singh graduated in mathematics from St. Stephen's College, Delhi, in 1984. She went to the Institute of Rural Management, Anand, for further studies and worked in the field of rural development for twenty years. In 1996, she wrote *The Last Frontier: People and Forests in Mizoram*. She has written two novels *Nine by Nine* (2008) and *The Sacred Grove* (2010), as well as *Strictly Personal: Manmohan & Gursharan* (2014) about her parents. She lives in Delhi with her husband, son and dog.

Gursharan Singh (1929–2011) was a well-known Punjabi playwright and theatre activist. In 1964, he founded Amritsar Natak Kala Kendra and introduced the best of world drama to Amritsar. From 1969, he took theatre to villages in Punjab. Since the early 1970s, he performed an average of 150 nights a year in Punjab's villages. Thousands came to see his plays, often travelling for miles on tractor trolleys, bicycles, bullock carts and foot to do so. He has authored close to 200 plays, published in seventeen books and seven collected volumes. Some of his prominent plays were 'Ek Kursi Ek Morcha', 'Ate Hawa Vich Latakde Log', and 'Chandigarh Puara Di Jarr'. Another play, 'Baba Bolda Hai', ('The Old Man Speaks') was written shortly after the anti-Sikh violence of 1984 and has been performed hundreds of times since its first performance in Delhi in early 1985. The play was translated by Tejinder Kaur and edited by Sadhu Binning.

Harvinder Paul Singh is a writer and theatre activist. He has written a number of plays as well as scripted a film, *Injustice*. He is the president of the Punjabi Rang Manch, Patiala, where he lives and works.

Known for his restrained performance in films like *Margarita with a Straw* and *Amu*, **Kuljeet Singh** is the founder and creative director of Atelier Theatre, a Delhi-based theatre group. He teaches English at the University of Delhi. He is a recipient of the Junior fellowship in Theatre (Ministry of Culture, GOI), Yuva Puruskar (Sahitya Kala Parishad, Government of Delhi) and Young Creative Entrepreneur Award (British Council, India). Singh has adapted and directed more than a dozen full-length productions for Atelier Theatre: The self-scripted *Goodbye Blue Sky*, Barrie Keeffe' *SUS*, Jean Anouilh's *Antigone*, Manu Bhandari's *Mahabhoj*, Neil Simon's *Laughter On The 23rd Floor* and *Rumors* (as 'Khusar Phusar'), Edward Albee's *The Zoo Story*, Badal Sircar's *Baaki Itihas* and *Saari Raat* and Ramu Ramanathan's *Collaborators*. *Goodbye Blue Sky* was awarded by the Sahitya Kala Parishad in 2006.

Jarnail Singh is a Delhi-based journalist and politician. He was born in Delhi in 1973. He acquired a Master's degree in Political Science from PGDAV College and completed a diploma in Journalism from the YMCA in 1994. He worked with *Dainik Jagran*, Delhi as a correspondent for ten years, covering the fields of Sikh politics and defence. He is the author of *I Accuse...: The Anti-Sikh Violence of 1984* (2011). He lives in New Delhi, with his wife and two children.

Khushwant Singh (1915–2014) was one of India's best-known writers and columnists. He worked as a lawyer in the Lahore Court for eight years, before joining the Indian Foreign Service in Independent India in 1947. He joined All India Radio as a journalist in 1951, and was the editor of the *Illustrated Weekly of India*, the *National Herald* and the *Hindustan Times* for several years. He was the author of several books, including the novels *Train to Pakistan, I Shall Not Hear the Nightingale, Delhi: A Novel* and *The Company of Women*; the classic two-volume *History of the Sikhs*; as well as numerous translations and non-fiction books on Delhi, nature and current affairs.

Khushwant Singh was a Member of Parliament in the Rajya Sabha from 1980 to 1986. He was one of the few writers who returned his Padma

Bhushan in 1984, as a protest against Operation Blue Star, when the Indian Army raided the Golden Temple.

Gautam Vegda is a poet and research scholar pursuing his PhD at the Central University of Gujarat. He has recently published a poetry collection, *Vultures and Other Poems* (2018) with a foreword by the poet Kathryn Hummel. Vegda's writing focuses on violence, caste-based oppressions, women's issues and social evils. He has an M.A. in English Literature.

Jyoti Verma is an undergraduate student in Chandigarh. She is currently compiling an anthology of short stories based on life in the slums. Her long-term project is to write a novel revolving around child-terrorism.

Satya Vyas is the author of three novels: *Banaras Talkies* (2015), *Dilli Darbaar* (2016) and *Chaurasi* (2018). He is a law graduate from Benares Hindu University, and currently a logistics professional. His first novel, *Banaras Talkies* was selected as one of the top five Hindi books of 2015 by Amazon India. His second novel, *Dilli Darbaar,* topped the Jagran-Neilsen survey for best-selling Hindi novel. He is currently working on a number of screenplays. He resides at Rourkela and can be reached at info@satyavyas.com.

N. P. Ashley teaches English at St. Stephen's College, Delhi. His areas of academic interest are performance analysis, youth culture and New Historicism. His plays have been screened at Edinburgh Festival Fringe and Brisbane World Theatre Festival. He translated the selected stories of O. Henry into Malayalam (Pappiyon Books, 2003). He has translated "The Dog of Titwal" (Saadat Hasan Manto), "The Ghosts of Mrs. Gandhi" (Amitav Ghosh) and Mukul Kesavan's articles on communalism and new politics into Malayalam. He works for inclusivism and egalitarianism through the voluntary organization, Dayapuram, in Kerala.

Jatindra Kumar Nayak is a translator, literary critic, columnist, editor and educationalist from Orissa. He has translated several works of Odiya literature into English, including *Yantrarudha*, a novel by Chandrasekhar Rath, as 'Astride the Wheel' that received the Hutch Crossword Book Award 2004 for Indian Language Fiction Translation. He is also a winner of the prestigious Katha Translation Award for his English rendering of Tarun Kanti Mishra's short story as 'The Descent'. Nayak is a co-translator of Fakir Mohan Senapati's Odiya novel *Chha Mana Atha Guntha*. The English translation of this book was first published in the US as *Six Acres and a Third*. He has also translated *Atma Jibana Charita*, the autobiography of Fakir Mohan, as *Story of My Life*. His other notable translations Jagannath Prasad Das's *A Time Elsewhere*. He has founded an organisation at Bhubaneswar called Rupantar, which is devoted to the cause of translation. Rupantar' has already published many volumes of Odiya books in English. Nayak teaches English literature to postgraduate students of Utkal University at Bhubaneswar.

Ganeshwar Mishra (1942–2015) translator and editor, was awarded a PhD by London University. He was the founding editor of the Odiya daily *Prameya*. He was conferred the Odisha Sahitya Akademi Award for Children's Literature for his book *Bilatare Babu O Papu*. He has published both fiction and non-fiction and has edited several texts in Odiya and English. He taught at Utkal University for many years. He was president, Odisha Sahitya Akademi.

Amritjit Singh retired as the Langston Hughes Professor of English at Ohio University. Before Ohio University, he taught for twenty years at Rhode Island College, where he was named the Mary Tucker Thorp Professor of Arts and Sciences in 1991-92. Singh has held visiting positions at New York University, Wesleyan University, College of the Holy Cross, and University of California at Berkeley. Singh's scholarly interests include African-american Studies, as well as inter-ethnic, migration, South Asian, and transnational studies. He has authored, edited, or co-edited over fifteen books. His latest book is *Revisiting India's Partition: New Essays on Memory, Culture, and Politics* (2016, coedited with Nalini Iyer and Rahul K Giarola).

Judy Ray was associate editor of *New Letters* magazine, a producer of the radio program «New Letters on the Air,» and the first executive director of The Writers Place. She has read her poetry at the Geraldine R. Dodge Poetry Festival, Arizona State Poetry Society, Knox College (Illinois), Vitalist Theatre (Chicago), and Kansas City Public Library. A recording of her poems is held in the Woodberry Poetry Room at Harvard University. She is co-editor (with David Ray) of the anthology *Fathers: A Collection of Poems*, co-translator (with Amritjit Singh) of *The Circle of Illusion*, by Gurcharan Rampuri, and co-editor of *The Whirlybird Anthology of Kansas City Writers* (2012). After moving to Tucson, Arizona, Judy was a volunteer teacher of English Language Acquisition for Adults in the community for several years, and some of that experience, including hearing of the murder of one of her students, is described in her book of essays, *From Place to Place (2015)*.

Acknowledgements

While working on the pilot project that became this book, as the outcome of seed-money support by Central University of Gujarat, Gandhinagar, we came across several people who supported this mission in numerous ways. I am grateful to the University and all the following people for letting me pursue this subject.

First and foremost, I'd like to thank Karnail Singh and Jaspreet Kaur, my cousins from Delhi, who took me to the Tilak Vihar Widow's Colony and helped me realize the truth. Their sincere concern and personal touch will always keep me indebted to them.

Heartfelt thanks to Prof. Rachel Bari, my mentor, who patiently listened and suggested that I should apply for a grant. I'd also like to acknowledge Prof. Atanu Bhattacharya, who took pains to read my project proposal and gave me valuable suggestions throughout. Prof. S.A. Bari not only approved the project, but also showed personal interest in the study, thank you. Prof. Sanjeev Dubey shared a short-story collection in Hindi on 1984 with me, which set the ground for my reading on this subject.

Many people contributed to this project, while others helped in establishing valuable connections. I need to thank my students Meghana Dalwaniya and Dharmanshu Vaidya. Prof. Amritjit Singh, University of Ohio, USA has been like a pillar, listening to my woes, as well as a motivator who often redeemed my fallen spirits. I really need to thank Urvashi Butalia, publisher of Zubaan Books, who helped restore my confidence; her words meant a lot to me. Prof. Charanjeet Kaur, who read my stories and listened to me whenever I needed her. Harinder Singh, Sikh Research Institute, USA and Devinder Pal Singh, Punjab Digital Library, need to be thanked for their support. Prof. Indira Dutta needs special mention as she has always been motivating and her positive energy is infectious. Prof. Girija Sharma, my supervisor, and Prof. Pankaj Singh, both taught me sincerity and commitment in whatever I do. Prof. Diamond Oberoi has always been there for me, whenever I have needed her.

Special thanks go to all the contributors who dedicated their time in writing particularly for this anthology. Each one of them has illustrated serious commitment and written with a special and personal responsibility. I am also grateful to the following authors and publishers for letting me use previously published material in this volume:

- Uma Chakravarti and Nandita Haksar, for interviews from *Delhi Riots: Three Days in the Life of a Nation* (Lancer International, 1987)
- Harper Collins India for excerpts from Daman Singh's *Strictly Personal: Manmohan & Gursharan* (2014)
- Harnidh Kaur, for poems from *The Brown Girl Magazine* (2016)
- Pashupati Jha, for poems from *Cross and Creation*, (Prestige Books, 2003)
- N.S. Madhavan and N.P. Ashley for the latter's English translation of 'When a Big Tree Falls' from *1984 in Memory and Imagination: Personal Essays and Short Fiction on 1984 Anti-Sikh Riots* (Amaryllis, 2016)
- Parvinder Mehta, for her previously published poems
- Bishnu Mohapatra, for poems from *A Fragile World*, (Poetry Connect, 2008)
- Penguin India for excerpts from Jarnail Singh's *I Accuse...: The Anti-Sikh Violence of 1984* (2011)
- Gurcharan Rampuri, for poems from *Circle of Illusion* (Weaver's Press, 2011)
- Gursharan Singh Yaadgaar Trust, for Tejinder Kaur's English translation of Gursharan Singh's play, *Baba Bolda Hai*
- *Sunday Observer* for Dhiren Bhagat's article 'Now All the Tears Have Dried Up' originally published on 25th November 1984
- Satya Vyas, for excerpts from *Chaurasi* (Hind Yugm)
- The affidavits included in this anthology have been reproduced from a CD titled 'Carnage '84: Massacre of 4000 Sikhs in Delhi,'

produced by the Delhi Sikh Gurudwara Managing Committee (DSGMC). The material was put together by Senior Advocate H.S. Phoolka, Prof. N.S. Bawa, Wing Commander R.S. Chhatwal and Commodore J.M.S. Sood. The consultant editor was Manoj Mitta, and it was designed and programmed by Simran Kaur & Hitesh Wadhwa in 2001. Legal and technical research was conducted by Satinder Singh. Thanks are due to the compilers of the CD.

Thanks are also due to my fellow associates and fellows at IIAS, Shimla, and the professors I met during my stay at Rashtrapati Bhawan in 2015 for the long discussions I had with them, especially Prof. Imtiaz Hasnain from Aligarh Muslim University, which helped bring this book to fruition.

Thanks are especially due to Kartikeya Jain, my editor at Speaking Tiger, for showing a keen interest and understanding the importance of the subject matter, and participating in the making of this book. Many thanks to Shalini Krishan for the valuable inputs while editing this book.

My mother Gurnam Kaur, and father Gursagar Singh Chaudhry need special mention as they took utmost precautions ensuring that we were secular at heart, instead of being fanatically religious. My thanks are also due to late Ravinder Randev, an unsung hero, who helped our family avert a mob attack in 1984 in Shimla. Our life today is his gift.

Last but certainly not the least, this work would have not been possible without my husband Avtar Singh and daughter Harsheel Kaur, and impinging on their time and space. Avtar has been my strength and utmost support. He has borne my moods, work commitments and woes. I thank him for being there in my life.

www.ingramcontent.com/pod-product-compliance
Lightning Source LLC
Chambersburg PA
CBHW051109230426
43667CB00014B/2507